Reflections on the future development
of education

Reflections on the future development of education

Unesco

Ministry of Education, Ontario
Information Centre, 13th Floor,
Mowat Block, Queen's Park,
Toronto, Ont. M7A 1L2

The designations employed and the presentation of material throughout this publication do not imply the expression of any opinion whatsoever on the part of Unesco concerning the legal status of any country, territory, city or area or of its authorities, or concerning the delimitation of its frontiers or boundaries.

Published in 1985 by the United Nations Educational,
Scientific and Cultural Organization,
7 place de Fontenoy, 75700 Paris
Printed by Imprimerie des Presses Universitaires de France, Vendôme (France)

ISBN 92-3-102152-4
French edition: 92-3-202152-8

© Unesco 1985
Printed in France

Preface

Following the twentieth session of the General Conference of Unesco, a prospective study was undertaken on the theme 'Reflections on the Future Development of Education'. Based on an analysis of the major trends in education during the 1970s and of socio-economic changes in the world and the foreseeable progress of science and technology, this study attempts to outline the prospects for education during the last two decades of the century and to identify the priorities for international co-operation in this matter.

Specialists from all over the world took part in this important task. Their participation has enabled the Unesco Secretariat to present a wider range of views as regards both the analysis of the trends that have marked the recent past and reflection on the future.

This study, then, is based first of all on the work of five symposia held in 1980 in Dakar, Bangkok, Beirut, Caracas and Paris, which gave specialists in various disciplines an opportunity to examine in depth present problems in education at the regional level and possible trends in its future development.

Besides this, an International Panel on the Future Development of Education was set up to advise the Secretariat. Comprising eminent people from the fields of education, science and culture, who represented all the regions of the world, this group met for the first time in Paris from 17 to 21 November 1980, in order to identify significant trends in the development of education throughout the world, to determine what factors were likely to influence it in the course of the next twenty years and to decide which of the main themes should be the subject of special studies.

The next stage was the preparation, by people of distinction in different countries, of more than twenty thematic studies.

At the second meeting of the panel, which took place in Paris from 30 November to 4 December 1981, all that had been done in the matter of reflection on the future of education was reviewed. The participants examined in particular questions such as the material, financial and human resources needed for education; the prospects for interaction between educational policy and cultural policy; the influence of scientific and technological progress on education; and education and the media.

The various documents relating to these meetings are reproduced in a special issue of the series 'Educational Studies and Documents', which complements this book.[1]

The International Panel on the Future Development of Education was composed of the following (those who attended only one of the two meetings are indicated by an asterisk): J. F. Ade-Ajayi (Nigeria), Ivan T. Berend (Hungary), R. Bjerregaard (Denmark), M. N. Chafiq (Jordan)*, A. W. Chahid (Syria)*, Chen Guo Mei (China), W. G. Demas (Barbados)*, A. Golubkov (USSR)*, L. K. N. Goma (Zambia)*, Henri Hogbe-Nlend (United Republic of Cameroon)*, P. Latapi (Mexico)*, K. A. J. Meesook (Thailand), J. Mentalecheta (Algeria)*, Gaston Mialaret (France), Milan Milutinović (Yugoslavia), I. F. Obraztsov (USSR)*, J. Pliya (Benin), M. K. Rasgotra (India), M. D. Ribeiro (Brazil)*, H. G. Shane (United States of America).

The thematic studies by the individual authors[2] constitute the major part of this publication. These original texts, grouped in chapters according to their themes, are each preceded by an introduction which, in order to give the reader an overall view of these very complex questions, attempts to isolate and synthesize a number of key ideas formulated at the time of the preliminary discussions organized in connection with the project. The names of the authors of the thematic studies are given in parentheses whenever their views are referred to. These introductions, dealing as they do with a subject as vast as the future problems of education throughout the world, of course make no claim to cover the whole question.

The ideas and opinions expressed in the thematic studies or reports are those of the authors and do not necessarily represent the views of Unesco.

---

1. *Reflections on the Future Development of Education*, Paris, Unesco, 1984. (Educational Studies and Documents, 49.)
2. Biographical notes on the authors are given in Appendix II.

Contents

Foreword by the Director-General of Unesco 9

PART ONE: RECENT TRENDS
IN THE DEVELOPMENT OF EDUCATION AND FACTORS LIKELY
TO INFLUENCE ITS FUTURE DEVELOPMENT

1 Recent trends

Introduction 13
*The development of mass public education: the lessons of history,
    by Ivan T. Berend* 27
Contemporary issues in education, by Torsten Husén 32
Trends and prospects in education, by Malcolm Adiseshiah 37
*Recent and current trends in the development of education
    in the developing countries and specifically in Africa south of the Sahara,
    by Jean Pliya* 45
*Reforms in education today and the challenge of tomorrow,
    by Shapour Rassekh* 51
The evolution of the content of general pre-university education, 1970–80 56

2 Factors likely to influence the development of education during the next twenty years

PART TWO: PROBLEMS AND CHALLENGES

3 Towards equal opportunity in education

Introduction 81
Education and democracy, by Ingrid Eide 93
Education and social justice, by Malcolm Adiseshiah 100

The democratization of education in Latin America,
   by Germán W. Rama and Juan Carlos Tedesco   103

4   The impact of science and technology

Introduction   113
Science, technology and educational change, by Denis G. Osborne   123
The evolution of science curricula, by Mircea Malitza   134
What the social sciences suggest for tomorrow's education,
   by Harold G. Shane   141
Science, technology and higher education, by Ivan F. Obraztsov   148
*The growing importance of science and technology education
   for national development*   152

5   Education and the media

Introduction   157
Education and the media: prospects for co-operation,
   by Michel Souchon   165
The impact of the media on general education, by Pierre Schaeffer   175
Interaction between educational, cultural and mass-communication policies,
   by Luis Ricarte Soto   187
The mass media: partners for development, by Asok Mitra   196

6   Interaction between educational policy and cultural policy

Introduction   203
Educational objectives and cultural values, by Andrzej Sicinski   211
Education and cultural policy in the developing countries,
   by Oleg K. Dreier   217
Education and cultural identity, by Nissanka Wijeyeratne   223
*The evolution of the notion of education
   and of its functions in African society*,
   by Jean Pliya   228

7   Material, financial and human resources

Introduction   235
The material, financial and human resources of education,
   by Jean-Claude Eicher   245
Educational resources, by Jean-Pierre Jallade   255

*Appendix I: School enrolment trends and projections
   by level of education and by age*   263
Appendix II: Bibliographical notes on the authors   289

Foreword

This work has its origins in the discussions of the General Conference of Unesco, which at its twentieth session recognized the need for a reflection on the future development of education with a view to promoting the establishment of long-term educational policies and plans by means of a forward-looking study. It is high time for such reflection: the forms, methods, contents and the very organization of educational systems urgently need rethinking, not only of course in the light of current reality, but also in regard to the ideals, hopes and efforts which all help to shape the future. Educational policies concern tomorrow's children just as much as today's, and should be aimed, with due regard for the social changes foreseeable from now until the end of the century, at giving all children equal access to education and the same chances of success.

Carrying out such a task raises particularly complex problems.

Concurrently with the calls made on education, often in countries with scarce resources, to deal with the immense difficulties resulting from population growth combined with the need for democratization, in all parts of the world it has also to face a significant challenge: that of expanding its field of action to adapt simultaneously to continuous advances in science, the growing impact of the mass media and the increasing mobility of employment to be found in most societies.

With this in mind, there is a need to make plans for a continuous process of education and training which will make it possible for each individual, at every stage in life, to fit without difficulty into the changing patterns of living and working conditions. Flexible, multi-directional lifelong education is likely to be one of the main demands in every society in the coming years.

It is also particularly important to develop, at all ages, methodical thinking and the critical faculty, which alone confer the ability to find one's bearings freely in a rapidly changing world and in particular to interpret and sift out what is necessary from a growing mass of increasingly diversified information.

Lastly, education should prepare the mind for the conscious acceptance of what gives each people its individuality, namely cultural identity, understood not as a sterile withdrawal into oneself, but as a fundamental dimension of one's being and future development; education should also stimulate attitudes and forms of behaviour adapted to the real situation in the world, based on respect for others and willingness to recognize worldwide solidarity.

These are the main problems discussed in this work, which attempts to make, as objectively as possible, a statement on the trends observed in education and the factors which will probably determine its development between now and the end of the century. However, the authors decline to make any forecasts or predictions. Their purpose is less ambitious: they simply wish to help decision-makers have a clear awareness of the options facing them.

It is hoped that this forward-looking study, which is intended to highlight salient features rather than present an exhaustive review, will contribute toward stimulating reflection by the international community in one of the main areas where, beyond any shadow of doubt, its long-term future is at stake.

AMADOU-MAHTAR M'BOW
Director-General of Unesco

Part One

Recent trends in the development of education and factors likely to influence its future development

I
Recent trends

Introduction

The development of education throughout the world during the 1960s and 1970s reflected all the dynamism and all the contradictions of the worldwide changes that took place in those two decades. The period was marked by the increasing rapidity of scientific and technological progress, which in turn had a profound effect on economic, social and political life; by the emergence of the group of developing countries, after many struggles, and their appearance on the international scene, along with the calling into question of the colonial system of international economic relations; and by irreversible processes of economic integration, the most obvious signs of which were the creation of interstate groups and the emergence of a new power, that of multinational corporations. It was a period of both fierce competition on a worldwide scale between opposing social systems and—for most of the period—détente in international relations. Many societies, particularly in developing countries, were to experience social tensions and changes in their political regimes. All these phenomena necessarily had repercussions on education, one of the oldest social institutions, which has never been untouched by the evolution of society.

HISTORICAL CONTEXT

The system of formal education as we know it today originated in the decades preceding the industrial revolution (Ivan Berend). Manpower requirements at the turn of the eighteenth century were responsible for the expansion of primary education. In the nineteenth century and even until the end of the First World War, compulsory and free primary education developed in several European countries in accordance with the ideals of certain social revolutions and with the prevailing currents of liberal thought. However, secondary and higher education were preserved as a class privilege. The second stage of educational development, which may be situated more or less between the two world wars and was notable for the social and technological advances that took place then, was distinguished by the expansion of secondary education. Primary education became universal where such was not yet the case, and higher education was extended, although it remained essentially élitist. The third stage began in the 1950s, with the scientific and technological revolution, rapid economic growth and decolonization. In a number of European countries, secondary education is tending to become universal, while with approximately one out of three people in the relevant age-group attending a higher education establishment, higher education has begun to turn into mass education. Education is becoming a more highly organized and integrated process, and at the same time more relevant and career-oriented than it was in the past.

Educational policies have reflected the main trends in each society's social and economic development. During previous decades, development strategies were based on the need for quantitatively defined economic growth, and so educational policies gave priority to the types and levels of education that seemed most likely to contribute towards such growth, mainly secondary and higher education. One of the most widespread notions in the 1960s was that of 'investment in human capital', and educational policies were frequently little more than policies for training the labour force.

When new conceptions of development emerged, in the 1960s and 1970s (integrated development based on man, for instance), educational policies were called into question, a situation accentuated by a marked increase in society's demand for education. Educational policies began to be based on the idea that society as a whole (and not just the educated élite) should participate in development and reap its benefits. Hence the need to provide everyone with an education to a certain level and the acknowledgement of the importance of mass education, literacy teaching and adult education. The democratization of education and lifelong education were salient features of the new educational policies. This inevitably led educators to seek solutions to questions such as how education and work are related, how to ensure the flexibility and coherence of educational systems, how to maintain the quality of education and how to make it relevant to the needs of socio-economic development.

QUANTITATIVE AND GEOGRAPHICAL EXPANSION

The most remarkable feature of the development of education over the past twenty years is its unprecedented quantitative expansion. School enrolment has increased almost twofold throughout the world, from 436.1 million in 1960 to 845.3 million in 1980.

This expansion is seen by observers as the result of various factors—demographic growth, increased needs for qualified staff owing to the scientific and technical revolution, the trend towards the democratization of education, literacy teaching and the provision of primary education for all in several developing countries, especially after decolonization. The closer link between

TABLE 1. Trends and projections of enrolment by level of education, 1960–2000

	Level of education	Number of pupils enrolled (thousands)					Average annual rates of growth			
		1960	1970	1980	1990	2000	1960–70	1970–80	1980–90	1990–2000
Industrialized countries	Primary	124 077	137 711	125 454	130 920	133 702	1.1	−0.9	0.4	0.2
	Secondary	46 429	70 519	80 574	81 087	86 734	4.3	1.3	0.1	0.7
	Higher	9 599	21 105	29 719	31 166	34 955	8.2	3.4	0.5	1.1
	Total[1]	180 105	229 335	235 747	243 172	255 391	2.5	0.3	0.3	0.5
Developing countries[2]	Primary	121 982	204 343	291 968	374 478	455 490	5.3	3.6	2.5	1.9
	Secondary	21 788	52 104	96 611	155 234	216 840	9.1	6.4	4.8	3.4
	Higher	2 625	7 037	16 763	27 942	39 946	10.4	9.1	5.2	3.6
	Total[1]	146 395	263 483	405 342	557 653	712 276	6.0	4.4	3.2	2.5

1. Totals and sub-totals may not necessarily add up correctly due to rounding of figures.
2. Not including China, the Democratic People's Republic of Korea or Namibia.
Source: Unesco, *Trends and Projections of Enrolment by Level of Education and by Age, 1960–2000*, p. 37, Paris, Unesco, 1983. (Current Studies and Research in Statistics.) (Unesco doc. CSR-E-46.)

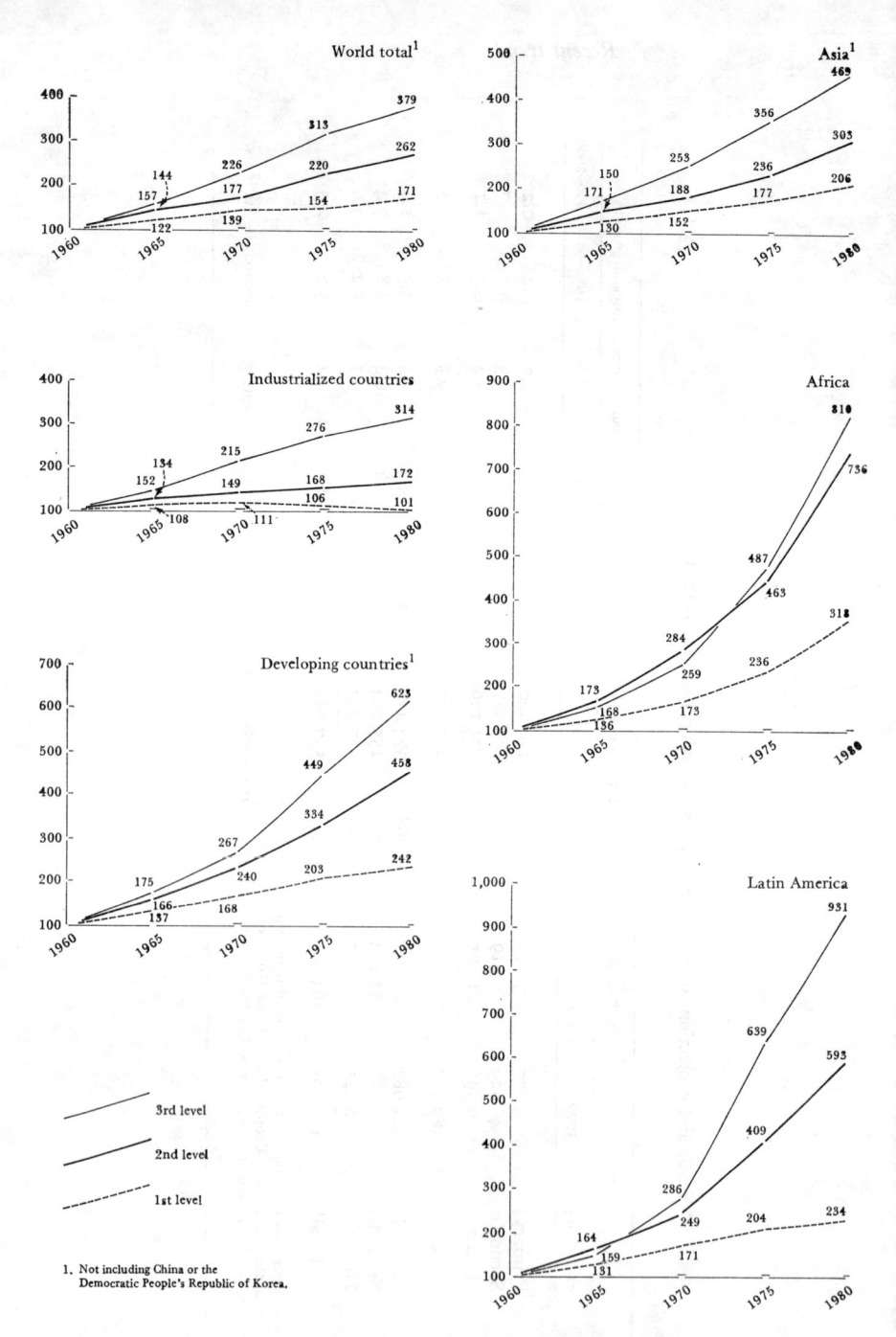

FIG. 1. Growth of enrolment by level of education using index numbers (1960=100) by region, 1960–80.

Source: International Conference on Education (38th Session, Geneva, 1981), *A Summary Statistical Review of Education in the World, 1960–1980*, pp. 21–2, Paris, Unesco, 1981. (Unesco doc. ED/BIE/CONFINTED/38/Ref. 1.)

education and job opportunities (Malcolm Adiseshiah), and the growing social demand for all types of education in the competition for the socio-vocational advantages that accrue from the possession of diplomas and certificates, which has been called the 'revolution of rising expectations' (Torsten Husén), were other important factors.

As can be seen from Table 1 and Figure 1, the rates of expansion were of course different for the different levels of education and in the various groups of countries.

Quantitative expansion was more moderate in the industrialized countries and was mainly due to the development of secondary and higher education. Between 1960 and 1980, enrolment at these two levels increased by 73.7 per cent and 209.3 per cent respectively, the enrolment rate in the respective age-groups having reached 78 per cent and 30 per cent.

In the developing countries, the increase was greater. In the same period, the increase in enrolment and the enrolment rates for all three levels (in percentages) were as shown in Table 2.

Although the regional goals (now often considered over-ambitious) that the Member States of Unesco set for themselves in the early 1960s for the late 1970s have not all been attained, considerable progress has been made. But perhaps the most important point is the fact that the expansion was accompanied by a number of phenomena likely to influence the development of education during the next twenty years.

First of all, in certain cases educational policies which were designed to promote secondary and higher education but did not adequately take into account the country's needs and resources led to the disproportionate development of educational structures, greater social inequalities and inefficient use of the resources available.

Second, attendance rates are often calculated on the basis of the enrolment rate, without taking into account the high drop-out rate—some 25 per cent of the pupils enrolled—or the repetition rate, which varies from 12 per cent to 14 per cent, depending on the region. Thus the actual enrolment rate is much lower than the figures imply, and varies considerably from one region to another; a greater effort to overcome disparities should therefore be made than seems necessary at first sight.

TABLE 2. Percentage increase in enrolment and enrolment rates in the developing countries, 1960–80

Level of education	Increase in enrolment from 1960 to 1980	Enrolment rates for age-groups in 1960	Enrolment rates for age-groups in 1980
Primary	139.3	47	68
Secondary	343.1	21	39
Higher	546.1	3.7	11.2

Third, the expansion of education has brought to light a number of problems and inequalities. For example, in some countries enrolment rates in rural areas are a third of what they are in urban areas; inequalities in access to education and in the chances of success, differences in the quality of education, due in particular to the many different types of education and to the varying level of the teachers' qualifications—these are only the most obvious examples of such disparities.

STRUCTURAL CHANGES

Many reforms and innovations of a structural nature have been undertaken during the past two decades. Most developing countries have endeavoured to make primary education, in one form or another, available to all, and some of them, along with most developed countries, have extended the period of compulsory education to the first level of secondary education. A number of developed countries, including the socialist countries, are in fact making second-level secondary schooling universal. Many developed countries, seeking to meet the needs of workers and acknowledging the educational importance of nursery schools which take into account the work schedules of parents, have made a considerable effort to develop pre-school education.

Most reforms in secondary and higher education have produced a greater diversity of courses and types of institutions, many of which are designed to provide vocational training. In developed countries, there has been a parallel trend towards providing 'common core' syllabuses, at least in certain parts of the system, which ensures that there is a certain unity amid the diversity. Some countries now provide several types of post-secondary education—short courses designed to train specialists or conventional courses of a more theoretical and more general nature, leading to research work.

The growing importance of out-of-school activities at all levels, within the framework of lifelong education, is another significant aspect of the development of educational structures in many countries. Many institutions, both public and private, provide adult education, vocational retraining and other educational services.

Another feature of the development of structures in the past two decades is the expansion of technical and vocational education; many people think that a strenuous effort will have to be made in the developing countries to improve this type of education in the next twenty years. This would meet the needs created by industrialization, the development of the services sector and, in general, changes in employment opportunities.

Finally, educational systems must be made more flexible by improving the internal coherence of their structures and courses, facilitating horizontal changes from one type of course to another, progressively eliminating 'dead-end' courses and making school and out-of-school services complementary.

CHANGES IN CONTENT

In a rapidly changing society, education, although it is an institution with deeply rooted traditions, is bound to change to some extent, especially as regards its content.

School used to be attended by children from the age of 6–7 up to the age of 13–14. They were taught only what they would need to know throughout their adult lives. But for some time now it has been difficult for the school to keep up with the progress in knowledge resulting from the current scientific revolution. Fresh information is piling up at an ever-increasing rate, and has quickly rendered obsolete the subject-matter of a number of disciplines. If the new data are not integrated into a particular subject or if information is not generalized and simplified so that it can be readily assimilated, the new material is often simply added on to syllabuses, instead of replacing the old. The ensuing risk of overloading syllabuses gives rise to the question whether the period of education should be extended or whether it should be made more specialized. Neither of these solutions is desirable, the first because it would place an additional burden on educational systems, and the second because of the danger that specialized knowledge would rapidly become out of date as a result of technological changes. The best way forward, no doubt, is for the school to provide specialized training co-ordinated with a general education; only thus will new knowledge be assimilated and self-education be promoted. In view of the gravity of the problem, the Unesco Symposium on the Evolution of the Content of General Education Over the Next Two Decades made the following observation:

We are in danger of sacrificing innovation, creative work, leisure, sport and, in general, training in how to achieve happiness and develop a well-balanced personality. In the years to come, we must try to determine which components of all this content are useful and necessary for the acquisition of knowledge and provide the best preparation for living in a world characterized by changing techniques and the development of information and communication media. In general, priority should be given to material that will develop the ability to anticipate and innovate—qualities essential both for survival in a world as yet unfamiliar and for making that world a more human place [1, p. 14].

The view is gaining ground that secondary education should provide the general education which will serve as a solid foundation for various types of post-secondary specialized education and in-service training. To the extent that specialization itself begins at the secondary level, to maintain a 'common core', efforts are made in order to ensure that specialization will not occur too soon, and before a minimal general basis has been laid down. In most cases, the same principle is applied to the development of higher education. The idea is that education, instead of being a matter of accumulating knowledge, as in the past, should enable the student to master the skills and methods by means of which he can search out, select from and apply newly acquired information; it would thus be related more directly to daily life and the environment. The student should be able to understand and interpret facts and phenomena as a whole, and this would be facilitated by an interdisciplinary approach geared to problem-solving.

Over the past few years, there has been growing interest in the renewal of education so as to take account of the values of society. This seems to be due to the fact that during the past two decades educators have had to cope with a breakdown in values which may be expressed by vandalism, violence, drug abuse, a feeling of frustration among certain groups of young people, or the loosening of family ties. The attitude of the school towards this problem varies from one country to another. Some educational systems, mainly in socialist countries, actively assume responsibility for social and moral education, others do not. Yet it is widely acknowledged that educational content should take into account the attitudes and values which are part of the most general aspect of human morality—a feeling for solidarity and justice, respect for others, a sense of responsibility, respect for human work and its achievements, attitudes and values concerning fundamental rights, the defence of peace, the preservation of the environment, and the cultural identity and dignity of peoples, as well as other social, ethical and moral values which can broaden young people's outlook on the world.

The role of the school in preparing young people for their working life and for the world of work, the link between manual and intellectual work and the fight against prejudice about work are other subjects of inquiry at present. Many countries have introduced productive or practical work into their educational programmes, both as a teaching method and as a means of relating education more closely to the world of work. For example, one way of linking general education with vocational training is to include socially useful work in general education and general education in vocational training; another is to alternate periods of study and periods of work. Socialist countries, for their part, have reasserted the importance of the part played by polytechnical education in familiarizing pupils with the world of work. Vocational guidance is also playing a greater role in the activities designed to prepare young people to enter the working world.

The content of education will also be affected by the greater attention now paid to interdisciplinary studies, the importance of general culture, the growing use of the mother tongue as the language of instruction, and physical education. All these changes are based on the idea that people must be prepared for the changes in store for them. To quote once more the conclusions of the symposium referred to above:

The idea of educating pupils for a changing future should be central to all thinking on the subject. Adjusting to change is no longer enough. Education, in all its forms, should enable pupils to foresee change, so that they can influence its direction and control it [1, p. 17].

The process of renewing educational content has special features in developing countries. In order to bring educational content into line with their own cultural and social context, such countries have to combine modern knowledge and theories with traditional values, customs and life-styles. Jean Pliya, for instance, believes that the type of school imposed on African society by colonization inevitably puts before its pupils a foreign model of civilization, and consequently can neither satisfy the basic needs of the various social groups who are trying to cope with the requirements of development nor help to give African children a balanced personality and adapt them to their social environment.

In general, the purpose of reforms in educational content already undertaken or planned is to find ways in which

general education can be made more relevant, more consistent and better adapted; more relevant *to the needs of each national community and to the demands of the international community;* more consistent, *i.e. with clearer links between the different subjects and a better balance within those subjects, following an* interdisciplinary *approach which makes allowance for scientific developments, manpower and production requirements and socio-political activities; and last,* better adapted *and more adaptable to future world changes* [1, Annex III, p. 2].

THE ROLE OF THE TEACHER

Along with modifications in content, innovations have been made in the teaching–learning process itself, sometimes resulting in the transformation of the role of the teacher and the placing of new responsibilities on the pupil. Thus, education based on the principle of memorization has gradually given way to methods designed to develop the pupil's capacities of observation, analysis and reasoning—in other words, his ability to learn. Since the 1970s, the desire to make education as active as possible and to stimulate the free expression of children and young people has led many teachers to adopt a non-directive method of education.

The enrichment and renewal of content and methods have enlarged the role of the teacher and made it more complex. As stated in the working document of the Third Conference of Ministers of Education of Member States of the Europe Region, the teacher must keep himself up to date about reforms in basic disciplines; in some cases acquaint himself with new subjects (information science, general technology); master new forms of teaching based on interdisciplinarity; keep up with mass media broadcasts, so as to be able to talk about them to his pupils, who are often greatly influenced by them; be able to show pupils how to select information and documentation, and use them with discrimination; acquaint himself with the problems of employment and economic life; study the techniques of adult education so as to take part in the task of lifelong education; gain some understanding of the major problems of the contemporary world (development, environment, human rights, peace, disarmament, international co-operation); collaborate with parents and the community, and so on [2, p. 18].

This evolution in the role of teachers in turn entails changes in their training. Most developed countries have extended the duration of initial teacher training and have instituted in-service training courses to help teachers keep their knowledge of basic subjects up to date and acquaint themselves with new training techniques. In most developing countries, the main purpose of teacher training has been to meet the needs created by increased enrolment. To increase the number of teachers from 4.8 million in 1960 to 14.7 million in 1980 (the world increase being from 12.6 to 28.8 million); it has sometimes been necessary to give teachers only relatively short initial training, which is expected to be followed by in-service training.

CHANGES IN THE MANAGEMENT OF EDUCATION SYSTEMS

In view of the quantitative expansion and qualitative changes in education over the past two decades, almost all countries have sought to improve the management of their educational systems, particularly by the implementation of reforms and innovations within the framework of coherent, long-term education policies, the adoption of a planned approach to the development of education and the improvement of administrative structures.

The magnitude of educational development has led many governments to formulate detailed policies and set targets for education in accordance with social, cultural and economic objectives, and also to define a structural framework, in conformity with the overall national development policy, for all types and levels of formal and non-formal education. Two main trends in educational policy have emerged over the past twenty years. The first is the universal will to democratize education, mainly by providing access to education for all social groups and all individuals and by ensuring that all pupils have an equal chance of success at school. The second trend, which is related to the first, reflects the awareness that education should be adapted to the socio-economic and cultural context of each country and to its development goals. The way in which such ideas are formulated and put into practice varies considerably from one country to another, but in many countries they have given rise to planning and reforms in the management of education.

The most striking thing about educational planning is the fact that many countries, instead of merely estimating staffing needs for the future, which was all they used to do, have adopted a broader outlook, and now take social, ethical and cultural aspects of education into account in their plans, as well as economic considerations. This general framework for educational planning largely determines whether the conception, scope and objectives of the plan, as well as its methodology and techniques, will gain acceptance. In socialist countries, it is an integral part of overall socio-economic planning. Local and regional education authorities, teachers and their trade unions, pupils and parents participate increasingly in the formulation and application of edu-

cational plans. Once adopted, the plans must be executed, although adjustments may be made from time to time. In market-economy countries, the scope, role and effects of planning are quite different. The plan, if there is one, is rarely mandatory and generally used merely as a guideline. However, in the 1970s, the need for social planning which was also applied to education was more widely acknowledged, and considerable progress was made in this respect. As for the developing countries, where educational planning did not begin until the 1960s, the main aim seems to have been to provide for quantitative expansion and consequently to meet the internal needs of the development of formal education. It was not until the mid-1970s that policy-making began to pay attention to the qualitative aspect and to the principal ways in which education is related to the economic and social life of countries (needs of disadvantaged groups, interrelation between education and employment, etc.).[1]

Aside from these differences, though, educational planning is now almost universally accepted as an essential part of modern administration. It seems to be becoming more flexible and more open to the participation of teachers, parents and other groups concerned. In certain countries it has greatly helped stimulate innovation and reforms in teaching.

The rapid expansion of education during the past twenty years has made it necessary to strengthen educational administrative systems, especially in developing countries. As the administration is the co-ordinating machinery set up by the state, it plays the main role in promoting and organizing both formal and non-formal education. The numbers of administrative staff have increased rapidly, but as well as this there has been a profound change in approaches and ideas regarding the structuring of the administration as well as its development. For instance, topics such as decentralization and community participation are commonly discussed by educational administrators today. In Asia, for example, the general tendency seems to be towards decentralization of the administration, while certain Latin American countries have set up new multi-sector participation machinery in educational administration, at both the regional and the local levels. The introduction of modern management techniques has helped many countries to reform their administration and introduce many innovations, such as systems analysis and the use of computers in the checking of stocks, timetables, accounting and wages, as well as data collection, storage, analysis and retrieval.

---

1. Mark Blaug describes the trends in education planning in developing countries, in the 1970s, as follows: 'Nowadays educational plans in the Third World consist largely of ambitious schemes: (a) to introduce work experience into the primary school curriculum; (b) to integrate adults with children in a more flexible system of first-stage education; (c) to vocationalize the curriculum of secondary schools; (d) to introduce a mandatory period of labour market experience between secondary and higher education; (e) to recruit the dropouts of the educational system into a national youth employment service.'

Recent trends

NEW EDUCATIONAL ACTIVITIES:
THEIR REPERCUSSIONS ON THE SCHOOL

One of the salient features of the recent evolution of education is the fact that educational institutions are offering new activities for different types of learners. Despite the rise in school enrolment, education today is not something for children and young people only; the proportion of adults who are students is growing rapidly. This trend is pronounced in industrialized countries, where the idea of lifelong education first appeared. Education is increasingly regarded as necessary to working life; persons who want to be competitive must take retraining or in-service training courses or one of the various kinds of formal and non-formal education programmes. In the Union of Soviet Socialist Republics, for instance, only 58.2 million of the 98 million persons engaged in studies in 1980 were pupils or students in conventional schools; the rest were taking various types of out-of-school or non-formal courses.

Such new educational services are provided either by schools (in addition to their usual courses), or by new kinds of institutions (centres, courses, all sorts of 'open' establishments, clubs and so on), which are actually only a complement to the school, since they cater for learners other than those who attend school. New ideas have been circulating in the past two decades; some people even suggest that the school should be replaced by another form of education. Some writers think that pupils who are unsuccessful in school should be educated by new educational services; others go even further, and question the school's right to exist. In the former case, the solution usually recommended is non-formal education, but that term has not yet been clearly defined, and it is often used to mean a more flexible, less demanding kind of school education, sometimes close to conventional teaching. The idea of replacing the traditional school—which, it is true, is costly and does not always reach everyone or provide everyone with a relevant education—by another kind of institution is of interest mainly to certain experts from developing countries, who hope that in this way they will be able to provide tens of thousands of people with the education they need. Malcolm Adiseshiah, for example, writes that with the appearance of new forms and methods of acquiring knowledge, education has moved from the concept of schooling to that of learning; and the process itself may be situated at home, in church, at the place of work, in cultural centres or elsewhere. He estimates that 30 per cent of children of primary-school age in Asia and Africa do not in fact go to school and that 60 per cent of those enrolled at school drop out before Class IV. He also says that school curricula are sometimes ill-adapted to actual socio-economic circumstances and that education is available only to the sufficiently rich. He concludes that in several developing countries schools have not succeeded in becoming centres of learning for the majority of the population, and that the school of the future will occupy a smaller place in the educational system. Consequently, all the other forms and methods of learning must be mobilized over the next twenty years in order to satisfy the increasing edu-

cational requirements. If the situation is considered from this angle, it is difficult to see why non-formal education should not be used as a temporary measure to provide basic education for people who are outside the school system. But if such education is regarded as an actual substitute for the school system, the result will probably be an ersatz school, which moreover may well be more costly.

The most daring thinkers among those who want a substitute for school have gone so far as to suggest the complete abolition of the school, that is, of any systematized, organized education (I. Illich, E. Reimer), an idea that the International Commission on the Development of Education has already termed 'intellectual speculation'. The idea of abolishing the school system seems to be out-dated, and suggestions such as replacing universities by 'free choice' systems, in which everyone chooses the knowledge he needs, are no longer taken seriously [3, p. 470].

Non-educational institutions, also, provide instruction and information. The development of the media, with their enormous capacity for disseminating information and propagating behaviour patterns and values, is of great importance to educational institutions; the action of the media has been compared to that of a 'parallel school'. The school must define the nature of its relation to this new institution and delimit their respective roles more clearly. However, there is no reason to believe that the role of the school will become less important than it is; on the contrary, it is quite likely to become more so as people become more capable of absorbing new information, analysing it and keeping it constantly up to date.

In the following articles, the authors analyse the distinctive features of the development of education in different groups of countries and also the problems that have had to be coped with during the past two decades amid all the diversity of situations and approaches.

REFERENCES

1. INTERNATIONAL SYMPOSIUM ON THE EVOLUTION OF THE CONTENT OF GENERAL EDUCATION OVER THE NEXT TWO DECADES (Unesco, Paris, 1980). *Final Report*. Paris, Unesco, 1981. (Unesco doc. ED-80/CONF.803/7.)
2. THIRD CONFERENCE OF MINISTERS OF EDUCATION OF MEMBER STATES OF THE EUROPE REGION (Sofia, 1980). *Education in the Europe Region: Trends and Future Outlook*. Paris, Unesco, 1980. (Unesco doc. ED-80/MINEDEUROPE/3.)
3. BERTAUX, Pierre. L'avenir de l'éducation. *Futuribles* (Paris), No. 8, Autumn 1976, pp. 467–77.

The development of mass public education: the lessons of history

Ivan T. Berend

History tends to show that a well-established educational system is a prerequisite for the economic and social change referred to in Europe as the 'industrial revolution'. There are no examples to indicate the contrary; that is, in all countries where the industrial revolution took place the educational system was a well-established one. During the British education revolution from the mid-sixteenth century to the middle of the seventeenth century, 40–50 per cent of the young generation became literate and about 10 per cent of the secondary school generation was enrolled.

Compulsory elementary education was introduced in Denmark at the end of the seventeenth century and in 1827 in Norway. In the middle of the nineteenth century illiteracy disappeared among those under 50 years of age. Only 10 per cent of adults remained illiterate in Sweden.

One could say, therefore, that basic mass education and a successful fight against illiteracy were prerequisites of the agricultural and industrial revolutions and of modern socio-economic change. Without education, society was not flexible enough, not mobile and not ready to absorb the new technological knowledge, or the new skills and know-how required to establish modern industrial production based on machines and to modernize traditional agriculture.

In general, between the end of the eighteenth century and the First World War, modern public education became a pressing necessity. This period marks the first stage in the development of the modern European educational system, characterized by the introduction of free and compulsory mass education.

From the early twentieth century onwards, European educational development entered a new phase, one of major qualitative changes.

The educational changes of this period were rooted in the new economic and social factors that had emerged. In the first half of the twentieth century, great structural changes were taking place in the economies of the most developed countries. With a more developed educational level, science and technology started to play a more and more important role in the development of new sectors of the economy. Two epoch-making inventions, electricity and the combustion engine, transformed the process of mass production, and led to changes in a great many fields. Industry itself was also profoundly transformed, with consequences of great significance for education. From the enormous progress in technology that has often been referred to as the 'second industrial revolution' came new branches leading to the predominance of heavy industry. The small private enterprise characteristic of the nineteenth century was to some extent replaced by managerial enterprises led by professionals; long-term decisions, planning and research became separated from the actual process of production. Mass production and scientific business organization came to dominate the industrial scene.

Other great changes taking place at this time in the developed countries were the infrastructural developments: railways were overshadowed by motor vehicles; electricity became the main source of energy; radio—and later television—became an important means of mass communication. During these years modern health services and mass sports facilities also emerged as parts of the infrastructure.

The established elementary school system, with its emphasis on the teaching of reading, writing and arithmetic, could no longer suffice. Secondary education spread quickly, and by 1950, in the developed countries, two-thirds to three-quarters of the age-group concerned had attended secondary schools. What had been a university-oriented élite education was gradually transformed to become an extension of mass education. We can thus speak of a kind of second 'educational revolution', in the sense of a general expansion of scope rather than that of an improvement in content. In these decades, compulsory free public education was becoming a reality in European countries.

From the mid-twentieth century on, development in education accelerated, and reached a third stage. The bearing that the new socio-economic background has on these changes too, is quite evident. The technological explosion that followed the Second World War, the advent of electronics, of computers, of space and atom technology, and of automation, and the unprecedented speed with which scientific results came to be employed in industry meant an extraordinary change in industrial technology and productivity. This was also the period of the industrialization of agriculture, of almost incredible increases in yield, of practically total mechanization, of the use of chemical fertilizers and of crossbreeding, and of the development of industrialized animal husbandry, all of which combined to bring agricultural employment down to a minimum. Consumption and the welfare services available to the masses changed greatly, as did social services, health care and the use of leisure time. The traditional service sectors of transport, communications and commerce all underwent a complete transformation. So the greatest changes and the most rapid growth took place not in the productive branches, but in the infrastructural service sectors. Two-thirds of all investment went to these sectors, and in quite a few countries they employ nearly 60 per cent of the working population.

The development of mass public education: the lessons of history

All these changes have increased the need for ever more highly trained manpower. The accelerating rate of economic growth, the need for rapid change-overs and the need for structural flexibility in employment, have set education a whole new series of training and retraining tasks.

Social developments represented another important pressure for educational change. One can point to the changed power structure resulting from the development of socialism. The destruction of colonialism; the fight for equal rights by oppressed groups and minorities; the progress in the emancipation of women in many regions of the world, or, for example, American blacks. Human rights became an important issue and reality. Several new forms of representative government besides traditional parliamentary democracy developed. Trade unions became much stronger. Community councils and workers' councils became more important and influential.

It is these influences that have given rise to the third phase of the development of modern education, since about 1950.

At their most advanced, the changes characterizing this new phase are quite spectacular. At first glance one notices mainly the quantitative changes exemplified by the expansion of secondary and higher education. Behind the statistics, however, one can see a new and important qualitative turning-point. During the last few decades secondary education has become as widespread as was elementary education at the turn of the century. Higher education has also started to turn into mass education. Whereas higher education involved only a small proportion of the 18–24 age-group until the 1950s, it is gradually becoming a natural continuation of basic education.

The educational revolution of the second half of the twentieth century means that in a number of more developed countries, most young people are receiving some sort of coherent, comprehensive, and at times, professionally oriented training up to the age of 18 or 19. In many countries, between 20 and 30 per cent of the age-group go on to graduate from an institute of higher education.

The longer years spent in school and the higher levels of education have also been attended by some changes in the content of education. Having become generalized, secondary education, for instance, began to give some kind of specialized vocational training. In a number of countries even today there are several types of secondary schools, comprehensive and vocational.

In the post-war decades, the educational structure has frequently come to reflect what has often been called the 'information explosion'. The ever-growing store of new information rendered the contents of traditional school subjects obsolete, and imposed the incorporation of new elements. Two types of solutions were tried: one was to prolong the period of education, the other to make education more specialized.

Too great a specialization in many cases led to an overemphasis on practical know-how soon rendered obsolete by technological change. Therefore, schools of all types began to concentrate on comprehensive education. As for intermediate and higher education, an idea emerged that it should be supplemented by flexible short courses of specialized training linked, if possible, to on-the-job experience.

Today, then, secondary education emphasizes mainly the acquisition of general knowledge, and specialized training has become increasingly the task of a variety of postgraduate and on-the-job training programmes. In this, we see the first steps towards an entire system of 'lifelong' education, which is a combination of training, further education and retraining programmes. The same kinds of conclusions were to be drawn from the demands of higher education. The fact that higher education had become the mass education of people with the most heterogeneous backgrounds also highlighted the need for a thorough general education, and for postponing specialized training as late as possible.

These changes developed in response to the needs of the post-war period in the most advanced economies. Also, education often became a means by which the relatively less-developed countries tried to catch up to economically more advanced countries. The averagely developed or developing countries cannot follow the same pattern as the industrialized countries. The distance they have lost in the area of education cannot be made up in three successive stages, as it is on today's world market that they must compete. It is not enough to make up for what has been missed in the past, for this will not yet prevent them from losing ground again. Doing away with illiteracy, essential though it is, will not in itself solve the contemporary educational needs of the less-developed countries. For concurrently they have to face tasks related to the use of modern technology in production, transport, and the military domain, or the needs of public health and welfare, for example. At the same time they face educational tasks which much of Europe had over a century and a half to solve, ranging from the fight against illiteracy to the creation of an appropriate system of higher education.

The history of the socialist countries is interesting in this respect. Most of them were slightly or averagely developed countries as late as the period between the two world wars, and were far from having done away with illiteracy. In spite of this, after the Second World War, they not only concentrated on elementary education, but also took part in the revolution of higher education. The Soviet Union, for instance, despite an illiteracy rate of almost 70 per cent prior to 1917, by using the ten-year system of general education, joined the top-ranking nations by the end of the 1970s, with 20 per cent of the relevant age-group receiving higher education. The ratio in Yugoslavia is similarly high. Special mention should be made of Cuba which, within the space of two decades, managed not only to do away with most illiteracy, but also to achieve a participation in higher education comparable to that of the average European country.

The development of mass public education: the lessons of history

However, in education, as in other areas of social development, it is impossible simply to skip a phase. Although we can affirm that the less developed countries are not purely following the same path that the more developed countries have already covered and are accepting different ways and roads in history, we still may stress the continuity of historical processes. If this seems to be contradictory, it is the dialectical contradiction of historical development.

No country can, for instance, aim directly at a comprehensive secondary educational system without first taking steps to prevent the reproduction of mass illiteracy. And yet, since the developing countries, amid their grave economic problems, are able to use but a fraction of their GNP to finance education—generally about half of the ratio allocated to education by the developed countries—instead of gradually catching up, they are falling ever further behind. Thus, only a realistic strategy based on international co-operation taking into account the demands imposed by continuous development can overcome this lag.

One of the lessons of the history of the more developed world is the close correlation between social progress and educational development. When social changes were very radical, as in the case of the socialist countries, the progress of education was accelerated and bridged the gap between past and future.

The less-developed countries could exploit the lessons of history to develop a strategy for coping with illiteracy and, at the same time, develop the intellectual infrastructure. They have to concentrate on the fight against illiteracy because general elementary knowledge and literacy are the basis for all further training, and for the willingness to change traditional methods in production and in social and political life. At the end of the twentieth century they cannot be satisfied with gradual advances but must mobilize all possible social forces. Concentrating to achieve general literacy, they have, however, to organize the development of the 'second' and 'third' stage of educational history—the development of a mass secondary and higher education.

One could, of course, pretend that historical experiences offer all the required solutions. The historical development of education in the developed part of the world is only an element of the experiences we can consult. History itself is not sufficient to find practical measures and policies. But without a thorough knowledge of historical trends, practical decisions may be irrealistic and distorted.

Education in the next few decades will therefore have to develop in a direction which is uniform with respect to its responsiveness to new trends, but which is differentiated enough to accommodate a variety of cultural heritages and levels of development.

Contemporary issues in education

Torsten Husén

A major problem shared by countries all over the world, both rich and poor, developed and developing, is the soaring social demand for formal education, the enormous pressure for more and more formal education. I have referred to this phenomenon as the 'revolution of rising expectations'. But there is an important difference between industrially developed and developing countries in the evolution of this demand over time. The enrolment statistics studied longitudinally are, indeed, revealing.

In Europe, enrolment in secondary and tertiary education, in terms of relative participation of the relevant age cohorts, rose very slowly from the turn of the century up to about 1950. Exponential growth of secondary and tertiary enrolment started in the early 1950s and reached its peak during the 1960s, when there was much talk about an 'enrolment explosion'.

Most developing countries have shown a different pattern of growth in their formal system of education. In the first place many of them have in a way jumped over the period of slow linear growth in secondary and tertiary education that was so characteristic of many of the industrial countries in the Northern Hemisphere over a period of almost a century. Although I shall not try here to make an analysis in depth of why there has been such a striking difference between North and South, one can point out several key factors. In the first place, education has been 'sold' to the Third World, not least by the aid agencies, as the main instrument in bringing about development and economic take-off. Secondly, education became an early responsibility of the state in the developing countries, whereas the costs for schooling in Europe and North America beyond the mandatory level had to be paid for by parents, which, of course, made the enrolment socially biased and put post-compulsory schooling beyond the reach of the masses. There is no doubt that political pressure, which in developing countries brought about an enrolment explosion at the secondary and tertiary levels even before primary schooling had become universal, will prevail in the next couple of decades. The financial implications of such a development are far-reaching, since a student in post-primary schooling in many poor, developing countries costs the public purse at least ten times as much as a student in primary education.

A review of some salient features of the educational system can help to broaden the perspective and perhaps give an idea of where the school as an institution is heading.

1. A decade ago the most conspicuous tendency was what at that time was characterized by the phrase 'educational explosion': more young people were staying in school longer. The school system, particularly in the industrialized countries, had also begun to absorb an increasing number of adults. Education tended to become part of the everyday life of most individuals, that is, lifelong. In Sweden by 1980 the number of part-time adult students in secondary formal education exceeded that of young people 18 years of age and under, in spite of the fact that secondary education for the young was practically universal. Many of these adults had only had six or seven years of primary school and wanted to upgrade their formal education by attending school on a part-time basis. In 1977, when the new University Education Act came into effect, about 60 per cent of those who enrolled at the University of Stockholm were at least 25 years old, and students of 'normal' undergraduate age were a minority.

2. In the early 1960s economists began to argue that education (and research) were major determinants of economic growth: it paid a country to invest heavily in education. Education increasingly began to be conceived by individuals as a career-determining factor. In addition to helping people to function in an increasingly complex society, education also provides skills and competencies that make people more easily employable when changes are made necessary by changes in the structure of the economy. The German sociologist Schelsky is quoted as saying that educated talent is modern society's substitute for distinction by family name and inherited wealth. In other words, one can note a clear tendency towards meritocracy. In spite of broadened opportunities and a big increase of available places in institutions of further education, competition, particularly for university entrance, has increased. This competition has tended to have strong repercussions all the way down the educational system, beginning with primary education. In order to secure a good place in the line of job-seekers one has to climb as high up on the educational ladder as possible, scramble for marks and achieve good examination results. This influences the teaching and learning process, so that students tend to learn for external rewards.

The meritocratic tendency emerging during the 1960s as part of the revolution of rising expectations has become stronger and could lead to an even more intense competition in the educational system, as a surplus of young people with advanced education enter a sluggish labour market.

3. Research and development has recently developed into a 'knowledge industry' which produces an exponentially growing amount of information. Since the number of scientific publications has doubled every five to seven years during the last three decades, the term 'knowledge explosion' is,

indeed, justified. In the 1960s the investments in both fundamental and applied research doubled every five years in some countries.

4. Young people increasingly stay on at school through their teens, both because of prolonged compulsory schooling and voluntary further education, whereas previous generations of young people at the same age were working and learning adult roles. This brings to the fore the two main issues educators are facing today: participation and relevance. The fact that these issues have not yet found solutions is witnessed by commonplace disciplinary problems, absenteeism and the failure by many young people to acquire basic skills in school.

5. The added number of years young people spend in school has tended to widen the scope of duties the school is expected to perform to encompass social and custodial ones.

In recent years the criticism and disenchantment launched against the school as an institution in several highly industrialized countries have led to a debate on the proper division of labour between the family and the school. The critics have accused the school of usurping duties that essentially should be performed by the family. However, shorter working hours, legal entitlement to paid vacation and the increased role of the father in child care at home are some signs of a possible renaissance of family life in these countries. The proper division of functions between school and family will no doubt remain a major issue for some time to come.

6. As recently as the 1950s the idea was widely held that by going to school the individual would learn what he or she as an adult needed to know. The school was supposed by and large to provide a fare of knowledge and skills to nourish a person for a lifetime. In a rapidly changing and highly technological society specific knowledge rapidly becomes obsolete, and an individual must keep learning in order to cope with the changes brought about by the technological application of new knowledge. Thus the skills which provide the competence to absorb new knowledge have become essential, in particular the ability to learn on one's own.

7. By the end of the 1960s the new educational technology, not least educational television, had raised high hopes for the possibilities offered of teaching an increasing number of individuals. New processes, such as programmed instruction mediated through teaching machines, were often perceived as panaceas that would reduce not only teaching staff but also costs.

By now we have seen both the rise and the fall of the gadgetry of educational technology. We have begun to realize that at the core of the educative process is the interaction between individuals, namely the teacher and the students. The teacher in close contact with the student must plan, implement and check on the progress of learning. The teacher's role is to provide the student with the adequate learning opportunities, and for this role to be carried out there must be a relationship of confidence between the two partners.

8. In recent years the expansion of the educational system has also meant an expansion of school size and of administrative units. Bureaucratization followed in the wake of enlarged administrative units and led to a weakening of the personal contacts between decision-makers and employees. The growth of school plants, particularly at the secondary level, can provide some advantages of economies of scale: broader offerings and programme options, diversified teaching staff and various specialized services.

In some countries the typical primary student now goes to a school with an enrolment of some 400–500 students as compared to some 30–60 a few decades earlier. The growth of school units at the secondary level has been similar.

There is no evidence that big schools provide more cognitive competence. There is, though, a social price paid for size: the bigger the school, the more it suffers from impersonal formality. The social climate easily becomes influenced by lack of stable relationships between the students and the school staff. Absenteeism, vandalism and harassment thrive in a social climate where direct social control is replaced by a system of formal regulations.

The tendencies cited above dominated the educational scene, certainly in the industrialized countries, more than a decade ago, and have in general prevailed in the 1970s. But there are some fundamental modifications that cut across them all. The futuristic perspective under which the current trends were observed in the 1960s was a growth-oriented, optimistic one. In the industrialized countries new features have emerged.

Economic growth has slowed down nearly to a standstill. During the 'golden years' of the 1960s the educational system in the industrial countries of the Northern Hemisphere was allowed to grow twice as rapidly as the economy at large and almost doubled its share of the GNP. It has now been forced to suffer cutbacks and to face what Kenneth Boulding refers to as a 'management of decline' [1, p. 8]. The stagnation is difficult to accept for people who have been forming their expectations and conducting their planning with uninterrupted growth in mind.

The educational euphoria of the 1960s has turned into criticisms and misgivings about what formal education can achieve and about the ways in which it is operated. Until the late 1960s, the school as an institution was by and large above criticism and attack. However, critical voices became louder in the 1970s. The school became vulnerable to attacks from both left and right. It was accused of being a factor of discrimination and of the preservation of inequalities. The standards of competence achieved were said to be falling. The mounting absenteeism and vandalism were pointed out.

A decrease in enrolment due to the falling birth rate has now begun to affect secondary and tertiary institutions. Many industrialized countries will have to face a surplus of trained teachers in the near future.

One has begun to discover that education is not the great equalizer that some nineteenth-century liberals hoped it would be and to realize that education, by making the poor more competent, does not automatically remove poverty. The high correlation between formal education and economic success, both at the individual and aggregate level, has been disputed. A problem of 'overeducation', with a particular reference to the surplus of university graduates, has emerged in some countries. In many countries, education no longer enjoys the solid political backing that it had until the early 1970s, and has tended to slip down the political priority scale.

In Third World countries, among the problems which are being aired the most pressing is the one of reconciling quantity and quality. Because of the strong political pressure for expanding enrolment above primary level there is a temptation to buy quantity at the cost of quality. Another overriding problem is the need to achieve more relevance in the content of curriculum. This is partly a problem of the colonial heritage, but is also one related to students' expectations of what education should provide in terms of subsequent status and income. Thus each stage in the educational system tends to be seen as preparatory for the next stage. The lower stages have no clear aims of their own and are seen only as being stepping-stones to the top stages. A third, and pervasive problem which many Third World countries are facing is the high costs caused by student numbers and by wastage in the form of repetition and drop-outs.

Over the next couple of decades, when the formal educational system will be facing a reduced margin for expansion and lower political priority, more realistic expectations must emerge about what education can achieve. Education cannot be a panacea for problems which are essentially social and economic in nature.

A reappraisal is called for in three main areas. First, a more equitable balance between primary education and secondary/tertiary education will have to be established. This is particularly urgent in the Third World where education absorbs a far larger proportion of public funds than in the rich countries.

Second, consideration must be given to greater flexibility in school attendance, both with regard to age of entry and number of days per year of attendance. Part-time attendance with teaching of higher quality would have to be considered.

Finally, the role of the teacher in the learning process will doubtless be subject to more careful consideration. Given the high proportion of staff costs and the shortage of well-qualified teachers, economizing the teacher's time can considerably reduce the unit cost.

REFERENCE

1. BOULDING, Kenneth E. The Management of Decline. *Change* (Washington, D.C.), Vol. 7, No. 5, 1975, pp. 8–9, 64.

Trends and prospects in education

Malcolm Adiseshiah

QUANTITATIVE EXPANSION

Since the 1960s education has recorded both a rate and volume of expansion which are unprecedented. Between 1960 and 1975, school enrolment in the world expanded by over 70 per cent, with over 100 per cent increase in the number of teachers, while the number of adult literates increased during the period by over 30 per cent. There are many reasons for this impressive quantitative expansion of education, the first and most obvious of which is demographic growth and the internal age distribution of that growth. From 1960 to 1975, the world population increased annually by about 2 per cent, from 3,000 million to over 4,000 million—with those of school and college attendance age within this growing population being a high 35 per cent and increasing from 30 per cent to 40 per cent during this time period [1-3].

Second, expansion was favoured by the political–social conjuncture which witnessed the liberation of colonial lands and peoples by the start of the 1960s, and the spread of the doctrine of democratization worldwide. Democratization of education was interpreted to mean free and unhampered access to educational institutions and facilities.

A third cause was the demonstrated link between education and employment, between education and earnings and the growing awareness among the masses of the importance of this phenomenon. The combination of economic benefits and prestige accruing from education has led to a growing queue for entry into educational institutions.

Fourth, in concert with other international agencies, Unesco assumed a certain leadership in encouraging the expansion of education. It has supported adult education from its founding days, with such initiatives as the Marbial Valley project in Haiti and, since 1967, the Annual World Literacy Day; in addition, as of 1954 there was a campaign for universalizing primary education which climaxed with the Asian (Karachi), African (Addis Ababa) and Latin American (Santiago) Plans.

Malcolm Adiseshiah

EXPANDING BEYOND SCHOOLING
TO LEARNING

In most countries education has long been equated with schooling. Such an equation was possible when there was a basic stability and continuity in society—when today was like yesterday and tomorrow was like today. Under such conditions, education became a matter of learning about the past, because the future would simply be a repetition of the past. Schools had a simple job of conserving culture and transmitting known and received knowledge, in particular to teach its pupils what we call the three Rs—reading, writing and arithmetic. Education was restricted to families who were wealthy, and who could permit their children to spend up to twenty years of their lives doing nothing but going to school. Until the beginning of this century in the industrialized countries and even later in the developing countries, education meant schooling, and schooling was restricted to those who could afford it—a tiny proportion of society.

Despite the movements towards democratizing education and constitutional provisions for equality of educational opportunities, the élitist monopoly of schooling in developing countries persists through a generally accepted distinction between quality schools which cater for the well-to-do and the ordinary run-of-the-mill schools for the majority. The magic which school diplomas and university certificates have acquired in the eyes of individuals and of society also contribute to the equation of education with schooling.

From the 1950s, however, the concept of education began to be broadened to include all forms, means and types of learning and to extend beyond the physical locales associated with formal schooling. The first major change was in the development of adult education, both of the general-education type which included study circles, folk high schools and people's colleges, and of the vocational-training type which included apprenticeship schemes, on-the-job and in-service training of workers, advanced training, orientation and conversion courses, management programmes, symposia, seminars and other organized forums for discussion and exchange.

The next development in broadening the concept of education was the development of various forms of non-formal education for those who had been denied schooling; who had to interrupt their schooling for economic reasons; or whose skills faced obsolescence. Thus arose the various forms of adult literacy programmes, the farmers' training and education schemes, the correspondence courses for those living at a distance from educational centres or those wishing to learn more or afresh. So, the concept of education has been expanded from more schooling to learning, a process for which the locales can be the home, the church, mosque or temple, the playing field, the work place, the club, the cultural centre in addition to the classroom in the school, college and university. Similarly the means of learning have widened from the teacher, the textbook, and the curriculum to other media, newspapers, books, libraries, museums, films, radio and television broadcasts, theatre, and the computer and micro-electronic technologies.

What can explain this phenomenon? One reason, perhaps the earliest one, was the inadequacy of the school to meet the learning needs for the individual. Various forms of adult education outside of the school framework, curriculum and discipline, were devised to meet individual learning needs which required learning methodologies radically different from the instructional techniques of the school and university and a flexible time-frame which did not require full-time learning.

Furthermore, the school system has failed up to now to meet even its limited quantitative goals. In the developing countries as a whole, the school is not able to attract and retain the majority of children through even four years of primary schooling.

Another cause for the expansion of learning beyond the school is the inability of the school with its curricular patterns, single-point entry with no exits, sequential movement upward and hierarchy to adjust itself to the fast changing, moving and developing world scene. The Club of Rome's study *No Limits to Learning* [4] refers to the world *problématique*, which is a complex of problems in the areas of population, food, pollution, energy and resources. There is now a call for a learning system which will do more than simply enable us to understand the fairly stable past and the changing present. In the past the school fulfilled this function through what the study calls 'maintenance learning'. What is now required, as was foreseen by Unesco's International Commission on the Development of Education, nearly a decade ago, is a learning system that is both anticipatory and participative [5]. Learning has to be anticipatory to permit people to understand and control the future. For instance if, as is now recognized, 70 per cent of jobs will be new for today's children and youth when they enter the employment market in ten or twenty years, learning today must help the pupil to anticipate and train for the as yet unpractised job. Learning has to be participative in the sense that it will not be hierarchical as in the school, but will be by consensus and extended to include what is called 'societal learning'.

These changes, together with various forms of interpersonal exchanges and communication, which are being harnessed in various innovative forms of non-formal and adult education, will extend the scope of the learning process and opportunities, improve the access to education for the majority of people of the poor countries and reduce the costs of education and learning.

Malcolm Adiseshiah

EDUCATION AND SOCIETY

Education's involvement in society is a many-sided one. The economic link has perhaps been the most pervasive and prominent one. There has also been a technical link, involving the outflow, impact and deployment of science and technology. Education has long-standing cultural facets and links; above all it has very deep involvement in the movement towards a society of justice or injustice, of equality or inequality.

Economic links

Economists have long regarded education as an instrument for the economic progress of society. A good deal of literature exists on the contribution of education to economic development which specifies the nature of the contribution, the means of measuring the contribution, and the balancing of educational costs against benefits.

To start with, the contribution of education to the economy was seen to be through its function of training middle- and high-level manpower for running the government, peopling parliament, and operating agriculture, manufacturing industries, mines and trade of the country. Two consequences followed. First, educational planning came to be associated with elaborate techniques for calculating the numbers of the different levels of skilled manpower that a country needed. Second, national and international resources came to be concentrated on the education of middle- and high-level manpower. The annual average rate of growth of national public educational expenditures from the early 1960s to the mid-1970s on secondary and tertiary education was from four to ten times the rate of growth of the expenditure on primary education.

This difference was economically justified through simplistic conclusions of manpower studies showing that the transfer of national resources to expand primary education and adult literacy would increase urban poverty and leave rural poverty unchanged [6]. At the international level, World Bank lending for education started in 1963 and from 1963 to 1969 84 per cent went to secondary education and 12 per cent to higher education. None went to primary education. From 1970 to 1974, the World Bank reports that 50 per cent of its educational loans were for the development of secondary education and 40 per cent for higher education [7].

By the mid-1970s, it became clear that there were two major defects inherent in the concentration of educational planning, educational finance and international credit and aid on secondary and tertiary education. First, this approach ignored the logical interrelation between the different levels of education. The second and more serious problem is that the concentration of educational resources on a growing army of educated middle- and high-level manpower benefited the rich minority and left most people with little or no educational facilities and opportunities. In India a sociological survey of secondary and higher education, which had expanded six to eight times as rapidly as had primary education, concluded that 80 per cent of those completing high school and university came from the top 20 per cent of society [8].

Since the mid-1970s, efforts have been made to change national planning methodologies to develop plans from the local level upwards, with the aim of reducing poverty, generating employment and reducing inequalities rather than simply trying to attain certain GNP targets. Simultaneously, educational planning also enlarged its focus on secondary and higher education, to include primary education, adult literacy and basic education for the masses at both the national and international levels. Educational planning methodology in turn has moved from use of manpower techniques to cost-benefits, rate of return and cost-effective techniques and methodologies.

In the future, the linkage of education to the economy will continue to give education special importance all over the world and will influence the content and methodology of learning in industrialized countries. The developing countries' head start in secondary and tertiary education will have to be consolidated in the next twenty years, and a special emphasis put on vocational and professional orientation and training. Additional efforts, involving fresh investments to ensure accessibility, full capacity use and relevant learning modules, will have to be made in primary and adult education, so that everyone has the basic tools and skills of learning by the year 2000.

Links with science and technology

Education is linked with society through science and technology. The school and the university are where science grows and matures; related or parallel research and development programmes in firms, centres and institutes are where technology develops. Science education is developing in all countries at the school level. Science education faces three problems. The first is enabling the student and teacher to keep up with the increasingly complex world of information which has emerged through scientific development. The constant review, revision and updating of the science curriculum is one answer, even though there is a continual time-lag between the changed perception of reality and the teaching and learning of science at school. The second problem is the time-lag between scientific breakthroughs and their application to the learning process and teaching techniques in school, which is disturbingly wide.

In too many cases breakthroughs are either ignored in the classroom or are tried out for prolonged periods on a pilot and demonstration basis only. Third, at the university and postgraduate level in the developing countries, there are too many science faculties teaching obsolete subjects and too few considering the new and emerging. In society, there is no such thing as chemistry or biology or astronomy or economics or sociology. The field of science must be viewed in its holistic reality; but there is also a need for interdisciplinary studies and in some cases trandisciplinary approaches to supplement and complement the disciplinary studies on which all schools and universities are founded.

Cultural links

Education is not only the birthplace and home of science and technology, it is also society's cultural focus. Today's school reflects society's culture in its dance, drama, language, literature, games and values; it also creates its own culture in the teacher–pupil relationship, and in some values and attitudes that it develops in all its members. The cultural function of the school is partly built into its curriculum and partly expressed in its 'hidden curriculum'. The teaching and diffusion of values through the school differ from the rapid, mechanized forms of learning which cybernetics and the use of the computer and electronic technology ensure.

The school faces several problems in discharging its cultural vocation. First, the overt curriculum is increasingly crowded both with new knowledge and the addition of many new areas, such as population education, family planning, environmental education, education for international understanding, education for national integration. As a result, there is no time and space in the school for the teacher and the student to reflect on the values being learned, nor to discuss these values, attitudes and behavioural patterns openly, fully and fairly. In the coming years, the schools and all other learning forums, particularly in the developing countries, will be thinning out their curricula in order to concentrate on learning how and where to learn what, and to give themselves more time for value orientation and cultural reflection.

Second, the cultural reflection and cultural creation of the school referred to earlier is also embodied in the common memory of the people—memory of history, geography, the life of the mind and spirit and the daily toil of its people. In the future, history and geography as expressions of culture will be made an essential part of all learning at all stages. They are increasingly being adopted not only at school but also at the post-secondary level.

Third, the values in the school are in part a reflection of the values of the society in which it is placed and in part the values which it creates itself. One of the major cultural values in most developing societies is tolerance, a tolerance reflected in the school by the coexistence of different facets of truth in philosophy, religion, art, science and tehnology. In this sense, culture is both humanist and universal. It is humanist because its centre is man, and universal because it comprises all manner of diversities, varieties and particularities. But this value of tolerance also leads to tolerance of the wrongs in society: its inequalities, injustice and inequities. The revolt against these evils is also part of the school culture. In the future, while schools will continue to embody the values of diversity and tolerance, they will also increasingly form the vanguard in the fight against all that is shabby and shoddy, and in righting the wrongs which man has inflicted on man.

Fourth, the culture which the school and college embody is the manifestation of the common life of the people, the people's culture. Hence, increasingly now and in the future, schools and universities in the developing countries will go out to the people, work with them, face their problems alongside them and use classroom and library learning to find the solutions to problems. In this sense, everything the schools and universities do to understand, elevate and transform the working conditions and products of the people is an act of cultural promotion.

EDUCATION AND INTERNATIONAL RELATIONS

It is well known that the per capita GNP gap between industrialized and developing countries is wide and widening; what is less known is that the gap is even wider in school expenditures between the two groups of countries. The thirty most industrialized countries, with 24 per cent of the world population, spend seventy-five times more per inhabitant on education than the twenty-three least-developed countries which also have 24 per cent of the world population. Consequently, the GNP disparity ratio is 25 : 1 as compared to an educational expenditure differential of 75 : 1 between the two groups of countries [9, 10].

The international educational inequalities contribute to and worsen the international economic inequalities which the New International Economic Order aims at correcting. For the future, the correction of international educational inequalities is part of the wider fight to correct international, political, social and economic imbalances to create a New International Order. Present and future action will be concentrated on improving and increasing investments in learning systems within each developing country, and to increased co-operation between developing countries. Following Leontief's [11] division of the developing countries into fifteen regions, which can be subdivided into a total of twenty-five or thirty subregions, co-operation between the education systems of countries in each subregion can promote self-reliance and stop the worsening of educational disparities. This co-operation can take the form of exchanges of research and teaching staff, and the joint production of educational materials and equipment, replacing the action of multinational corporations. The learning systems in the industrialized and developing countries need to train personnel for the New International Economic Order and to join the fight for its realization. The present silence of the school and university system on the struggle for the New International Economic Order needs urgently to be replaced by information, study and participation in the fight.

REFERENCES

1. *Unesco Statistical Yearbook, 1978–79*, Tables 1.1 and 1.2. Paris, Unesco, 1980
2. INTERNATIONAL BUREAU OF EDUCATION (IBE). *Educational Trends in 1970: An International Survey*, Table 9. Paris/Geneva, Unesco/IBE, 1970.
3. WORLD BANK. *World Development Report, 1980*, Table 23. Washington, D.C., World Bank, 1980.
4. BOTKIN, J. W.; ELMANDJRA, M.; MALITZA, M. *No Limits to Learning: Bridging the Human Gap—A Report to the Club of Rome*. Oxford, Pergamon, 1979.
5. FAURE, Edgar et al. *Learning to Be: The World of Education Today and Tomorrow*. Paris, Unesco, 1972.
6. COLLAUGH, C. *Education Expansion or Changes: Some Choices for Central and Southern Africa*. London, 1974.
7. WORLD BANK. *Education Sector Policy Paper*. 3rd ed. Washington, D.C., World Bank, 1980.
8. NATIONAL COUNCIL OF EDUCATIONAL RESEARCH AND TRAINING (NCERT). *Field Studies in the Sociology of Education*. New Delhi, NCERT, 1971.
9. UNITED NATIONS. STATISTICAL OFFICE. *Statistical Yearbook, 1978*. New York, United Nations, 1979.
10. *Unesco Statistical Yearbook, 1978–79*. Paris, Unesco, 1980.
11. LEONTIEF, W. et al. *The Future of the World Economy: A United Nations Study*. New York, Oxford University Press, 1977.

Recent and current trends in the development of education in the developing countries and specifically in Africa south of the Sahara

Jean Pliya

INABILITY OF THE SCHOOL TO MEET CURRENT EDUCATIONAL AND OVERALL DEVELOPMENT NEEDS

In the developing countries the idea of education has become broader in scope and richer in meaning over the past twenty years; it makes new demands on educators, education specialists, states, bodies that use the services of those trained by the educational system, and also on the family. As we know, the very nature of the school today, its aims, structures and methods, fail to meet the major needs of various social classes that are faced with the dual exigencies of development and survival.

In the case of young people, the spectacular increase in the school-age population in countries in Africa south of the Sahara has given rise to acute problems: the educational infrastructure is overloaded, educational facilities are inadequate and there is a shortage of qualified teachers.

The cultural ambitions of young people and their wishes regarding their education (for example the increased demand for training for legal, economic and scientific careers) do not always coincide with the concerns of political decision-makers and planners, who have to take into consideration the requirements of economic development as well as the international economic situation. Furthermore, the school is failing in its duty to educate young people for living as well as to give them knowledge and teach them skills; it seems unaware that they need a balanced personality as well as knowledge if they are to attain socio-cultural well-being and economic success. Failure to provide an adequate education in morals and civic affairs, together with widespread indifference or openly hostile attitudes towards religion, will do nothing to develop the child's will-power, emotions and altruistic moral values, or to satisfy his spiritual aspirations.

The school, therefore, does not develop the child's personality in a balanced way, nor does it make him an integrated member of society. It does not enable him to take responsibility for his own health, knowledge or conscience about work, and it does little to foster patriotism and a feeling for national and international solidarity.

The educational needs of adults in both rural and urban areas are considerable, but the educational system is incapable of meeting them. Farmers would benefit from functional literacy teaching, which would enable them to upgrade their traditional technology or to take advantage of innovations, and craftsmen and other workers could improve their position by further training, but the school has virtually nothing to offer them, either for lack of funds or because it has no fresh ideas.

These educational needs are part of the process of independent, self-managing development, which is both conditioned by and dependent on them. Unless formal and non-formal education of good quality is provided, it will be impossible to achieve agricultural and industrial development, by which the vital needs of the masses can be met, to improve the quality of life, to attain self-sufficiency in food or to combat malnutrition, unhealthy conditions and famine.

The main function of the school should be to train as many qualified people as are required. In point of fact, unfortunately, schools are still selective and élitist, and they still perpetuate and accentuate the gap between antagonistic social classes, just as the purest colonial domination strategy did.

Increased competition in socio-economic life brings with it new selection criteria, which means that persons who are considered incapable are shut out. New barriers are being set up, so that education may rightly be said to be an obstacle race; the selection process is discriminatory from the outset, for with few exceptions the children of rural dwellers or under-privileged people are automatically excluded, since the material, financial and cultural resources needed for education are not available [1, p. 34]. An increasing number of those who have attended school are frustrated or unemployed. The content of school education is often unsuited to solve the problems that arise. So it comes about that the school as it is today encourages the exodus of young people towards urban centres or abroad, and creates a highly mobile work-force. Its facilities are too costly or too sophisticated for it to cover its own running costs. In countries where the school, having been reorganized, is trying to do so, results have been uneven [2, p. 43]. Lastly, the school does little to safeguard national cultural identity, for it turns the child away from the family, the traditions of his people and the aspirations of his nation. On the other hand, it brings the developing countries into touch with the world and its knowledge, and gives them some degree of technological expertise, which is all to the good.

However, trends in formal education are developing in the 1980s and can be expected to be more marked by the year 2000. These trends are the result of reforms undertaken to give effect to national decisions, or are due to a desire to imitate foreign educational models.

Syllabuses, for instance, have been lightened in order to avoid cramming pupils' heads with facts. Steps have been taken to reduce the number of screening examinations and to make the method of appraising pupils' work less arbitrary and fortuitous by introducing a system of continuous assessment. Hitherto the languages of the former colonialists were used mainly or even exclusively, but now the importance of national languages is being emphasized; this means that there is less interest in foreign languages, and less time is given to teaching them. Consequently, more care is taken in selecting textbooks than in the past. In cases where this reaction against the study of foreign languages is carried further, the result is a shift of emphasis from literary to scientific careers. The decision having been taken to emphasize scientific and technological education, the best students are selected and given a sound training. Moreover, international co-operation programmes are in line with this tendency, for they assign priority in funding to educational projects or institutions centred on scientific studies which can have direct repercussions on development studies such as medicine, agronomy and economics. The decision taken by several countries to Africanize history, geography, literature and sociology syllabuses, for example, and to diversify the foreign languages taught has certainly not been encouraged by bilateral co-operation with former colonial powers. Another point to note is that young people tend to choose careers that bring prestige and are well paid. Steeped as they are in the civilization of the West, where money is supreme, they prefer careers which will rapidly bring them affluence: they want to become managers of companies or banks or of state-controlled or private businesses, or to be international civil servants. More and more students are training for such careers, and the resultant imbalance is jeopardizing all attempts to make national plans. No one wants to train for demanding and poorly paid jobs, the very archetype of which is teaching. It is extremely difficult to get students to enter teacher-training schools, whether at the lower or the higher level, and in both scientific and literary branches. Teaching seems to be the principal career that students of the humanities can take up, and more of them are entering this profession than students of the sciences, who move into more profitable fields. Sometimes special incentives must be offered or coercion must be used in order to encourage or persuade students to enter teacher-training schools. This situation exacerbates the tendency for people with higher or medium-level qualifications to leave the country—a serious loss for the country that has provided their training and a considerable advantage for the countries they go to, which are quick to offer most attractive working conditions.

NEW PROSPECTS FOR THE DEVELOPMENT OF EDUCATION

For some twenty years now, conferences of African ministers of education have examined the question of the need to reform educational systems and also the question of how education should be related to employment, society and culture. The Lagos conference, held in 1976, clearly demonstrated the interaction between education and productive work, and declared that it is by actually producing things that the pupil learns to be a producer in the community. These summit meetings have sparked off a movement towards the harmonization of educational goals in Africa, although some countries tend to go their own way. Nowadays, 'the primary objective of educational policies in African countries is to achieve an integrated and overall development of their standard of living' [3, p. 9]. This can only be done by meeting the growing demand for a good education to be provided by the national and local communities.

The constant increase in the number of school-age children creates a need for greater investment, more classrooms and the provision of suitable teaching materials. In some cases it is difficult to allocate a larger proportion of the national budget to education, but existing resources must be managed more carefully, and in meeting the various educational needs priority must be given to those young people whose training will have a more lasting impact on development and also to the safeguarding, at all costs, of cultural identity, which will be the dynamic basis of a new type of school.

African cultural values are not being integrated into educational systems inherited from the colonial period as rapidly as is desirable. The school should be the principal means of safeguarding cultural identity, but a policy of state support is also needed, to stimulate cultural workers of all types, artists, writers and researchers, protect them and encourage them to create a new African humanism.

Education for development will also be an important educational priority in the coming years—perhaps the most important one. 'Educate in order to produce, educate whilst producing, train efficient agents for general development, such is the new challenge to Africa in regard to this second decade of development, because a set-back in development is specifically accountable to the failure of education for productive work' [2, p. 26]. All states are in agreement on this point; in the future, however, not only must productive work be effectively integrated into education, but education must help to solve development problems; it must be a community affair, in which all those working for development play their part. Another important goal which the school of tomorrow must keep in view is that of *new relations with the local and national communities*, by providing community education designed to bring together the different components of the community which were separated as a result of colonization and also to integrate formal and non-formal education. In this way, formal education, which was once used to tear apart the social fabric, will be used to repair it. We shall therefore do well to examine the experiments that have been carried out in some countries, in education for development, as well as the attempts being made to demarginalize the school and to make of it a centre for activity and the mobilization of effort. This means

Recent and current trends in the development of education in the developing countries and specifically in Africa south of the Sahara

that we shall no longer use artificial terms such as child or adult education, or speak of functional literacy teaching for a category of society deemed uneducated and incapable, or of lifelong education, since formal and non-formal education will be closely linked together, as Amadou-Mahtar M'Bow, the Director-General of Unesco, has said. The school must be able to 'transmit the values of its environment and its time, it must become a centre where people acquire technical skills and also master the art of living' [4, p. 55].

Inter-African co-operation and international co-operation will reinforce national efforts. If such co-operation is to be effective, states must pool their resources and help one another by exchanging teachers and researchers and by making concerted use of the external bilateral or multilateral aid provided by bodies such as the Association of Partially or Entirely French-Speaking Universities (AUPELF—Association des Universités Partiellement ou Entièrement de Langue Française) and the Agency for Cultural and Technical Co-operation (AGECOOP—Agence de Coopération Culturelle et Technique). Through its Regional Education Office for Africa, Unesco is able to play a bigger part, not only in assisting states to frame interdependent educational policies, but also in the exchange of educational innovations, and above all in seeing that decisions are put into effect. The more clearly the situation is understood at the national and inter-African levels, the more obvious it will be that African states can indeed be genuine partners in a new international cultural order.

Whether it be within the framework of contracts for mutual support or within that of special co-operation agreements, the African states must retain the initiative in decision-making, and they must themselves determine the educational priorities which are to receive international aid.

These states are faced with complex problems: they have to provide education for as many people as possible, and at the same time train qualified persons who can work to bring about real development. They often have difficulty in deciding which of the many and urgent educational needs should take precedence, especially as all three major areas of concern are interdependent. The improvement of living and working conditions for parents and workers has repercussions on the equilibrium of the family and also on the quality of the school and out-of-school education provided for children, whose success and harmonious integration into the community will lighten the responsibilities that parents have to bear. National development will take place smoothly, without unnecessary agitation, because it will have the support of citizens who are anxious that it should do so. The pre-eminent role is that of the state, which has the greatest power, in educational matters, to give the people the democratic choice of the kind of society they wish and to take measures to bring it about. It can affect educators, their living conditions, their working facilities and the content of education for good or ill. It is desirable that priority should be given to the education of young people over that of adults, that the judicious use of national languages in education should be introduced without delay, and that care should be taken to see that foreign languages are studied as working tools, for reasons of technical expediency, and not to serve the purpose of neo-colonialists. Whatever the means at the disposal of African states, they should be better managed, and states should rely primarily on their own resources to fund vital sectors. They should lay down the terms according to which foreign aid will be accepted and used. Such aid should be merely a supplementary contribution, to be used in sectors designated on a sovereign basis at the national level. Foreign aid—even that granted within the framework of a contract of mutual support—should not be a determinant factor in budget forecasting for national development planning. In any case, the achievement of basic educational goals should not be contingent on foreign aid. The influence of industrialized countries which is inherent in such aid must not be allowed to jeopardize the African countries' chances for self-affirmation and self-expression, or to compromise the goal they have set for themselves—that they should have a real system of education for community development by the year 2000.

REFERENCES

1. *Programme national d'édification de l'école nouvelle en République populaire du Bénin.* Cotonou, Office National d'Édition, de Presse et d'Imprimerie, 1975.
2. PLIYA, Jean. Concept, Experiences and Alternative Orientations in Africa. *Final Report of the NEIDA Regional Seminar on Education and Productive Work, Porto Novo, 1–12 October 1979*, pp. 25–55. Dakar, Unesco Regional Office for Education in Africa, Network of Educational Innovation for Development in Africa Co-ordinating Unit, 1980. 201 pp.
3. *Final Report of the NEIDA Regional Seminar on Education and Productive Work, Porto Novo, 1–12 October 1979.* Dakar, Unesco Regional Office for Education in Africa, Network of Educational Innovation for Development in Africa Co-ordinating Unit, 1980. 201 pp.
4. HOUETO, Colette. Éducation et société. *Éducation béninoise*, Institut National pour la Formation et la Recherche en Éducation (INFRE) (Porto Novo), No. 4, 1978.

Reforms in education today and the challenge of tomorrow

Shapour Rassekh

The studies undertaken by international organizations on major problems of today and the investigations on world prospects carried out by various individuals or associations in the early 1980s show that the world cannot proceed as it has done hitherto and that there must be a profound change in structures, mentalities and behaviour if mankind is to survive.

The state of the world is changing, and we must expect constantly recurring crises; since the 1970s awareness of this fact has induced many officials and experts in education to suggest large-scale reforms.

In the 1950s and 1960s, efforts were mainly geared towards expanding educational systems, but since the 1970s more attention has been given to the fair and equitable distribution of educational services. Again, in the 1950s and 1960s one might almost say that too much trust was placed in labour planning and in balancing supply and demand by promoting technical and vocational education. In the 1970s doubts arose as to this conception of planning; the idea emerged that the actual operation of the labour market should be more carefully analysed, by making follow-up or other studies in order to improve the planning of human resources; and, lastly, the suitability of technical and vocational education was called into question, especially in the case of Third World countries where the traditional and informal sectors play a predominant part in the economy.

In the 1950s and 1960s, education and development were seen from an economist's point of view; it was thought that the system should above all be adapted to market needs. In recent years the social, political and cultural dimensions of education have been considered to be as important as its quantitative development.

The concern for profit and the bureaucratization of planning often led to the centralization of decision-making. In the past few years, however, increasing attention has been paid to decentralization, community participation and even learner participation in the educational process (through active education, individual learning, programmed education and so on).

Among other recent innovations lifelong and recurrent education have been given greater importance, particularly in developed countries; new techniques and the media are being increasingly used in education; and educational services have been provided in out-of-school institutions, such as industrial enterprises and workers' universities.

Reforms have been undertaken in all these new fields. Programmes to ensure that all pupils enjoy equal opportunities have been only partially successful in schools whose structure is based on inequality, as many radicals (Gentis, Bowles, Carnoy, Levin) have shown. There has been much progress, however, in the adaptation of educational content to advances in science and technology.[1] Some of the reforms designed to make education contribute to development (and among other aspects to economic growth) have had good results, while others have had practically no effect at all.[2]

Generally speaking, the reforms carried out in developed countries have been more realistic, given their 'backward-looking' nature, that is their emphasis on solving problems that have been observed already, whereas the forward-looking nature of the reforms undertaken in most developing countries, which have sought to make large-scale changes, may explain why their ambitious goals have not always been attained, except in cases where there were corresponding changes in the rest of society.

On the basis of such experiments, national and international experts have seen these new developments as indicating the direction in which education will move in the future (see Table 3).[3] If we examine most of their studies we have the general impression that they are a projection of existing trends into the future rather than proposals for a completely new or revised educational system. It is reasonable to think that the importance and gravity of the problems arising in an uncertain future are not adequately taken into consideration and that the solutions suggested are not commensurate with the problems to be solved.

There are of course other challenges that education will have to meet in the future. For instance, educational policies must give high priority to the problems of absolute poverty among rural peoples in certain parts of the world and to those of disadvantaged city-dwellers, who make up almost one-fifth of the world's population; reforms designed to strengthen the link between education and production will contribute to this end. Another aim of education should be to promote the wise exploitation of land in those parts of the world that are threatened by famine. Nor should it ignore the rapid deterioration of the environment, which calls for the training of experts in ecology and environmental conservation, as well as the dissemination of general information on the biosphere. And it must take into account the problems that are damaging the social climate to an

---

1. John Simmons (*Lessons from Educational Reforms*, Washington, D.C., World Bank, 1979) is sceptical about the good effects of such reforms on educational achievements, but the issue remains controversial.
2. Ibid.
3. See also the Bibliography at the end of this article.

Reforms in education today and the challenge of tomorrow

TABLE 3. Major educational problems and proposed solutions

Problems	Solutions
1. Considerable increase in the demand for education despite budgetary constraints	(a) In developed countries, development of post-compulsory education in order to meet the social aspirations of young people rather than manpower needs (b) In developing countries, priority for basic education and literacy teaching (c) Investigation of new ways of funding schools (by the family, community, employer) and new forms of education that will be less costly than at present, though of the same quality (d) More efficient management of education
2. Rapid progress in knowledge	(a) Constant updating of the scientific content of education (b) Continuous training of teachers (c) Introduction of an overall, interdisciplinary, problem-centred approach (d) Improvement of teaching methods and training of original, inventive researchers
3. Insufficiency of jobs available for the educated young people seeking them	(a) Measures to counter the tendency to attach too much importance to paper qualifications (b) On-the-job training, after basic education (c) Schemes for intermittent education, such as part-study, part-work arrangements (d) More emphasis on education for an occupation and integration of productive work into the school (e) Training for self-employment
4. Inequality of opportunity, not only in society and on the employment market, but also at school	(a) Awarding of scholarships for disadvantaged social groups (b) Abolition of élitist educational systems (c) Pre-school training and other 'compensatory' arrangements (d) Application of the principle of lifelong education and elimination of the rigid linkage of age and education level (e) Diversification of the educational system combined with strengthening of the counselling and guidance system
5. Bureaucratization, centralism and rigidity of structures and methods	(a) Decentralization and participation (b) Increased attention to non-formal and informal teaching methods and to improved co-ordination between formal and non-formal education (c) More frequent use of educational media (d) Transformation of the role of the teacher from that of an authoritarian, repressive figure to that of a counsellor or guide
6. Politicizing of education	(a) The school must not be politicized; young people must be better educated about politics (b) Promotion of international understanding and solidarity in education

TABLE 3 (*continued*)

Problems	Solutions
7. Changes in national strategies concerning aid to education	(a) Promotion of education with a view to self-sufficiency and endogenous development (b) Strengthening of the cultural identity of each people (c) Promotion of international co-operation in research and development, on a basis of equality
8. Increased importance of new technologies	(a) Wider use of new audio-visual media, their content being adapted to the needs of each group (b) Greater use of information service (computers) in education (c) Introduction of a technological revolution in education (d) Changes in the role of teachers and greater participation of learners in the educational process (e) Individualization of education, through the use of video, teaching machines, etc. (f) Greater emphasis on individual learning

increasing extent (for example violence, drug abuse, delinquency), which means that greater attention should be paid to the ethical and spiritual aspects of education. It it is to fulfil all of its tasks, education must undergo a radical transformation, so that it can carry out its increasingly important mission—the building of a better future.

BIBLIOGRAPHY

BENGTSSON, Jarl, et al. *Does Education Have a Future?* Vol. 10 of *Plan Europe 2000, Project 1: Educating Man for the 21st Century.* The Hague, Martinus Nijhoff, 1975.
COGGIN, Philip A. *Education for the Future: The Case for Radical Change.* Oxford/New York, Pergamon Press, 1979.
FAURE, Edgar, et al. *Learning to Be; The World of Education Today and Tomorrow.* Paris, Unesco, 1972.
FRAGNIÈRE, Gabriel (ed.). *Education Without Frontiers; A Study of the Future of Education from the European Cultural Foundation, 'Plan Europe 2000'.* London, Duckworth, 1976.
HUMMEL, Charles. *Education Today for the World of Tomorrow.* Paris/Geneva, Unesco/IBE, 1977. (Studies and Surveys in Comparative Education.)
HUSÉN, Torsten. *Education in the Year 2000.* Stockholm, National Board of Education, 1971. (Mimeo.)
——. *The School in Question: A Comparative Study of the School and its Future in Western Society.* Oxford/New York, Oxford University Press, 1979.
JENSEN, Stefan; TINBERGEN, Jan; HAKE, Barry. *Possible Futures of European Education; Numerical and Systems Forecasts.* The Hague, Martinus Nijhoff, 1972.
REUCHLIN, Maurice. *Individual Orientation in Education.* Vol. 2 of *Plan Europe 2000, Project 1: Educating Man for the 21st Century.* The Hague, Martinus Nijhoff, 1972.

Reforms in education today and the challenge of tomorrow

SCHWARTZ, Bertrand. *Permanent Education.* Vol. 3 of *Plan Europe 2000, Project 1: Educating Man for the 21st Century.* The Hague, Martinus Nijhoff, 1974.
SHANE, Harold Gray (ed.). *Curriculum Change Toward the 21st Century.* Washington, D.C., National Education Association, 1977.
TOFFLER, Alvin (ed.). *Learning for Tomorrow; The Role of the Future in Education.* New York, Random House, 1974.
VIAL, Jean. *L'école cap 2001.* Paris, Éditions ESF, 1977. (Science de l'éducation.)
WAGSCHAL, Peter H. (ed.). *Learning Tomorrows: Commentaries on the Future of Education.* New York, Praeger Publishers, 1979.

The evolution of the content of general pre-university education, 1970–80[1]

Education as teachers and pupils know it in daily experience is different from the education that we read about in official texts. The differences arise, paradoxically enough, either because teachers are poorly trained or because they have a lot of initiative, also because the pupils' receptivity and intelligence vary. Political, economic and social factors that upset plans or slow down their application are also responsible for such differences. However, analysis of the data obtained from official sources shows that in the years 1970 to 1980 the content of education changed in accordance with new overall trends. A distinction must be made, however, between the situation in the developed countries and that in the developing countries, whose circumstances are different.

THE DEVELOPED COUNTRIES

In the developed countries, the changes that are now taking place in the content of education can be described as attempts to overcome the effects of disturbances in the system resulting from previous structural reforms. The principal changes occurred in the 1950s, when it was decided that selective educational systems should be changed so that the need for both educational democratization and economic development could be more effectively met. The most striking effect of this decision was the introduction of a common core syllabus; its duration varied, but in general it was taken by pupils up to at least the age of 14 or 15, the period of compulsory attendance being extended to the age of 16 or 18. These

1. This study, which is reproduced in much abbreviated form, was prepared for the participants in the International Symposium on the Evolution of the Content of General Education Over the Next Two Decades (Paris, Unesco, 7–11 July 1980). It was based on the answers to a questionnaire sent to thirty institutes and other bodies engaged in educational research. The data were analysed by specialists in the fields investigated, who also used the reports drawn up by Unesco, in particular those prepared by the International Bureau of Education, as well as a number of studies and documents published by the Organization itself.

decisions had considerable repercussions on the content and methods of education. For example, the elementary school, which until then had been the only type of school attended by most people and which was responsible for educating both citizen and producer, became a school which prepared everybody for secondary education. Everything that was intended to prepare pupils for practical life was therefore gradually removed from the syllabus and the elementary school became a preparatory school providing a general education and covering a relatively short period. At the same time, the extension of the period of compulsory schooling meant that vocational training was not begun until the age of 16 and that the content and methods of education for all were brought into line with those of the traditional secondary schools, which were regarded as the best available and which until then had been reserved for a socially privileged minority. Material of a purely cultural nature was also introduced, replacing the practical and pre-vocational courses which had until then been provided for pupils of this age-group (12–16 year olds).

However, changes which took place in all the developed countries had unexpected effects. The technological and economic development of society, which owed much to the above-mentioned educational reforms, brought with it infrastructural changes. The increase in productivity resulting from the marked division of national and international labour and from automation gradually reduced the size of the primary sector of the economy. At first the secondary sector was strengthened by the creation of more unskilled industrial and commercial jobs; but these jobs were gradually abolished and the result was a dichotomy between highly skilled jobs on the one hand and unskilled jobs—or no jobs at all—on the other. This state of affairs has increased the effects, described above, of the provision of a general education for all. The training of highly qualified personnel is consistent with the trend we have mentioned, but the low level of qualifications for unskilled jobs means that a large number of young people are without qualifications—those who, even if they are able to get the best out of the new content of education, very often fail to turn it to advantage for the purposes of finding a job.

Consequently, governments have sought to modify the educational system itself, in the hope of remedying these unexpected effects. The more or less systematic measures that have been taken can be divided into four categories.

Reaction against excessive formalism

Steps are being taken to make general education more practical and relevant to modern life, as a reaction to the excessive formalism which successive reforms of the various subjects had brought about. The syllabuses and teaching methods used in the basic subjects had been modelled on those of the secondary school, and this hastened the trend towards irrelevance and formalism. It meant that the less gifted pupils—those whose cultural background had given them little inclination to acquire knowledge for its own sake—were apt to opt out, and it led to a growing loss of interest in education among young people. For this reason experiments are now being undertaken that may be regarded as a step towards the rehabilitation of the basic skills of reading, writing and arithmetic. For the same reason changes are being made, often extensively, in natural and social science syllabuses in order to take greater account of modern technological and economic conditions; the media are being more systematically used; and educational content is being made more realistic to facilitate the development of interdisciplinarity. Concern for the environment has a similar origin: local conditions are being studied as systems requiring the collaboration of different disciplines which are brought to bear on natural and human conservation projects.

The reinstatement of work as a part of education

Another important measure is the reinstatement of work as a subject of study and as an integral practical aspect of general education. It is being reintroduced more or less systematically, for more or less clearly stated reasons. In countries with planned economies, for example, the introduction of pupils to the world of work is an important part of general education. Arrangements are made for pupils to visit places of production at an early stage, and technology is studied. Other countries make such arrangements only for their more practically minded pupils, but teach everyone the theoretical aspects of technology. Similarly, vocational information is being made available to all pupils. Education for leisure, which is related to artistic activities, is another aspect of the reintroduction of manual work into the curriculum, but little has been done as yet in this type of education.

Preparation for lifelong education

In a world dominated by mass media and the rapid advance of knowledge, young people cannot be educated once and for all at school. Pupils must therefore 'learn how to learn'; they must be prepared for lifelong education, whether the studies they undertake are of practical use or not, and they must be educated for both individual and group leisure. Therefore new methods are being worked out: experiments are being made in independent work for both individuals and groups; pupils are being taught how to use reference material; and the 'credit' system of examinations is being introduced, so that pupils can make full use of lifelong education. Here too, there universal trends have come up against the

*The evolution of the content
of general pre-university education, 1970–80*

didactic and dogmatic traditions of the formal school. As a result, some countries rely on out-of-school activities for this aspect of education, pupils being given the opportunity to develop the desired skills by joining various kinds of clubs.

Making more room for individual differences

A fourth area of reform concerns both the structures and the content of education: the introduction of optional as well as common core subjects for 11 to 16 year olds. The purpose of these optional subjects is as much to encourage pupils to make independent decisions as it is to take account of the diversity of school populations brought together by previous reforms. This is an attempt to return to the diversification of education without the loss of the social benefits of unified school systems. The optional subjects are mainly technology, handicrafts, the sciences and the arts.

THE DEVELOPING COUNTRIES

At first sight, it may seem that the content of education in the developing countries is being changed for the same reasons—because of the desire to make education more relevant to real life (the study of local conditions, the environment, etc.) and to develop the teaching of scientific subjects. There is also the same desire to cater for individual needs and to make pupils self-reliant. But while the words are the same, they do not always mean the same thing. While similar demographic and economic conditions give rise everywhere to comparable scholastic situations, the nature of political regimes cannot but affect the effort to develop educational systems. Generally speaking, in the developing countries the coexistence of two types of education is still the rule: first, a system of primary and secondary education reserved for a minority, which is comparable to the systems prevailing in the developed countries and which from afar conforms to changes in those systems; and second, an elementary school system with major problems of enrolment capacity and staff shortages, particularly in rural areas.

In secondary schools, the content and methods of the former colonial system are often perpetuated, even when the ex-colonizing countries themselves have abandoned them or are in the process of doing so. Whenever an innovation is introduced, it follows the same trends as in the developed countries, with a few years' time-lag. These innovations include the modernization of the teaching of mathematics, the introduction of linguistics into language teaching, the promotion of independent study and the use of reference works. But neither the educational system nor its content attains its object, and the only effect the system has had is to produce young people with diplomas, but no skills that can be used in an employment market which is still rural or heavily dependent on manual skills. Another consequence has been a tangible and often dramatic fall in standards, particularly in language proficiency, in cases where schools continue to teach the language of the former colonizer as the basic language of education.

At the elementary level, the major problem is still how to provide literacy teaching for children and adults. The relative failure of previous efforts, which has been due either to demographic problems (too many pupils, too few teachers, too little money) or to the pupils' lack of interest in an abstract type of education which they consider to be useless, has led to experiments in functional literacy teaching, as it is called, in Asia, Africa and Latin America. This is another example of the awareness that local needs, particularly those of rural development, should be taken into account. Literacy teaching is, first and foremost, a matter of meeting technological and practical needs; reading and writing are but a means to that end. Experiments carried out in Asia and in Latin America have shown that this is the path to genuine development. Such experiments, however, are still rare, and they have come up against that spontaneous sociological movement which impels the inhabitants of the countryside to migrate to the towns, where they swell the ranks of the illiterate and the unemployed.

The most passionate desire of the developing countries in the past decades, however, has been to reclaim their indigenous culture, and therefore their local language. Most of these countries still use imported foreign languages, such as those of the former colonial powers, in their educational systems. This is one of the major factors that impedes the work of democratic literacy teaching. The problem, therefore, is to teach people not only how to write but how to write in the language or languages of their own country; hence the widespread effort to transcribe oral languages and sometimes also to select a dominant local language which is acceptable to all—the more difficult task of the two. It would seem that bilingualism or even trilingualism (one language for communication and two local languages) will be common in the future.

As regards secondary education, those countries which have cut themselves off most decisively from the former colonial regime have undertaken a radical change of a similar nature: they are taking measures to promote the national language and to introduce scientific and technological subjects that serve the needs of economic development and help to consolidate national independence. By so doing, these countries will probably succeed in avoiding the difficulties faced by some developing countries, where the abstract nature of the subjects taught and their irrelevance to real life accompanied by a de facto democratization resulting from urbanization, has given rise to even more serious problems then those facing the developed countries at the present time. An education of a quite original nature, which seems to be progressing in a promising manner and from which the developed countries themselves could benefit, is thus coming into being.

INTERDISCIPLINARY EDUCATION: A WORLD-WIDE TREND

While we have distinguished between the developed and the developing countries in order to indicate more clearly what the specific concerns of the two groups are, a number of trends, deriving from the general evolution of educational principles and methods, are common to both. The growth of interdisciplinary studies is one of these trends. The organization of schools has long been based on the compartmentalization of the subjects taught; each has its own timetable, syllabuses and teachers, and there is no communication between them. Pupils think of knowledge they have to acquire as a collection of juxtaposed but separate components, the cleavage between disciplines being particularly evident at the secondary school level. It is obvious, however, that all these components are interconnected in one way or another, in a system of relations or interactions, just as they are in the real world: physics or technology cannot be studied without mathematics; history without geography; zoology without ecology and so on. One of the principal aims at present is to give pupils an overall view of the way in which subjects intermesh and interact, to take account of this fact in teaching, and to refashion a unity in diversity, so as to give young people a clearer perception through an understanding of the relations and interactions of different disciplines. Obviously this aim, which runs counter to traditional ideas, calls for a precise definition of objectives at each stage, the consequent adaptation of syllabuses, and the provision of suitable training for teachers, who must refuse to be locked up within the walls of their own disciplines, and begin to build bridges and establish links with subjects taught by other teachers. The formation of educational teams in schools is also required to co-ordinate the work of teaching in order to attain these aims. The experiments that have been carried out and the results achieved augur well for this new path in the world of education.

2
Factors likely to influence the development of education during the next twenty years

The trends analysed in the first chapter are the result of the internal development of education, and sometimes they are quite good indicators of some of the changes which may affect it in the future, such as greater flexibility in school attendance with regard to both age of entry and number of days per year of attendance; a better balance, in the developing countries, between primary education, on the one hand, and secondary and higher education, on the other; and harmonization of the various educational requirements, whether traditional or pragmatic, of the need for both equality and quality, and of the action of the various groups involved in the day-to-day operation of the school (Torsten Husén).

While recognizing the importance of these factors in the internal development of education, we must also note that the development of education is in general the result of complex interactions with different sectors of society—with economics, politics and social or cultural life. If education is examined in its social context, it will be seen to centre round four main ideas: education as an institution; education as a series of educational measures (educational process); education as a body of knowledge and behaviour (content); and finally education as the result or product of educational measures (criteria of ability to meet the needs of society). It is impossible to analyse the future of education in all its dimensions unless we also take into account factors which influence it, but which lie outside the direct control of those responsible for education.

It is probable that the role of education will become more complex in the future, because some of the problems of contemporary society are of increasingly universal significance: the maintenance of peace; disarmament and international security; the many different aspects of social, economic and cultural development (the elimination of poverty and of the disparities between rich and poor, industrialization, etc.); the control of scientific and technological progress; and the protection of the environment. Energy, unemployment, the struggle to overcome famine and desertification are other problems which education will need to deal with more directly than it does now. Education must accordingly train research workers who will specialize in these questions and staff able to put into effect the solutions

Factors likely to influence the development of education during the next twenty years

adopted; it must transmit the necessary knowledge and skills, and ensure that all those concerned with such problems are aware of the facts and develop their sense of responsibility; and finally it must in general encourage the development of attitudes likely to promote active participation by all.[1]

Certain forecasts, mainly of an academic nature, have been made as to which factors or trends are likely to have an influence on education, though without entering into details or establishing links between such factors and actual changes.[2] We shall endeavour to enumerate the main factors which seem likely to influence education in the future, although we do not claim to have covered them all.

DEMOGRAPHY

Demographic changes would appear to be the most important factor influencing the development of education. According to the middle variant of the United Nations estimates (1980) the world population will increase by about 40 per cent between 1980 and the year 2000, rising from 4.4 to 6.2 thousand million. This growth will be very unevenly distributed among the major regions of the world, ranging from 5.8 per cent in Europe to 81.5 per cent in Africa. The total population of the developing countries will increase by almost a half. The growth in population will give rise to an increase in the school-age population which will be, on average, of the order of 1.9 per cent in the developed countries and 40.1 per cent in the developing countries, i.e. twenty times greater than in the developed countries. The rate of increase will be even greater in the case of Africa—84.6 per cent.

The rapid rise in the number of school-age children will bring with it a

---

1. Mr Prem Kirpal, a former Chairman of the Executive Board of Unesco, in a speech given during a United Nations training programme in 1980, classified the factors which will affect the future of education as follows: three developmental 'explosions' (of population, knowledge and aspirations); three critical problems (war and peace, man and the environment, culture and technology); three deep-rooted conflicts (between man's soul and the external world, between science and the world of the spirit, between individual liberty and social organization); and, finally, three disparities (between the developing countries and the developed countries, between knowledge and wisdom, and between power and love). *Towards an Education for the 21st Century; The Global Prospects*, New Delhi, 1980.
2. McHale identified some societal trends which seemed to him likely to have a substantial impact on education now and in the future. These trends include: (a) a slowing down of population growth, alleviating the problem of numbers; (b) an ageing society as people live longer and population growth dwindles; (c) a movement from an attitude of material growth to human growth as the economy continues towards lean times; (d) a concern for quality beyond economic utility, which denies that more is necessarily better; (e) a shift in human values, aspirations, and expectations which places human beings and the physical environment above material goods, and reflects changes in life-styles and models of legitimacy. *Education: A Time for Decisions; Selections from the Second Annual Conference of the Education Section of the World Future Society*, p. 52, Washington, D.C., World Future Society, 1980.

*Factors likely to influence the development
of education during the next twenty years*

considerable increase in enrolments, even if the enrolment ratio remains unchanged—an increase of almost half, for example, in the case of primary education. No country, however, expects these ratios, whose projected future trends are shown in Table 4, to continue unchanged or to fall. The combination of the projections of the increase in the school-age population and of enrolment ratios would mean a much greater increase in enrolments. In the case of primary education, an enrolment ratio of 100 per cent in the year 2000 would result in a increase of 63 per cent in the numbers enrolled. In order to reach a more realistic ratio, estimated by Unesco as 96 per cent by the year 2000, the developing countries would have to increase their enrolments by 55 per cent between 1980 and the year 2000. According to this hypothesis, as is shown in Table 1 (see page 15) enrolments at the primary school level would rise from 291.9 million pupils in 1980 to 455.4 million. Such a rise may seem difficult to imagine, but we shall see

TABLE 4. Projections of enrolment ratios by level of education and by age-group (percentages)

Region	Year	Adjusted gross enrolment ratios[1] First level	Second level	Third level	Enrolment ratios by age-groups 6–11 years	12–17 years	18–23 years
Industrialized countries	1980	107	78	30.0	93	83	32.2
	1990	106	85	34.2	93	91	36.4
	2000	105	87	37.6	93	90	39.8
Developing countries[2]	1980	86	31	7.4	68	39	11.2
	1990	92	42	9.9	75	46	14.6
	2000	96	49	11.8	79	51	17.3
Africa[3]	1980	78	21	3.2	63	37	7.9
	1990	88	35	5.1	74	48	12.0
	2000	93	43	6.4	80	54	15.1
Latin America and the Caribbean	1980	104	44	14.3	81	64	22.2
	1990	107	59	21.0	86	73	29.5
	2000	109	67	25.9	89	77	35.2
South Asia	1980	83	31	6.7	66	32	9.1
	1990	89	40	8.5	72	38	11.3
	2000	93	47	10.1	77	42	13.4
Least developed countries	1980	57	15	1.7	43	24	3.3
	1990	71	23	3.1	55	32	5.7
	2000	82	32	4.4	63	40	8.1

1. The adjusted gross ratios are calculated according to the relationship of the total number of enrolments at a given level, independently of the age of those enrolled, to the volume of the population which should be enrolled at that level. These ratios may be interpreted as an indication of the potential 'capacity' for enrolment, in the absence of repetition and late entries.
2. Not including China, the Democratic People's Republic of Korea or Namibia.
3. Not including Namibia.

Source: Unesco, *Trends and Projections of Enrolment by Level of Education and by Age, 1960-2000*, p. 35, Paris, Unesco, 1983. (Current Studies and Research in Statistics.) (Unesco doc. CSR-E-46.)

Factors likely to influence the development of education during the next twenty years

that it is quite within the bounds of possibility if we remember that, for example, the number increased by 163.5 million (139.3 per cent) between 1960 and 1980. On the other hand, the results of extrapolation of the trends in enrolments in secondary and higher education seem unrealistic.[1]

In the industrialized countries, enrolments at the primary school level may increase by barely 8 million (i.e. 6 per cent) between 1980 and the year 2000. In secondary education also, enrolments will rise very slowly, increasing by only 6 million by the year 2000. The increase in the number of students in higher education will probably also be quite small in these countries: an additional 1.4 million during the 1980s, and 3.8 million during the 1990s. The projections indicate that total enrolments throughout the world at the three educational levels will increase by about 51 per cent between 1980 and the year 2000, rising in absolute terms from 641.1 million to 967.7 million (excluding China). The major part of this increase of 326.6 million will be in the developing countries (where enrolments will rise from 405.3 million to 712.3 million) whereas in the developed countries the increase will be moderate (from 235.7 million to 255.4 million).

This quantitative increase is only one of the signs of the influence which the demographic factor will have on education in the future. There will undoubtedly be others. The structure of the population, for example, will determine the size of future demands for educational services. In the industrialized countries the decline in the birth rate has brought about a change in the proportion of the population which is of school age: in 1980 this was of the order of 40 per cent (the group aged 0–24 years), but it will be only 36 per cent in the year 2000. On the other hand, the adult population, among which there is considerable demand for out-of-school education, will increase. Likewise, the increase in life expectancy and the

---

1. If past trends were to continue in the developing countries the numbers enrolled in secondary education would rise from 97 million in 1980 to 217 million in the year 2000, i.e. an increase of about 120 million or 124 per cent. The increase would be of the order of 284 per cent for Africa, 115 per cent for Latin America and 99 per cent for South Asia. Despite such a sizeable increase, the projected enrolment ratio of 49 per cent in secondary education in the year 2000 would be less than the 55 per cent attained by the industrialized countries in 1960. In addition, the disparities in the enrolment ratios at this level among the developing countries themselves would continue to be considerable: 67 per cent in Latin America, as against 47 per cent in South Asia, 43 per cent in Africa and 32 per cent in the thirty least developed countries.

The greatest relative increase in enrolments in the developing countries would occur in higher education, if the trends were to be maintained. On this basis, between 1980 and the year 2000 the number of students would increase from 3.7 million (i.e. 274 per cent) in Africa, by 8.6 million (i.e. 166 per cent) in Latin America and by 11.1 million (i.e. 113 per cent) in South Asia. Taking into account such factors as the high unit costs of higher education, the widening of the gap in many countries between essential needs and the resources available for education, the efforts made to give priority to providing basic education for all and the increase in unemployment rates among graduates, there is good reason to wonder whether the growth rate of higher education in the developing countries could in fact continue in line with past trends.

general ageing of the population could lead to a considerable increase in the provision of educational services for elderly people.

As regards the developing countries, the proportion of their population which was of school age in 1980 was 60 per cent (in Africa 64 per cent) and will be only 53 per cent in the year 2000 (in Africa 62 per cent). An age structure of this kind means that a relatively small adult working population would need to generate an increasingly large income in order to provide subsistence for a large population of young people and finance an educational system which would be constantly expanding.

Some experts are trying to make forecasts of school enrolments that take into account the combined effects of demographic, economic and technological factors which are likely to influence the socio-vocational structure of the population in the future. Thus, Asok Mitra anticipates that during the next twenty years 60 per cent of the population of the Indian sub-continent will live in a technologically simple environment, similar to that which now exists in agriculture and rural industry. Only 35 per cent of the population will need to use intermediate technology, which requires nine to eleven years of general or technical education; while activities in the field of advanced technology, research or the upper levels of administration will involve no more then 2–5 per cent of the population. This writer assumes that education beyond the age of 14 would have to be highly selective and conditioned by the needs of technology or of the development of society.

Population drift from the countryside to the cities is another factor to be taken into account. By the end of this century, 80–90 per cent of the population of the industrialized countries, which are already highly urbanized, will live in the cities, but the developing countries will probably be even more affected by this trend. It has been estimated, for example, that by 1990 about 70 per cent of the population of Latin America will be living in urban areas. We shall witness the appearance of huge 'megalopolises' inhabited by tens of millions of people. Rapid urbanization in the developing countries often gives rise to over-populated shanty towns and leads to environmental pollution, the distortion of the labour market, social and cultural dislocation and an insufficiency of essential services such as schools. However, despite this move to the cities, in many developing countries the rural population is continuing to increase in absolute terms. Such trends are obviously important for the future of education, particularly with regard to the geographical distribution of educational facilities.

THE ECONOMY

Thanks to the progress made in educational economics and planning during the last two decades, we now understand much better how education and the economy interact and how the development of one is conditioned by the other. It is now generally accepted that the prospects for the development of education have been affected by the recession in the world economy and that adjustments will therefore need to be made in educational planning so as to meet the new situation. The recession has been accompanied by a worsening of the problem of unemployment, by high inflation and by the appearance of severe financial constraints (including constraints on educational expenditure). The situation seems likely to become even worse, especially in the developing countries. The Organisation for Economic Co-operation and Development's (OECD) report *Facing the Future* predicts that by the year 2000 only about 12 per cent of the world population, people with a per capita income of $2,500 and above (at 1976 values), will escape underdevelopment, while the group of low-income countries (per capita $250) will contain 2,000 million people, so that 28 per cent of the world population will be living in conditions of absolute poverty in the year 2000 [1, pp. 202, 230]. The economic constraints experienced by the developing countries are likely to worsen, because of the deficit in their energy balance sheet, which will be almost three and a half times larger than in 1975—except for the Oil Producing and Exporting Countries (OPEC)—due to food shortages. The same report predicts that the shortfall in cereals will increase from 40 million tonnes (10 per cent of consumption) in 1977–78 to 140 million tonnes (18 per cent of consumption) [1, pp. 237, 246]; because of the impossibility of reorganizing traditional agriculture, on which more than three-quarters of the population will directly or indirectly depend. Industrialization, on which many developing countries have pinned their hopes, will enable industrial production to increase from 7.1 to 7.4 per cent, though the same OECD report expresses the fear 'that the present direction of world industrialization is tending towards a wastage of both capital and labour' [1, p. 259]. The Director-General of Unesco has described the existing situation in the developing countries in the following terms:

In the Third World, things appear differently. There, progress and prosperity are but isolated islands in an ocean of want, swept by famine and epidemic, by drought and by flood. There, the problems of the quality of life are encountered above all in terms of survival. After immediate relief, the most urgent priorities are the acquisition of scientific and technological resources and the provision of education and training by which peoples will gain control of progress so that it serves their most essential needs [2, p. 2].

Such prospects are far from favourable for education, both from the point of view of the social and economic demand for education and training and also from the point of view of the resources which could be assigned to them.

In the developed countries, the continued growth of the service sector, which is often accompanied by a proportionate reduction in industrial manpower, should continue. It is not yet clear if this trend will continue until the end of the century but, at least in the immediate future, it would be wise in any event to prepare most pupils and students for employment in this sector.

However, the problem of providing employment will probably continue for some years to be a source of anxiety for most governments. In the present situation of recession common to most market economies, insufficient new jobs are being created, particularly for well-qualified young people. Thus, as we have seen, the increase in youth unemployment has become a major problem which, it would seem, cannot be solved, and still less avoided, by either expanding vocational training or 'vocationalizing' general education.

However, unemployment and underemployment cannot be attributed to the recession alone. Technological progress has reduced the need for labour in all the subsectors of the economy, especially in agriculture and industry, thereby tending to reduce the status of certain jobs, while at the same time raising the level of qualifications required for others. Even if there is an upturn in economic activity, structural unemployment seems unlikely to be reduced through an increase in the number of jobs, as the rate at which jobs are created is generally lower than the rate of economic growth.[1] Educational systems will therefore need to be able to meet rapidly these new needs in the labour field, provide new types of training, and prepare men and women to adapt to a labour market in a constant state of change.

Education will also need sufficient resources to be able to cope with another change which will affect the labour market—the expansion in the demand for jobs, which promises to be greater than ever in the next two decades. According to International Labour Organisation (ILO) figures, the working population of the world will reach 2,500 million people by the end of the century, i.e. 900 million more than in 1975. At present 450 million people are reckoned to be unemployed or underemployed. ILO estimates that to end unemployment would require the creation by the year 2000 of 1,000 million jobs, of which 880 million would need to be in the developing countries. It is mainly young people, more highly educated than in the past, who will be affected by the problem. The Director-General of Unesco has spoken on this subject in the following terms:

Certain problems which are generally acknowledged to be particularly serious lay special responsibilities upon education. Prominent among these is unemployment, which is affecting more and more young people. May I express my deep concern

---

1. Some writers predict that the millions of underemployed (as distinct from the unemployed) will have somehow to create their own demand for their own services. See for example G. Psacharopoulos, 'Towards an Atomistic Model of Education', *Prospects—Quarterly Review of Education* (Paris, Unesco), Vol. X, No. 4, 1980, pp. 456–61.

at the despair which has come to affect increasing numbers of young people throughout the world. If this situation should continue unchecked, if unemployment should be the fate of more and more young people in the prime of life, there is every reason to fear that we shall see exceptionally serious upheavals, tensions incomparably greater than those that we are at present striving more or less successfully to hold in check, and, to speak plainly, a new form of violence likely to have a severe impact on many societies [3, pp. 4–5].

It would seem that, quite apart from the extent to which the market will be able to absorb the available labour, contact between education and the world of work is likely to become even closer. That presupposes, first of all, a strengthening of the trend, which emerged in the 1970s, towards expecting the school to instil into its pupils an appreciation of all forms of human creative work, to eliminate verbalism and to reduce the gap between the acquisition of knowledge and its application. However, the main feature of this closer contact with the world of work during the next twenty years may well be that education is more definitely slanted towards employment. This means not only introducing technical and vocational subjects into general education and providing better vocational guidance for school leavers, but also redirecting educational policies so as to achieve the rapid development of vocational education as a preparation for exercising a trade or profession, which could give it greater relative weight in existing educational structures.

As far as the developed countries are concerned, this statement reflects the series of measures, taken towards the end of the 1970s in order to promote vocational and technical training, which will soon begin to bear fruit. In the case of the developing countries, since it is likely that unemployment will become even worse, it may become a major social, economic and educational imperative to give priority to technical and vocational education. The General Conference of Unesco at its eighteenth session stressed the fact that 'given disparities that may exist between formal education, whether secondary or tertiary, and the employment and career opportunities available, the highest priority should be given to technical and vocational education which prepares young people to exercise occupations...' [4, Paragraph 24]. This is confirmed by experts who have emphasized the probable increase in the role of technical and vocational education (M. Adiseshiah, A. Mitra and others).

In conclusion, therefore, it would seem that education can no longer be planned on the assumption that there will be rapid economic growth and an abundance of cheap resources. Through its content, education might be required to modify the consumer mentality in the developed countries and replace it by a more realistic view—an awareness that the high costs of production require more rational consumption, reasonably limited, economical in the use of resources, and based both on ecological principles and on solidarity with the countries producing raw materials. Education cannot be held responsible for unemployment, which is likely to become

Factors likely to influence the development of education during the next twenty years

even more widespread, but neither can it ignore the problem, and it will have to introduce schoolchildren to various kinds of productive work, stimulate the spirit of initiative which can create jobs in the non-formal sector, and help young people adapt more easily to structural changes in employment.

THE PROGRESS OF SCIENCE AND TECHNOLOGY

The increasing part played by science and technology in the daily life of the individual and of society makes it necessary for people not only to have a scientific understanding of the universe but also to be introduced to the use of techniques which are constantly being improved. It is the duty of education to enable people to comprehend the world and to master the ways of transforming it which are made both necessary and possible by science and technology. The final quarter of the twentieth century seems to mark the dawn of a new technological era characterized by the extension of the uses of nuclear energy, electronics, telecommunications, computer technology, automation and cybernetics, all of which have or will have an effect on education. As this question is dealt with in a separate chapter, we shall look at only one aspect of the problem.

Because of the scale and speed of scientific and technological advance, together with the social changes and the changing economic situation which are profoundly altering the conditions of employment, further training and in-service training for new responsibilities or new careers are among the major tasks of education. As was stated in the final report of the first meeting of the International Panel on the Future Development of Education, 'a really innovatory educational process should prepare children and young people for change and enable them to cope more effectively with their environment' [5, p. 8].[1]

Socio-professional mobility will be accentuated during the next two decades by the robotization of certain branches of industry. Thus, it has been forecast that at General Motors, in ten years' time, robots will have replaced people in 60,000 jobs, and at Renault they will be doing the work in 12 jobs out of every 100. Education will clearly be affected by this situation. First and foremost, it will have to face up to the restructuring of

---

1. It is interesting to note that the capacity, both of the individual and of society, to adapt to the process of change was placed second among the global needs (after the need for peace and international harmony and understanding) in the IBE questionnaire which Member States answered during the preparation of the 38th International Conference on Education. They were followed by the reduction of socio-economic inequalities, economic development, the development of the full potential of the individual, etc. (International Conference on Education, 38th Session, Geneva, 1981. *Development of Education in the Future in the Light of Global Needs and World Problems*, p. 3, Geneva, Unesco/IBE, 1981. (Unesco doc. ED/IBE/CONFINTED/38/3.))

the labour market in the future, which will give greater priority to graduates. It will also have to provide initial and further training for the existing workforce. At the present time, the introduction of a robot at Renault requires three men to be trained for 670 hours; in 1980, 240,000 hours of training on the use of automation were provided [6, p. 71]. In some cases, initial and further training may become an essential and permanent part of work. An engineer at IBM spends 10–25 per cent of his working time attending courses; during the first five years of service, training occupies thirty-three weeks a year [7, p. 244].

The progress of science and technology can therefore be expected to accentuate the trend towards the expansion of lifelong education. Furthermore, particularly in the developing countries, it will impose additional tasks on education because of the need to create or strengthen scientific potential—the establishment of a social climate favourable to the development of science and technology and to their application, the popularization of scientific knowledge, the improvement of science teaching at all levels, the encouragement of creativity among learners and the training of a sufficient number of research workers and technicians (see Chapter 4).

THE ENVIRONMENT

Unlike the societies which have preceded it, modern industrial society has brought about profound and rapid changes in the physical environment as a result of the irrational exploitation of natural resources, which is linked to systems of production and forms of consumption based on the creation of artificial needs, and also as a result of the uncontrolled use of pollutant technologies. This situation, which affects all countries whatever their level of development, has raised further questions about the philosophical and ethical foundations of the relations between man and nature. New attitudes have arisen towards the strategies of economic development, which are increasingly criticized when they threaten the natural environment.

This new ecological ethic is of fundamental importance for education. It seems certain that in the future ecological factors will receive much greater attention and will have to be given a central role in the educational process, so that everyone may come to understand the complexity of the biosphere and be ready to support action for its protection and rational management. With these ends in view, education might encourage a general awareness of the dangers to which the environment is subject, of their gravity, their causes, their consequences and of the measures needed to deal with them. Much more than in the past, education is expected to be able to provide scientific knowledge on environmental problems and to encourage attitudes of appreciation of and respect for the natural environment, especially among those who are responsible for taking decisions which might affect it (administrators, engineers, scientists, architects, members of health services). By taking account of ecological conditions and ethical principles, education could also help to promote the necessary changes in the patterns of consumption. In connection with this problem, attention should also be drawn to the growth of artificial environments, particularly in large cities. With their artificial lighting and air conditioning, their vertical and horizontal means of transport (lifts, escalators, moving walkways, underground railways, etc.), these micro-environments consume large quantities of energy and resources and contribute to the imbalances in the environment. This new type of environment and the secondary effects of urbanization—totally unplanned urban growth, traffic jams, overpopulation, all kinds of pollution—affect the behaviour and values of the people living there. Such changes can hardly fail to exert an effect on the school, the conditions of whose operation will also change in line with the growth of urbanization.

SOCIAL AND CULTURAL FACTORS

Closely linked with the demographic, economic, technological and ecological factors is a whole range of socio-cultural factors which are peculiar to each society. They interact profoundly with education; they are subject to its influence, but education also serves to reproduce and perpetuate them. Examples of such factors are people's views of the world, systems of values, religious beliefs and types of behaviour.

There is unfortunately no doubt that millions of human beings will continue to live in atrocious material conditions. According to the estimates given above, by the year 2000 the number of those who will be living in absolute poverty (i.e. with an income below $300 a year) will amount to about 30 per cent of the world's population. Poverty is not only an economic reality; it is a social fact which is often characterized by malnutrition, physical deficiencies, shortened life expectancy, fear and despair. Here, too, in the years to come, education must meet the particular needs of those who are the victims of such misfortunes.

The social dynamic of the process of democratization will certainly be maintained and may even accelerate. In some countries, the advance towards equal rights for underprivileged groups—women in particular—will perhaps slow down, but there is every reason to believe that in the long term the advance towards equal opportunities will continue. In such circumstances, educational services will have to respond to new social pressures for equality of access and of opportunities of success (see Chapter 3).

Another important factor is an increasingly marked awareness and assertion of the cultural identity of ethnic, linguistic and religious groups and sometimes even of nations, which are demanding respect for their cultures, their ways of life, the expression of everything which marks their identity and, in many cases, greater freedom of action or even administrative autonomy. Educational structures will have to show a far greater capacity to adapt to the different demands of these groups, while at the same time seeking to ensure equal opportunities and equal chances for all. This tendency, which has already had some influence on the content of education in many countries, has given new relevance to the teaching of people in their mother tongue. As long as this does not prejudice the use of the major languages of communication or the importance of universal values, it may considerably strengthen the cultural component of education and improve its quality and effectiveness.

At the present time leisure is an important aspect of life in the developed countries and, if present trends continue, its role will probably be even greater in the future. The working week will be considerably reduced, thanks to increases in productivity and technological advances, holidays will be longer and people will retire earlier, although they may remain active longer. Perhaps leisure, recreational activities and values associated with them will finally come to occupy in man's life the place which is at present occupied by work and the work ethic. If these forecasts are borne out the increase in leisure time will have far-reaching repercussions on education.

POLITICAL FACTORS

The development of education in the future will be affected, as it has been hitherto, by many political factors whose influence will be all the more varied because they themselves are often the result of very different economic and social forces which act differently in different societies. Thus, *Facing the Future* [1] takes the view that on the socio-political level the countries with market economies are evolving towards societies which might be characterized by a double fragmentation, one with a social dimension and the other concerning people's participation in political life.

These fragmentations could take the following forms. On the one hand, we should probably see the continuation of the tendencies and cleavages of the post-war period, marked by the search for equality by some and the defence of their advantages by others, which would result in constant conflicts over the distribution of the national income and lead to greater state intervention and to the growth of bureaucracy. On the other hand, changes in values would be reflected in the development, within the 'middle majority' or on its periphery, of a number of minority groups whose need for liberation and the establishment of roots are a response to demands for decentralization and participation [1, p. 109].

As far as the first of these possibilities is concerned, the response of education will probably depend on changes in the relationships between different forces within society. The report of the first meeting of the OECD

Factors likely to influence the development of education during the next twenty years

Committee for Education (1978) clearly showed that divergences exist in the definition both of educational policies and of the nature of the relationships between education and employment. The Trade Union Advisory Committee, for example, emphasizes that the educational system should not be directed towards training élites and that the main aim of all countries should be to guarantee every young person a job, a place in a vocational training centre or the opportunity to continue studying full-time. On the other hand, the Business and Industry Advisory Committee, which reflects the viewpoints of the employers' federations, calls into question the feasibility and practicability of attempting to provide indefinable and unrestricted social guarantees of education, training or work for all young people. The view has been openly expressed that a far greater number of graduates, in particular those who possess qualifications of too general a nature, will have to be prepared to limit their vocational ambitions. Reservations have also been expressed concerning the possibility of alternating education and work in the second level of secondary education and concerning society's obligation to enable all young people to obtain full technical and vocational qualifications, or to provide education above and beyond compulsory schooling [8, pp. 30–8].

As far as the second fragmentation is concerned, several other studies forecast the further growth of the tendency towards increased participation by local people in the decisions which affect them, particularly in the educational field. It is certain that such participation could become an important factor in the political control of education; besides, education could make a considerable contribution to the political maturity of the population and to the development of its capacity for active and responsible participation in public life.

In publications dealing with the future, there are dozens of forecasts of a political nature which, in specific circumstances, might become factors affecting education. *Facing the Future* predicts, for example, that 'major conflicts are brewing in the advanced industrial societies, concerning the stake that the share of public expenditure in national income constitutes for the different social and economic groups' [1, p. 178] and that there will be difficulties affecting the operation of political institutions (poor co-ordination of governmental activities, insufficient control of the bureaucracy, ineffectiveness of parliaments, conflicts resulting from demands for decentralization and participation, etc.) [1, p. 189]. Because of the large number of forecasts of this kind and the uncertain nature of their influence on education, we shall not attempt to deal more fully with this phenomenon.

In the developing countries, there are certain specific factors in addition to the political factors which have just been mentioned. In such countries education generally depends to a far greater extent on a reasonably strong political commitment and on stable institutions. In some countries, political instability has given rise to violence and the terrorism of totalitarian authority, whose impact on education is even more disastrous than social imbalances. If the number of people who live in conditions of absolute poverty increases and if international conditions for the socio-economic development of the developing countries do not improve, we can be sure that political instability in the developing regions will continue, with all the disastrous consequences for education which that would entail.

INTERNATIONAL RELATIONS

The effect that the economic and social forces mentioned above will have on education may be either increased or lessened according to the nature of the decisions and political actions taken at the international level. It is obvious, for example, that prospects for development in all countries depend to a large extent on the world economic situation and on international trading relationships. Although international economic competition seems to have become keener during the last few years—often at the expense of the developing countries—little progress has yet been made within the framework of the General Agreement on Tariffs and Trade (GATT) and the United Nations Conference on Trade and Development (UNCTAD) towards the elimination of trade barriers. Regional economic groups such as the Andean Pact, the Association of South-East Asian Nations (ASEAN), the Council for Mutual Economic Assistance (CMEA) and the European Economic Community (EEC) will no doubt continue to develop and help to create new economic, social and cultural situations, possibly even a certain degree of political integration—all of which are factors having important effects on education.

We should also note the importance for the development of education of the efforts which governments need to make to settle their differences peacefully and achieve détente through the improvement of relations in various fields. If the process of détente were to lead to disarmament, or even merely to a halt in the arms race, education in many countries could make use of some of the resources which would become available as a consequence. Conversely, education would suffer greatly from failure in the task of securing peace. Its own role in this task is constantly increasing. As part of the contribution to the maintenance and strengthening of peace, education can provide knowledge on the problems of peace and disarmament, on co-operation and international relations, and on the threats to peace and the catastrophic consequences which a nuclear war would have for the whole of mankind. Education should contribute towards a greater knowledge, a better understanding and a more just appreciation of other peoples and of other cultures, develop and inculcate values favourable to peace, and promote attitudes in keeping with respect for the rights of other peoples and other cultures, together with determination to participate actively in the maintenance and reinforcement of peace.

Factors likely influence the development of education during the next twenty years

Finally, as has already been stated, the improvement or worsening of the international climate will depend to a very considerable extent on progress in international economic relations. Any educational measures intended to promote values which foster international solidarity and which are likely to bring about a new commitment in this field will help not only to improve international relations, but also to create the conditions needed for the development of education.

REFERENCES

1. *Facing the Future*. Paris, Organisation for Economic Co-operation and Development, 1979. 425 pp.
2. INTERNATIONAL MEETING ON NEW AIMS FOR MANKIND (Madrid, 11 December 1981). *Address given by Mr Amadou-Mahtar M'Bow, Director-General of Unesco*. (Unesco doc. DG/81/49.)
3. INTERNATIONAL CONFERENCE ON EDUCATION (38th Session, Geneva, 10–19 November 1981). *Opening address given by Mr Amadou-Mahtar M'Bow, Director-General of Unesco*. (Unesco doc. DG/81/46.)
4. GENERAL CONFERENCE OF UNESCO. Revised Recommendation concerning Technical and Vocational Education, Adopted by the General Conference of Unesco on 19 November 1974. *Records of the General Conference, 18th Session, Paris, 1974*. Vol. 1: *Resolutions*. Paris, Unesco, 1975.
5. MEETING OF THE INTERNATIONAL PANEL ON THE FUTURE DEVELOPMENT OF EDUCATION (Unesco, Paris, 17–21 November 1980). *Final Report*. Paris, Unesco, 1981. (Unesco doc. ED-80/FUTURED/4.)
6. Robots: le revers de la médaille. *Futuribles* (Paris), No. 47, September 1981, pp. 70–1.
7. *Education on the Move*. Paris/Toronto, Unesco/The Ontario Institute for Studies in Education, 1975.
8. *Future Educational Policies in the Changing Social and Economic Context*. Paris, Organisation for Economic Co-operation and Development, 1979.

Part Two

Problems and challenges

3
Towards equal opportunity in education

Introduction

The statistics, policies, plans, studies and reports which document the development of education over the past two decades reveal a universal tendency towards greater democracy in education, which is both a consequence and a cause of growing social demand for education. Nearly all governments have committed themselves to democratize their educational systems and numerous reforms and measures have been set in motion to this end, some of which will make their impact known only in the 1990s or later.

Although sometimes thought of as a goal in itself, the democratization of education is really a process which takes different forms in different social contexts and which can be promoted to attain various social goals and educational objectives. It is essentially a political process giving substance to the fundamental human right to education which, in turn, is an indispensable condition for the full enjoyment of other human rights and for the development of society. Experience has revealed the democratization of education as a far more complex process than originally imagined, capable of generating intricate problems and much controversy.

The democratization process appears to have a strong momentum both in the developing countries and in the industrialized countries, but the prospects for its further impact on the development of education will no doubt be somewhat different for each of these two very general categories. For example, one can readily imagine that the expansion of access to education, including the struggle against illiteracy, will be high on the agenda of most of the developing countries, whereas the industrialized countries, in which access to the first two levels of education is nearly universal, will no doubt give relatively more attention to meeting the particular educational needs of various population groups.

As the concept of education has broadened over the years, there has been a parallel evolution in the meaning attached to the democratization of education. Thus, equal access to education—a fundamental aspect of democratization—no longer means access only to schooling. People today want access to educational opportunities of all kinds throughout their lifetime. Furthermore, equity is no longer perceived merely in quantitative terms. The International Panel on the Future Development of Education observed that 'the universally accepted right to education, manifested by strong popular demand, seems to be understood by the people as a right to quality education' [1, pp. 3–4]. The international community has come very recently to accept that the democratization of education also involves equal opportunity to succeed within an educational system. Beyond the provision of sufficient classrooms, non-formal programmes and teachers, democratization implies improvements in the content of education, the teaching–learning process, the organization and structure of educational services, and the participation of learners and the local community in the decision-making, planning and administration of those services.

The concept of democratization will no doubt continue to evolve in the years ahead. In view of the considerable gap between concept and reality, however, the process of democratization will probably continue to focus largely on equalizing access, with gradually increasing attention being given to improving achievement.

EXPANDING ACCESS TO EDUCATIONAL SERVICES

The common denominator of all strategies to democratize education is the equalization of access to education. This is usually accomplished through measures designed to provide educational services to more people and population groups by eliminating such barriers as onerous school fees and restrictive admission criteria and by establishing new services and facilities. Since opening access to education does not, in itself, necessarily result in the utilization of the services available, many educational policies also provide for some combination of incentives and compulsion to encourage those people who would not otherwise take advantage of available educational opportunities to do so. In this connection, the prolongation of the period of compulsory education is both a significant trend and policy issue in many countries. Thus, for example, the countries of Latin America and the Caribbean have fixed as one of their common objectives, by 1999 at the latest, the provision of a minimum of eight to ten years of general education for all children of school age.[1]

Further democratization will entail, first of all, a continuing expansion of educational services to accommodate the growing school-age population. Figure 2 indicates the magnitude of the effort that will be required to keep pace with

1. See the Declaration of Mexico adopted by the Regional Conference of Ministers of Education and Those Responsible for Economic Planning of Member States in Latin America and the Caribbean (Mexico, December 1979). The expansion of primary schooling, as an essential condition for the democratization of education, was adopted much earlier as a common objective by the first Unesco-sponsored regional conferences of ministers of education (Karachi, 1960; Addis Ababa, 1961; Santiago de Chile, 1962; and Tripoli, 1966).

Towards equal opportunity in education

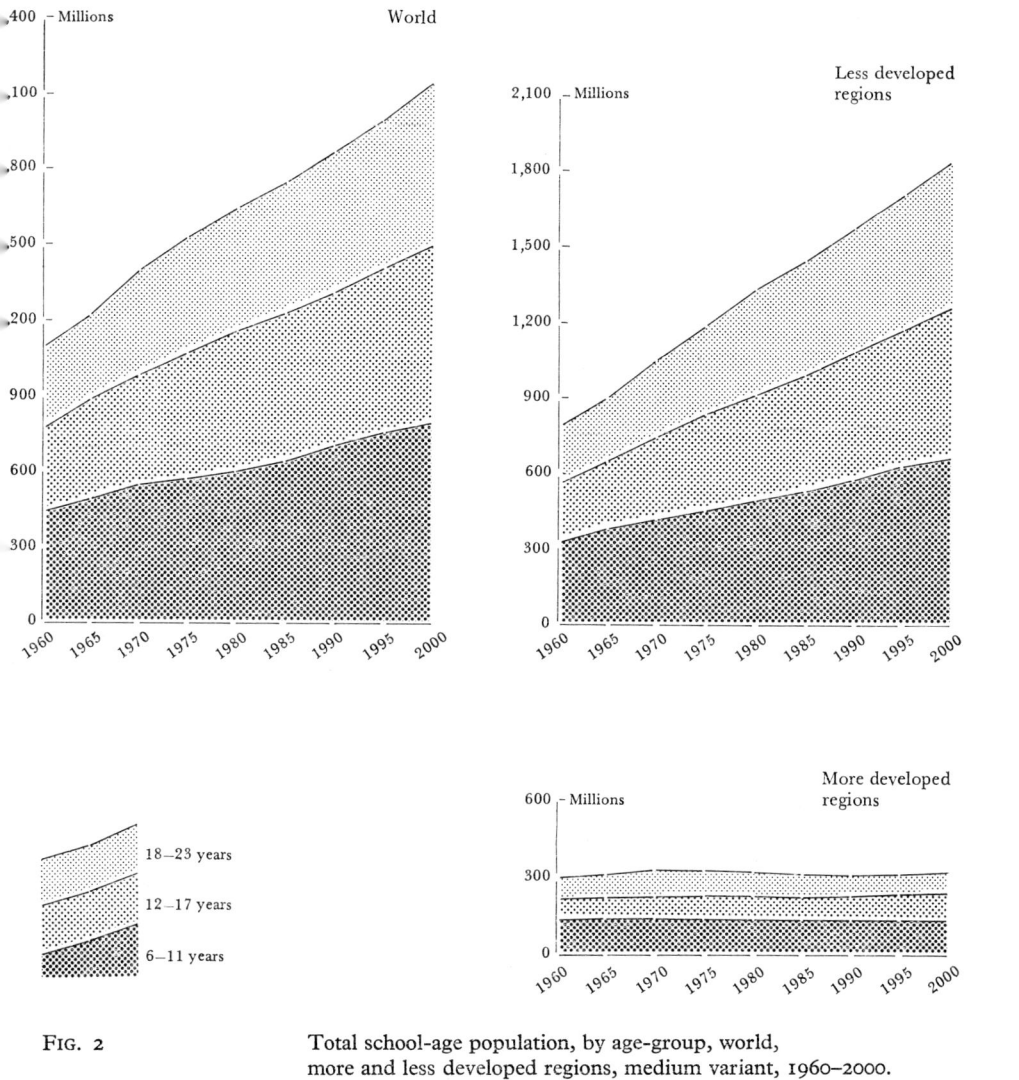

FIG. 2   Total school-age population, by age-group, world, more and less developed regions, medium variant, 1960–2000.

Source: World School-age Population until Year 2000: Some Implications for the Education Sector, p. 50, Paris, Unesco, 1981. (Current Studies and Research in Statistics.) (Unesco doc. CSR-E-39.)

population growth, particularly in the developing countries, where the 6–17 age-group is expected to grow by 30–50 per cent during the next twenty years. By the year 2000, the developing countries will account for approximately 85 per cent of all children and youth in this age-group. These countries would need to increase their primary-school enrolment by nearly 50 per cent in twenty years merely to maintain their current enrolment rate of 86 per cent, according to recent Unesco estimates. More complete figures are available in Appendix I.

Merely keeping pace with population growth—though requiring an enormous effort—would not be sufficient to eliminate the most glaring symptom of inequality in education: widespread illiteracy. Primary-school enrolments would need to be increased substantially, and energetic action would need to be undertaken to provide basic education for the vast population of adult illiterates, a population which is declining in relative terms but continues to grow in absolute numbers along with the general population. Unesco estimates that in 1980 there were 824 million illiterate adults (of whom 60 per cent were women), and most of the 240 million children in the 6–14 age-group who are not now attending school will join their ranks. If present trends continue, the number of illiterate adults in the world may reach 912 million (one person in five) by the end of the century, according to recent Unesco projections. Three-quarters of them would be living in Asia, but in terms of illiteracy rates at regional level, Africa would have the highest rate (35.2 per cent) and approximately half the adult population of the thirty-one least developed countries would still be illiterate.

Such an evolution of the situation, although highly possible, would be flagrantly unjust in a world which recognizes the right to education. Furthermore, it would also constitute a serious obstacle to socio-economic development in those countries with a large illiterate population. Yet these same countries have very limited resources to allocate to primary education and to literacy campaigns. Some countries, including Burma, Cuba and the United Republic of Tanzania, have demonstrated, however, that significant progress in the fight against illiteracy can be achieved in a relatively short period, given very high priority by the government and wide popular support.

Some observers argue that as societies become increasingly permeated by the computer and telecommunications, reading and numeracy skills will become less important: the non-reader able to recognize a limited number of symbols (such as international traffic signs) will be able to live quite adequately with the help of 'intelligent' machines. This argument, of course, leaves aside the larger issue of education and its contribution to the full development of the individual. Other observers foresee a growing need for computer literacy, without which the individual will be handicapped in seeking employment, in pursuing advanced study in certain fields, and in social life generally. However, these forecasts appear to be more relevant to technologically advanced countries, at least during the next twenty years, whereas illiteracy, in the current sense, will certainly continue to be a major problem for those countries with the largest number of illiterates today.

The fight against illiteracy is no doubt the most urgent task in democratizing education, but much else remains to be done to expand and improve access to education. People living in rural areas, who are the vast majority in developing countries, often have access at best to run-down, poorly-equipped schools staffed by underqualified teachers, some having sixty or more pupils in a class, which offer only the first few years of primary education. Educational opportunity in the rapidly growing urban slums is seldom much better, and in some countries migrant workers, nomads, refugees and ethnic or linguistic minorities are unable to benefit fully, if at all, from educational services available to the general population. Handicapped children in very many countries are denied access to regular schools and often have little or no alternative learning opportunities.

Furthermore, large numbers of children enjoying nominal access to education are in fact eliminated from the school system during the first few years because they do not perform adequately, then repeat, and finally drop out. Mary Berry, an American sociologist, writes in a study prepared for the International Panel, 'Despite problems the trend toward democratization is not likely to be abandoned, but democratization may mean only opening access for students at all levels and not quality or choice for the disadvantaged.' Local customs which tolerate child labour and a restricted role for women also take their toll. Other children are obliged sooner or later to drop out of school when their families can no longer afford the cost, even of 'free' public schooling. These various forms of educational wastage are not readily evident in official enrolment figures, which alone are not reliable indicators of democratization.

The disparity of educational opportunity between boys and girls continues to be a serious problem of equity and a handicap for economic and social progress in many developing countries. Table 5 shows the gradual improvement in the enrolment of girls in school since 1960 and the remaining disparity,

TABLE 5. Girls as a percentage of total enrolment by level of education

Region	First level 1960	First level 1970	First level 1980	Second level 1960	Second level 1970	Second level 1980	Third level 1960	Third level 1970	Third level 1980
Industrialized countries	49	49	49	49	49	50	35	41	46
Developing countries[1]	39	42	44	28	34	39	24	29	34
Africa[2]	36	40	44	29	32	38	17	23	27
Latin America and the Caribbean	48	49	49	47	48	50	30	35	44
South Asia	36	40	41	25	31	36	24	27	31

1. Not including China, the Democratic People's Republic of Korea and Namibia.
2. Not including Namibia.
Source: Unesco, *Trends and Projections of Enrolment by Level of Education and by Age, 1960–2000*, p. 15. Paris, Unesco, 1983. (Current Studies and Research in Statistics.) (Unesco doc. CSR-E-46.)

particularly at secondary and higher levels. In view of the importance of providing access to education for girls and women, the International Panel recommended that 'all efforts to this end must take account of the socio-economic role that women play, both in the context of child education and in the national economy'. Development activities of various kinds, such as those aimed at improving nutrition, crop yields, and family planning, have demonstrated again and again the key roles which can be played by educated women.

To some extent, adult education, whether in formal evening schools or non-formal programmes, can provide a remedy for inadequate access to education during the years of formal schooling. This remedial function of adult education applies to education at all levels, including university courses. In addition to giving the adults concerned a second chance, adult education also affects the democratization process by producing better-educated parents who are more likely to provide the home support so crucial to the achievement of young children in school and who are more likely to participate in the public management of education. In view of the growing world demand for adult education opportunities, access to education will no doubt be increasingly recognized as an issue applying to all age-groups and concerning educational services offered outside, as well as in, the schools.

IMPROVING EDUCATIONAL ACHIEVEMENT

Equal access to education, by itself, does not ensure equal educational achievement or outcomes. Certain population groups enjoy social, cultural and economic advantages that enable them to benefit more from the educational services available, and which in many cases seem designed to perpetuate those very advantages. In this connection, the International Panel observed that 'the provision of equal opportunities to unequal social groups merely leads to the reproduction of social inequalities' [1, p. 5]. Efforts to overcome the effects of such inequalities often require promoting equality in education by providing special services to disadvantaged learners. Current measures range from compensatory and supplementary programmes with individualized instruction, to positive discrimination, such as quotas, reserve lists, and earmarked scholarships, all intended to benefit disadvantaged pupils. According to some observers, this relatively new and challenging aspect of democratization will become much more important in the next twenty years.

Although certain countries have gained useful experience and have registered some progress in this direction, present efforts to equalize chances for educational achievement have proved a problem. Disparities in educational achievement due to material difficulties, such as lack of textbooks and teaching aids, or to the unequal distribution of educational services and facilities within a country, can be reduced by appropriate—and often costly—measures within the control of the education authorities. However, the social and cultural factors which contribute to disparities in educational achievement, such as parental or community attitudes and prejudices, cannot be totally counterbalanced or equalized by corrective measures within the educational system alone. The effect of such factors can best be moderated by policies and action to promote social equity, cultural development and more equal income distribution.

Perhaps the most important factor affecting achievement which the educational authorities can influence is educational curricula. Much of the formal curricula in schools around the world is irrelevant to the learning needs and social context of pupils. Thus, in many developing countries, the textbooks in use were designed, sometimes decades ago, for the children of the urban élite and are totally unrelated to the realities of the rural population and to national development objectives. Such irrelevance no doubt accounts for much of the lack of interest and motivation underlying scholastic difficulties and dropping out, which eliminates from school systems large numbers of pupils, usually from low-income families. In this connection, the International Panel was of the opinion that 'contents, methods and techniques reflecting the relevant needs, interests and problems of children will ensure their involvement, bolster their motivation and increase their chances of terminating a full course of studies. Greater retention resulting therefrom is thus another factor of democratization' [1, p. 4]. Yet, relating educational content to the learners' socio-cultural milieu, while contributing to better educational opportunity, may also serve to reinforce the distinctions between certain social groups and hinder social mobility.

Furthermore, some textbooks in current use still propagate ethnic, racial and sex stereotypes, as well as other messages, sometimes called 'the hidden curriculum', which are inconsistent with democratic values and behaviour. Designing curricula which are socially relevant and egalitarian, which stimulate the development of abilities and attitudes conducive to democracy, and which are consistent with the cultural context of a country, is a demanding and continuing task requiring political as well as technical skills. Even in those countries where the political will for such far-reaching curricula reform exists, the sheer magnitude of the task, the shortage of persons skilled in curriculum design, the cost of producing new textbooks and other learning materials, and the effort required to retrain teachers, constitute formidable obstacles. Many developing countries continue to adopt the easier alternative of depending on imported textbooks with their built-in curricula, despite their frequent irrelevance and possible harmful effects.

Closely related to this aspect of democratization is another which concerns the classroom situation, particularly the pupil–teacher relationship. If that relationship is essentially authoritarian, as is often the case, there is little likelihood that the pupil will be able to develop and practise at school important components of democratic behaviour such as free and independent inquiry, creativity, tolerance of other viewpoints, search for consensus, and respect for majority decision. Although calls for 'democracy in the classroom' obviously must be appropriate for the age-group involved, the social milieu of the school, that is the behaviour patterns and social relations practised within it, constitutes a very important hidden curriculum, which may be consistent or inconsistent with democratization.

A significant part of this hidden or implicit curriculum is the language of instruction, which structures thought processes and conveys an inherent set of cultural values and a perception of the world. The International Panel felt that instruction given in a foreign language constitutes an obstacle to democratization in some regions, since children and adults obliged to learn in a language other than their own are often put at a considerable disadvantage, which can compromise their chances for educational achievement. The importance of the mother tongue for educational achievement again underscores the significance of the home environment, particularly for young children. As mentioned earlier, adult education can contribute indirectly to improving the educational achievement of children by raising the general educational level of their parents. This intimate link between the educational prospects of children and the educational level of their parents, though long recognized by educators, has not yet been fully taken into account in educational policies. No doubt this link, the language of instruction, and other factors affecting the pedagogical situation, will be given more attention in future research with respect both to their contribution to effective learning and to the democratization of education.

EQUITY IN DIVERSITY

As a result of democratization, educational systems today are serving greater numbers of pupils and students, from more diverse socio-economic and cultural backgrounds, from all age-groups, and with a wider range of learning needs. The growing size and diversity of the population using educational services can cause strains on educational structures and standards, which often have not evolved in relation to new socio-economic conditions and learning requirements.

Problems linked to the expansion of educational systems and the heterogeneity of their clientele are not new but may be expected to become more acute in the future. They will require imaginative solutions to satisfy the requirements of social equity and managerial efficiency. Thus, for example, structures designed to prepare children from higher income groups for posts in public administration and commerce are unable to satisfy the more varied learning needs of other social groups or to prepare young workers and farmers for new economic roles in a developing economy. Similarly, socially integrated classrooms sometimes generate educational and disciplinary difficulties which can be traced to social inequities, intergroup relations and cultural phenomena prevailing in society as a whole. Such difficulties can no longer be quietly avoided by manipulating selection criteria and segregating social groups in separate classrooms or schools.

A large and diverse educational clientele does provide new possibilities, still largely unexploited, for enriching education. For instance, the schools in

Towards equal opportunity in education

many countries now contain for the first time a virtual microcosm of society comprising various social groups, each with its particular values, customs and life experience. Likewise, the larger numbers of pupils and students in secondary schools and higher education institutions now make feasible a much wider range of courses than ever before.

In order to meet the wider range of learning needs of individuals in various age categories and social groups, many countries have made significant changes in the organization and nature of their educational services. Differences in the social demand for education have led to a diversification of educational structures, and the former identification of education with the schooling of the young has generally given way to the broader concept of lifelong education. In addition to offering several types or streams of education (e.g. general, technical, vocational) within the formal school system, many countries now provide other services designed to make education more widely available to specific population groups: pre-school children, school drop-outs, young and adult workers, women, slum dwellers, rural inhabitants, immigrants, handicapped persons, senior citizens, ethnic and linguistic minorities, etc. Such services may take many forms: adult education, on-the-job training and apprenticeship schemes, correspondence courses, educational radio and television programmes, literacy campaigns, kindergartens and nursery schools. The impressive development of educational services has particularly influenced the growth of pre-school programmes. Since it is well established that the pre-school background of a child is very important in determining his or her performance in school, the International Panel found that 'pre-school education may, under certain conditions, constitute one important means of equalizing educational opportunity' [1, p. 4]. This appears to be the case in the industrialized countries, where pre-school education has become widespread, whereas in certain developing countries, the relatively few kindergartens either do not yet fulfil any significant educational role or in fact serve to provide yet another advantage for the children of privileged groups.

While a certain variety of educational services seems to be desirable, if not necessary, for democratizing education, too much variety or too many options may in certain circumstances contribute to unequal educational results. It has been found that specialization at too early an age tends to reinforce social inequities by segregating pupils according to supposed ability, which is closely related to the advantages or disadvantages of the pupils' socio-economic origin. Consequently, there is now a trend to postpone specialization until quite late in the compulsory education period. Similarly, various measures are being tried out to increase the flexibility and responsiveness of educational systems and in particular to permit mobility between hitherto hermetic divisions within secondary education, some of which have led to scholastic and employment dead ends. Such measures have generally been introduced with a view to equalizing educational opportunities, and further experimentation and reforms in this direction can be expected.

MANAGERIAL REQUIREMENTS FOR EQUITY

Efforts to democratize education will also encounter numerous management problems, some caused or exacerbated by the expansion of educational systems. The range of solutions to this kind of problem will depend to a large extent on the priority accorded to education by governments and the public, in terms of human, material and financial resources (see Chapter 7). Overcrowded classrooms and poor administrative support are common complaints in many countries, but it is likely that most developing countries will have to continue to cope with shortages of educational personnel, buildings and teaching aids. As in the past, some countries will resort to recruiting inadequately prepared teachers and administrators and to using whatever facilities are available in an effort to keep pace with expanding enrolment. Others will attempt to improve the distribution of educational services, which currently favours urban areas.

The distribution of the resources provided for education, regardless of the quantity, can have an important positive or negative effect on the democratization process. It is obvious, for example, as Mary Berry has pointed out, that 'it costs more to educate poor, disadvantaged, handicapped, non-English-speaking children, immigrants and illiterate adults than it does to educate children or adults who do not have these problems'. Resources allocated to those kinds and levels of education and to geographical areas which benefit the more privileged population groups are necessarily not available to the less privileged groups. For example, in many countries a disproportionate share of the educational budget goes to secondary and higher education, both of which cater largely for privileged groups. However, in very recent years there has been a noticeable trend in favour of expanding and improving basic educational services, notably primary education, literacy programmes, and adult education, both for better social equity and in support of national development efforts. This trend has gained the support of the international community and will probably become much more prevalent.

Mass schooling has usually led to big educational bureaucracies and a consequent weakening of personal contacts between decision-makers and employees. Because of the size and impersonality of educational systems and institutions, it is not uncommon for individuals, families and whole communities to feel that they have no responsibility for or influence on education. Centralized decision making from above has generally not proved conducive to stimulating the creativity, initiative, experimentation and dialogue which appear to be prerequisites for developing education in harmony with its social context.

Nevertheless there is a nascent demand, already quite advanced in several countries, by parents, teachers, students, employers and other social groups, to have a voice in determining various educational matters, particularly those most keenly felt at community level. Some observers believe that real progress in developing and democratizing education can be ensured only when suitable means are found to mobilize effective popular participation in education.

This issue of participation in the decision-making and managing of education again draws attention to the crucial importance of social context for the democratization of education.

LOOKING AHEAD

Although a look at current problems and trends in the democratization of education does not yield a clear picture of what lies ahead, it does provide a number of clues. Firstly, there appears to be no reason to believe that during the next two decades people will demand less education than they do today, nor that governments will cease to respond to this social demand. On the contrary, faith in education as a means of individual improvement and social mobility is widely shared among diverse cultures, and the Member States of Unesco have time and again reaffirmed their commitment to making the right to education a reality for all people. The recent history of education demonstrates that equity has become an accepted norm and objective nearly everywhere and that enormous efforts have been made in this direction. As a policy and a process, democratization will certainly continue to be a major characteristic, indeed a driving force of educational development, into the next century.

As the dynamics of socio-economic development and the accelerating pace of knowledge make lifelong learning important, or even imperative, for increasing numbers of people, the concept of equity in education will continue to broaden, together with our understanding of the democratization process. While consensus on fundamental points grows, due in part to more widespread communication between peoples made possible by modern transport and media, no doubt there will still be controversy over specific policies and practices.

From a global perspective, the provision of equal access to education will certainly remain the major preoccupation of educational authorities, especially in the developing countries. The education of children will generally be given priority for public funding, notably in those countries which have not yet assured universal primary education, but an increasing number of adults will also demand educational services. With or without public funding, adult education will have to expand significantly to cater for ageing populations in the industrialized countries. Many governments, inspired by innovation or necessity, will seek to use the mass media and other non-formal means to supplement the school and university in order to provide at least minimal educational services to as much of the population as possible. In some countries, the private sector can be expected to supply various services to meet part of the demand for education, in particular demand from higher income families and certain religious groups. Although this will help expand access to education, it may also contribute to inequities of educational opportunity.

Concern over the efficiency of educational systems will take on more political importance where there is inadequate funding for education. Increasingly, people will come to expect schools and other educational programmes to *produce satisfactory results, so more attention will be given to the quality of education and the actual achievement of learners.*

Early childhood educational programmes may be expected to continue spreading rapidly in urban areas, but more slowly in rural areas. Various old and new means to help disadvantaged learners will become standard features of educational systems in most countries, though not without some controversy. Developing countries will gradually increase the period of compulsory education as their means permit, although secondary education will remain largely selective and non-compulsory. The further development of secondary and higher education will be characterized by greater diversification and flexibility, thus offering a wider range of choice to individual learners. However, unequal social status and economic rewards will continue to make certain options more attractive than others, posing problems of access and selection.

In general, growing social demand for education and awareness of the problems relating to equity will create conditions in many countries conducive to greater community participation in the governance of educational institutions and programmes. Whether or not public authorities will in fact delegate or share such responsibility at community level will of course depend on the political structure of the country. The prospects for the democratization of education are intimately related to the broader process of democratization in each society.

Finally, an extrapolation of present trends suggests that some progress, at least in relative terms if not in absolute numbers, will be made in the next twenty years towards eradicating illiteracy and providing universal primary education, twin goals which are well within mankind's reach today. However, unless the many governments directly concerned, with the generous support of the world community, are willing and able to mobilize the enormous resources needed to back their stated policies, universal primary education will still remain an elusive goal in many parts of the world in the year 2000, and mass illiteracy will continue to be a shameful legacy of an unjust world system which is unable to secure education as a birthright of all men and women.

In the following articles, certain aspects of the democratization of education are discussed more fully. Each draws on the particular experience and prospects of one or more countries. Ingrid Eide explores the relationship between education and democracy, including the challenge of providing mass education of a high standard. Malcolm Adiseshiah argues that education is not yet fulfilling its role in advancing social justice in the developing countries. Germán W. Rama and Juan Carlos Tedesco present an analysis of social transformations in Latin America and their implications for the further democratization of education.

REFERENCE

1. SECOND MEETING OF THE INTERNATIONAL PANEL ON THE FUTURE DEVELOPMENT OF EDUCATION (Paris, 30 November to 4 December 1981). *Final Report.* Paris, Unesco, April 1982. (Unesco doc. ED-81/FUTURED/4.)

Education and democracy

Ingrid Eide

Democratization of education can perhaps be described as having a horizontal and a vertical dimension. Along the horizontal plane we would classify all efforts to secure access to educational institutions for increasing numbers of individuals for an increasing number of years and purposes. Along the vertical plane a different set of phenomena would be considered: how educational institutions actually interact with other aspects of life, learning and production, and more particularly, how educational institutions themselves operate. Throughout the twentieth century democratic states have concentrated on opening up and expanding educational institutions so as to provide access for all.

Along with this process individuals and society have increased their dependence on the educational system, mainly, but not only, for learning purposes. The result of this opening up and expansion of education, identified here as horizontal democratization, is that about a quarter of the population in our societies is engaged in the educational sector. The significance of a sector of this magnitude is evident. Questions abound concerning, on the one hand, the functions, cost and contributions of educational institutions, and, on the other, their compatibility with prevalent goals in society. In modern democracies some of these functions will be intended and even planned, costs will be publicly maintained, contributions or results empirically checked, and goals, when conflicting, will be politically debated. These activities imply a deeper concern for what was referred to as vertical democratization of education.

One basic assumption of this article is that during the next two decades more attention ought to, and will be, devoted to vertical rather than horizontal democratization of education. The challenge will be to act along either dimension in ways that also promote progress along the other.

Ingrid Eide

MECHANISMS FOR DEMOCRATIZING EDUCATION

In order to achieve the ideal of democratizing education, many structures have been devised: universal, compulsory and free education; geographically accessible educational institutions; one, and only one, school for all children of school age within a given district; cross-district intake of students to reduce social segregation in the school-age population; comprehensive schools; postponement of differentiation; changed criteria of admission; elimination of blind alleys in the system of educational institutions permitting individualized combinations and increased mobility within and between educational institutions; adult education; active encouragement of specific groups to continue school beyond the compulsory level; subsidies and scholarships; individualized educational programmes; changes in teaching methods, content, materials and organization; external and internal democratic control; developing educational institutions to meet demand; expanding educational institutions to accommodate all applicants.

The structures can be placed into two categories, representing steps referred to as horizontal and vertical democratization respectively. The latter category of structure—or of steps taken—has sometimes been required because the horizontal move was considered insufficient to obtain the desired degree of democratization. This should remind future educational reformers that combinations of structures rather than 'one step at a time' strategies are normally required in this field. Democratization of education is neither easy nor automatically arrived at. The financial cost is formidable, representing a great problem to potentially stagnant economies; in fact, financial constraints will probably in the years to come seriously challenge the ability to maintain and the will to expand democratization of education in Europe. Less costly structures would find many buyers on the political market.

The most recent and very dramatic change taking place is that age is played down: everybody, irrespective of age, is encouraged to seek more education. Society takes care of younger children in school-like institutions, sometimes called pre-school or kindergartens. Society likewise encourages children to spend more time at school than the minimum required by the law, and adults, whatever their age and previous school experience, are encouraged to re-engage in educational pursuits, and new contexts for learning are created to this end. While the inclusion of new age-groups can be seen as movement along the horizontal dimension of democratization, it has clear effects on the vertical dimension as well. There is of necessity a search for new approaches to education to take into account the points of view of the small child and the adult. In both cases established teaching methods, selection of content and other aspects of learning and schooling have to be revalued and revised.

Already new learning contexts are being created or rediscovered, with the traditional school, though dominant, as only one of many possible forms. In the history of education in Europe over the years, clear demarcations were established between the various areas of human activity: home, school, workplace.

The fact that learning takes place in all areas, and that they are actually interdependent and interact, has been frequently overlooked. With an increase of the very young and adults entering education, it seems that both the demarcation lines between areas, and the divisions of labour among then, are deliberately being blurred.

By establishing a variety of new learning contexts another basic characteristic of our societies is attacked: the clearly drawn lines between leisure, work and rest. All over Europe schools have been organized to be both a preparation for work, and for the young the functional equivalent of work. But the possibility that education can be obtained elsewhere, at other times and in other ways than at school, reduces the significance of classifying time as leisure, work and rest in connection with educational pursuits.

Compulsory education has ensured that nobody is left completely behind in this process of equalization. But beyond the compulsory level, differentiation begins once more, and it is a well-established fact that educational institutions provide the rationale for a new differentiation, new inequalities, which are more compatible with modern economies than with the ideals of modern democracies. Some democracies have been particularly active in their attempts to counteract this trend, and although they have never entirely succeeded, correlations between family background and educational career are being reduced, according to the most recent statistics.

Groups who previously were almost outcasts of the educational system— the handicapped, migrants and minorities—are admitted to and, in varying degrees, truly integrated in it.

Beyond the compulsory level, democratization of education has been launched on the assumption that individuals will grasp educational opportunities if they are offered on realistic conditions, that is, if formal and informal barriers surrounding educational institutions are adequately removed or overcome. But new sets of incentives and disincentives seem to operate in the modern world leading to new questions on how far and in what sense democratization of education will be successful beyond the compulsory level, where individual choice enters the stage and determines the success and failure of educational policies.

In Europe at present, with nearly 30 million unemployed, work may seem scarcer than educational opportunities for young people. The ethos of 'deferred gratification' may take on a different meaning in this situation: education is deferred, while young people start a career in the labour market, directly, without delay, so as not to be left out. The fact that work, leisure and rest are no longer clearly separated in time, place and function makes the choice between labour market and education for the individual concerned less dramatic than before.

There is no reason to expect a uniform set of reactions to the new situation in the labour market. Some young people will definitely invest in more education with a view to improving their employment chances. The education sought will be geared to a specific range of jobs, and the perceived probability of future success will influence the motivation for educational achievement. Others will calculate that the labour market is so uncertain that their education might just as well be geared to their own private interests and abilities, whether relevant to work or not. National policy, finances permitting, will probably attempt to satisfy a wide range of educational adjustments to the labour market and mass unemployment. Among these attempts some will strongly emphasize the intrinsic values of education and self-realization as a democratic right.

It may not be conditions in the labour market *per se* that most strongly attract young people to paid rather than unpaid but free education. The life-style of modern society is characterized by instant consumption rather than deferred gratification. This cultural atmosphere is not conductive to long-term and concentrated effort demanded by most educational institutions.

Women face special problems. Increasing with their level of education, sex roles within and outside the school community influence women's choice and achievement. Most probably, women will in the years to come be more actively encouraged than before to develop their talents independently of the traditional division of labour between the sexes. Not to explore and exploit this reservoir will be considered wasteful by a society increasingly dependent on specialized knowledge and research. Among women, new divisions will be created, contrary to the ideals of equality proclaimed by modern feminism.

Concern for the demographic balance of society, however, will increase the tolerance for interrupted educational careers due to maternity, child-rearing and family roles in general. Leaves of absence and facilitated re-entry will be institutionalized in ways that represent a fundamental challenge to, if not a fundamental break with, traditional division of labour between the sexes in family life and in education, and relative to the labour market.

In general, the numbers of women who obtain an education and hold positions in fields previously totally dominated by men will increase. This may provide examples to encourage other women to break down similar barriers. Democratization, in the sense of a more equal intake, may result, even if it is not the driving force or the dominant motive.

For the labour force, and particularly industrial labour, present-day changes in society seem no less fundamental than they are for the majority of women. Methods of learning have changed alongside changes in technology, production, organization and ideology. Democratic society has taken over the basic responsibility for the entire range of occupational training, but nowhere as yet is there a fully developed set of institutional solutions to carry out this task. The solutions sought will probably involve new combinations of formal and informal, individual and group training, and use both schools and work-places as arenas. But until solutions are found, there remain large groups of young people trapped in a situation of uncertainty, competing for still scarce opportunities to obtain an education and learn an occupation, either at school or at work. They are threatened with unemployment and the stigma of being social outcasts.

MASS EDUCATION

It is frequently argued that democratization of education means mass education, and that mass education threatens academic standards if it is not accompanied by some kind of segregation within or between schools. But it has also been argued that academic standards are not, or need not be, threatened. Schools have been given more resources to cope with the situation of a more varied student population, and still maintain academic standards. Longer hours, better trained teachers, teaching assistants, smaller classes, teaching equipment, individualized teaching materials, grouping, individualization: a whole range of initiatives have been suggested and launched so as to allow schools to apply the resources necessary to make integration policies succeed.

According to sceptics, the integrated classroom slows down academic progress, but on the other side stands the argument that a successfully integrated classroom provides a more productive learning atmosphere. With students from different backgrounds, with different abilities and potentials and varying ambitions—and some have special handicaps—teaching and learning have to be more varied, taking into account the wider range of experiences and challenges represented in the class or school. Students may actually learn to solve different kinds of problems involved in the learning process of fellow students. If students are allowed to help each other and to co-operate, academic achievement may gain momentum by being socially supported in the students' culture.

School authorities have also argued that academic standards are not the only measures to be used when evaluating the educational system. Equally important is the ability to function adequately in society, made up of people who are different in many ways. By integrating all individuals into one school, whether elementary or comprehensive secondary schools, social learning would improve.

Mass education has increasingly come to characterize all levels of the educational system. For higher education this experience has been almost revolutionary. Although expansion was planned, it appeared overwhelming when it came. The new situation demanded drastic changes so that in many places it was virtually impossible both to maintain all activities hitherto engaged in, and adjust physically, organizationally and educationally. Universities were openly politicized by these adjustments, and time and energy were obviously diverted from more traditional academic pursuits. University government in most places was democratized in the process. Probably the future will prove that the freer, less formal atmosphere created will also be more innovative and conducive to academic achievement, particularly its research aspect.

LEARNING AND DEMOCRATIC SOCIETY

Educational planning, old and new, has always been an arena for politics, particularly in democracies. The reasons are obvious. Education affects all and integrates the individual into the collective in a number of ways. It is one of the major vehicles of distribution and redistribution in society, and the heated debates over whether it produces, reproduces or corrects inequality bears witness to the crucial role attributed to education.

Education for all is a means of equalizing learning opportunities. But learning habits and learning products are established long before the school takes over in the life of the individual. And it is perhaps this 'takeover' by the school that produces both learning and non-learning, both creativity and passivity, in schools. Today's criticism of schools from a democratic point of view has raised precisely this question: have schools and other educational institutions monopolized learning with the result that too many still take it for granted that school is the only place where learning takes place, that children and young people of school age are the only ones who learn, and that teaching is for professional teachers alone?

A new consciousness seems to be under way, focusing on the conditions of learning, reactivating households and parents, communities and places of work, emphasizing lifelong learning, and not only opportunities for lifelong education. It seems reasonable to consider this as a new wave of democratization, very different from previous horizontal democratization. This wave implies that more people should take on the teacher's role, and not only that of the learner; it implies that schools should be opened up to use more local material. This may raise another debate about politicization of schools and by schools.

The traditional, hierarchical organization of most schools, the cleavage between youth and adults, between learners and temporary teachers and more permanent members of the school community—the externally determined law and budget—all these factors are not easily reconciled with ideas of internal democratic control. But a variety of models have been tried, finding different answers to the eternal question of democratic organization. Whatever the form of democracy chosen, it is its content and purpose that determines its potential for success. All participants will be disillusioned if they are invited to perform empty rituals. Participation must make a visible difference; it must provide a changed experience which is perceived as meaningful.

The continued interest in democratization of education must have many supports, both old and new. Horizontal democratization will represent a major effort. To be complete, it will have to be both fragmented and individuated. Modern information and communication technology will facilitate this development which both attacks and opens up new avenues for educational institutions and for learning.

More thought needs to be devoted to vertical democratization, to the social functions and the social functioning of educational organization. Democratization of education was intended to help lay the foundations for a democratic society. The opportunity to learn was also an experience of togetherness in learning, and interaction conducive to critical examination and organization of impressions, when educational institutions were at their best. A sense of individual growth was combined with the collective experience.

Democracy refers to relationships between individuals and between groups. It depends on people having learnt the rules as well as the roles of the game. It depends on people having a sense of purpose in their own lives and for society. It depends on the ability of individuals, groups and institutions to work out non-violent solutions to the conflicts within and between nations. Will education assist us in this endeavour?

Education and social justice

Malcolm Adiseshiah

The fact that the school system in developing countries is not able to attract and retain the majority of children, that is the rural poor, is a source of disillusionment with the school as a centre of learning. At least 30 per cent of the children of primary-school age in Asia and Africa are outside the primary school, and of the remaining 70 per cent enrolled in school, at least one in five will drop out before Class IV (i.e. the fourth year of schooling), which is the point at which Unesco has established that the permanent tools of learning are acquired. This dropping out and pushing out process continues until only about one child in three in the 12-17 age-group is still enrolled. Girls and women suffer a particular handicap: in Africa and Asia, even within the school residue, girls form less than 40 per cent of the class at the primary level, and 20-29 per cent of the class at the university and college level [1]. During the last fifteen years there has been no improvement in the capacity of the school to attract and retain children from the majority sector of society—the poverty sector—and in the enrolment of girls, a marginal 0.3 per cent rate of increase is recorded.

One explanation for this failure is that the schools were set up by the colonial authorities to train a certain number of clerks and subordinate officials for the ruling foreign government. With the countries' independence, the same schools, with little or no change, were unable to take over their assigned tasks of universalizing primary education. The main failure of the school to serve as the learning centre for the majority of people is due, however, to the fact that only when its clients are comparatively well off are the benefits higher than the opportunity costs. Thus, those who can afford schooling are around 30 per cent of the population in developing countries.

Consequently, the educational system in the developing countries contributes to political, social and economic inequalities. First, the content of school and university education reflects the values and interests of the dominant, well-to-do social class. Second, the degrees, diplomas and certificates of the educational system form the entry qualification for employment in the organized sector, resulting in a high degree of correlation between future incomes and school or college completion. The large majority of completers are from the richer sections of society. In fact, since school wastage (all children from poor families) constitutes 60 per cent of enrolment, and 40 or 50 per cent of the population is below the poverty line; educational inequalities are worse than economic inequalities. Through reservations, scholarships and other incentives, some poor people enter the meritocracy, but nothing is really changed. The old criteria of wealth and social status are replaced by new norms of 'educability' and 'educated intelligence', while the traditional and inequitable forms of social selection are maintained intact in the guise of meritocratic prerogatives, conserved and transmitted from one generation to the next.

Thus, the educational system promotes inequality spatially, between urban and rural areas; sexually, between males and females; generationally, between youth and adults; socially, between the rich and the poor; and fiscally, as a conduit for transfer of subsidies from the poor to the rich. Increased education and increased educational expenditures in the name of equality of opportunity and the even more dubious objective of equality of educational outcomes, have in effect been another hidden way of the poor subsidizing the rich. One study points out that schools in the USA, for example, are an almost perfectly regressive form of taxation, since the public cost of schooling the poorest tenth of the population is $2,500 per pupil over a lifetime, while the education of the richest tenth costs about $35,000 per pupil [2]. In India, the highest social group benefits four times as much as the poorest group which, however, pays 80 per cent of education costs through the system of indirect taxation [3]. Another study shows that private schools and colleges, which are the preserve of the children of rich families, are financed to the extent of 70 per cent through public subsidies and tax avoidance [4]. Even more serious, the school and the university, through the system of values, attitudes and aptitudes that they help to develop, also help to mould and condition the student to fit into and unequal and unjust society. Thus the major social function of the educational system in the developing countries seems to be to legitimize unequal and unjust social systems.

What then of the future? It is necessary to remind oneself that education by itself cannot bring about equality in an unequal society or justice in an unjust social order: in so far as it is part of society, it will in fact mirror all the features of the society. This is one of the dangers in linking education closely to rural and urban realities. In the future the educational system's role in actively promoting or worsening inequalities can and will be corrected by changing the access formalities and requirements, by bringing the hidden curriculum into the open for study and discussion in the school and outside, by reforming the system of degrees and certificates, and above all by breaking the link between school certificates and degrees, and employment and employment requirements.

The adult and non-formal learning is not so closely tied to power structures and the wealthy élite; in developing countries about to make a fresh start, the slate is still relatively clean [5]. Although the school will continue to be an important locus of learning, it will in the future occupy a smaller place in the total learning system. This is particularly important for the developing countries who have a commitment to increase their institutional forms of education.

The school system constitutes a bottleneck to social advancement in the developing countries from two points of view. First, in the low income countries, the massive poverty which is a consequence of inequalities in the distribution of wealth and income is exacerbated by the school system. The school retains the children of the wealthy minority, who can afford full-time day schooling, and rejects or excludes the children of the poor majority, who have to work alongside their parents to supplement the meagre family income. The vast majority of adult illiterates are in the poor countries. The school system is thus closed to the majority of people in these unequal societies. Second, there is a physical bottleneck related to the numbers in the developing countries who have to be provided with learning opportunities in the next two decades, estimated at 1.8 billion. Schools cannot be built fast enough, nor teachers trained, nor libraries and laboratories installed within the time span, even if the necessary funds were available.

Hence, all forms and media of learning will have to be mobilized and put to use for the developing countries in the coming two decades. This may be what leads some writers to say that important educational developments and innovations may come in the next two decades from the develloping countries [6]. Certainly, expanding out-of-school learning opens up some important areas and dimensions for innovation.

REFERENCES

1. *Unesco Statistical Yearbook 1978–79*, Table 2.4. Paris, Unesco, 1980.
2. REIMER, E. W. *School is Dead: Alternatives in Education.* New York, Doubleday, 1972.
3. ADISESHIAH, M. S. *Financing of School Education.* Madras, Government of Tamil Nadu, 1978.
4. TOWNSEND, P.; BOSANQUET, N. (eds.). *Labour and Inequality: Sixteen Fabian Essays.* London, Fabian Society, 1972.
5. ADISESHIAH, M. S. (ed.). *Adult Education Faces Inequalities.* Madras, Sangam Publishers, 1981.
6. HAWES, H. W. R. *Planning the Primary School Curriculum in Developing Countries.* Paris, Unesco/International Institute of Educational Planning, 1972. (Fundamentals of Educational Planning, 17.)

The democratization of education in Latin America

Germán W. Rama and Juan Carlos Tedesco

HISTORICAL HERITAGE AND RECENT TRENDS

In Latin America, the first efforts made towards universal and popular education in the last third of the nineteenth century were associated with the notion of a unified national society, equitable and democratic. The functions of education were defined from a double perspective, political and economic. Thus, for the Mexican President Benito Juárez, 'education is the first foundation of the prosperity of people and at the same time the safest means to make impossible the abuse of power' [1, pp. 11-12].

From the political perspective, the peculiarity of Latin America consisted, precisely, in the design of strongly homogeneous educational systems: the common public primary school, the slightly diversified secondary school and the university centred in the traditional professions. Defined in this manner, the nucleus of the educational struggle in the region revolved around the inclusion–exclusion axis. Contrary to Europe, where differential and stratified forms of educational inclusion were articulated, in Latin America the option was to be educated or to be excluded.

Apart from some limited sections of the traditional and emerging middle class involved in the development of state activity, the productive system did not require an educated labour force. Most labourers learned essential skills empirically on farms and in artisan workshops. Even as recently as 1950, census data show that approximately 50 per cent of the population over the age of 15 was illiterate. The gross enrolment rate of primary schooling at that time for the entire region was 48 per cent, with wide variations between countries, e.g. Uruguay 92 per cent, Bolivia, Guatemala and Honduras 20 per cent, while Brazil, the country with the largest population, had a primary school enrolment of 31 per cent. Secondary and higher education were restricted to the élite with gross enrolment rates of 6.9 per cent and 1.9 per cent respectively [2].

The three decades from 1950 to 1980 constituted a period of social and educational transition of enormous significance for the future. From a structural point of view, three processes have operated to varying degrees in most societies: urbanization, industrialization and the development of the services sector. The urban population, which towards 1950 was 40 per cent, rose to 64.3 per cent by 1980, whereas the total population—due to high birth rates—increased from 164 to 373 million. Latin America is being transformed due to the emergence of a chain of cities, fed by rural emigration, in which the population passes from 'face to face' parochial socialization to an experience of modernization and to a situation of political availability, as the old mechanisms of social control cease to operate. Thus people experience a true revolution of expectations concerning education and social participation.

Industrialization, most evident in larger Latin American countries, tends to concentrate manufacturing in centres of a certain magnitude and progressively introduces modern technology into the units of production related to the traditional market. This phenomenon is taking place in a period during which industrial technology is reaching an advanced stage all over the world. This explains the fact that the process absorbs only limited amounts of workers and, contrary to what happened in those countries which began industrialization early, an important development of services is taking place from the beginning of the process, especially in the social services under the responsibility of the state.

The predominance of urbanization transfers social problems from rural to urban areas, with the formation of vast marginal population groups without employment and, therefore, without possibility of integration. The advance of industrialization implies the increase of the internal market, a better relative distribution of income and the extension, at certain levels of society, of participation in power. This transition has led to a crisis for the model of oligarchic domination, the loss of importance of land as the base that sustained power, the definition of new social groups (bourgeoisie, middle class, proletariat) and the loss of the old mechanisms of socialization and of ideological control.[1] Instability is the predominant sign: no system of power achieves legitimate dominion, and the dominant sectors are forced to compromise with other social groups, establish alliances or use repression to hold on to power.

Between 1950 and 1980, the population of Latin Americans aged between 5 and 24 years increased from 67 to 158 million and total enrolments at all levels of the educational system increased from 16 to 87 million. The educational services were confronted simultaneously with the pressure of population growth and social demand. The latter explains why the expansion of the different levels has been so unequal: primary enrolments up from 14 to 66 million; secondary, from 1.5 to 16 million; higher from

---

1. Among the vast literature on the subject, refer to F. H. Cardoso and E. Faletto, *Dependencia y desarrollo en América Latina*, Mexico City, Siglo XXI S.A., 1969. Also, F. H. Cardoso, 'El desarrollo en capilla', in : Instituto Latinoamericano de Planificación Económica y Social (ILPES)/Fondo de las Naciones Unidas para la Infancia (UNICEF), *Planificación social en América Latina y el Caribe*, Santiago de Chile, UNICEF, 1981.

250,000 to 5 million. This unequal expansion of the levels was not planned—the quantitative goals of education plans were surpassed in most countries—but due to the unequal power of social groups. As a result of the interplay of forces, an educational system was formed with democratic characteristics with respect to the dynamics of its expansion, but not with respect to its selective action leading to the exclusion of half the population from completing primary education, nor to its superposition of segmented educational cycles that reserve cultural and scientific education for the upper social classes.

All the recent quantitative diagnoses reveal that in the first three grades of primary school, a 'filtering' process is carried out that leaves a large portion of the newly incorporated groups very close to the situation in which they were before gaining access to school. Repeating grades [3], premature school leaving, and low level of achievement in terms of learning the basic cultural codes are the most outstanding features of this stage of compulsory basic schooling. In this sense, one of the central problems around which the democratization of basic schooling revolves at present is the concurrence between the quantitative expansion of enrolments and the deterioration of the capacity to learn writing [4].

The expansion of schooling to include the traditionally excluded social groups is being carried out without modifying the cultural model that the schooling system has traditionally used. In other words 'the failure of schooling can be explained by the fact that the system is being extended but continues to demand a basic cultural capital that is an exclusive heritage of those social sectors that traditionally had access to the system' [5, p. 69].

The tendency to produce the existing social structure is evident in the constitution of an educational system that is incapable of providing a cultural basis common to all the population, while the post-primary levels of education have developed enormously, sometimes benefiting from resources out of proportion to those dedicated to basic schooling. Furthermore, the expansion of secondary and higher education has been characterized by progressive internal stratification. In this way the upper class and the upper middle class have received advanced cultural and scientific education in excellent secondary schools, generally private. Less fortunate pupils were discouraged from aspiring to continue their studies at the third level, after attending establishments that were not equipped to teach up-to-date technology which presented science and the humanities in a dogmatic form, with obsolete contents, using methods based on memorization. While the privileged students could enter a high-level university, most others were relegated to the 'massified' universities, which are increasingly discredited due to the lack of human and material resources and affected politically by the frustration of the students as to their social expectations. The lower-middle groups have received only a semblance of university training at private or public provincial night schools [6, pp. 45–94].

Education, considered as cultural capital, has been subjected to the same unequal distribution applied to other social goods in almost all societies. But in Latin America, the factors mentioned above have created a peculiar socio-educational structure. For example, those in power formally accepted the successive demands of different social groups but, far from establishing a basic schooling cycle for all the population, they responded to each group with an educational offer at the level requested, but awarded unequal resources, according to the social importance of the group. Each group thus obtained an offer corresponding to its power to channel its demands: the groups with less power received a school with only the formal appearance of what it should be, whereas others were able to obtain a school of adequate quality in terms of equipment, teaching, curricula, and so on. Instead of channelling the demand for secondary and higher education through systems of specialized training, as was done in Europe [7], the option chosen was the 'massification' of the former élitist education.

In spite of these structural imbalances, recent educational expansion has perhaps been the most important development of social democratization in Latin America, and this is reflected in the following indicators of cultural transformation.

By 1970 illiteracy in the 15–24 age-group had been reduced to 18.2 per cent, although the distribution of illiteracy was very uneven, for example 31.1 per cent in rural areas and 4.5 per cent in the capitals of seventeen countries of the region [8]. This indicates that the acceleration of urbanization is and will be parallel to that of literacy.

The extension of secondary education in relation to the 13–19 age-group increased from a modest 6.9 per cent in 1950 to 26.5 per cent in 1975, reaching 30 per cent in 1980.

The expansion of higher education covered 16 per cent of the respective age-group in 1975, compared to 1.9 per cent in 1950.

PROSPECTS FOR DEMOCRATIZATION OF EDUCATION IN LATIN AMERICA

Historically, the expansion of access to education has not been the result of concessions but of conquests. A similar comment can be made concerning the content of teaching. Historical analysis also shows that the educational system has not been on the sidelines of the debate and of the dynamics of the ideological confrontation that exists within the framework of society as a whole. Theories of the educational system as a reproductive apparatus tend to ignore the present crisis in schooling which is fundamentally the crisis of its reproductive role in society. In this respect it is possible to summarize as follows the features that define the present link between school and bourgeois culture, on the one hand, and school and the structure of the work force, on the other.

With regard to culture, it seems evident that the evolution of industrial capitalism has provoked a series of significant changes. In the area of production, the intense pace of technological change has increasingly tended to create a dichotomy between types of human labour, as creativity is concentrated among a decreasing proportion of people and of activities and an ever-increasing number of tasks are simplified. Hyper-specialization, for its part, is making impossible an overall comprehension of phenomena, despite growing trends towards interdisciplinarity. The expansion of micro-electronics and their application to communications are creating a new type of language and new forms of cultural control. In the political arena, the crisis of traditional forms of participation is evident, with the organization of popular forces on one side and growing transnational power on the other. There is also a tendency towards the marginalization of vast sections of the population, especially youth, which is manifest even in developed economies. In respect to social relations, changes in forms of family socialization are notorious, particularly those concerning the role of authority and of permissiveness.

Facing this panorama, it is evident that the school has not responded in a dynamic way. Studies confirm that the pedagogical action of schooling is characterized by its archaism and its growing autonomy when confronted with external changes. The bureaucratization and rigidity of the school system, which successfully resists all attempts at change and reform, are ample proof of this phenomenon.

Regarding the relation of education to the labour force, the most significant fact of recent decades is that the expansion of education and trends in the labour market to save on manpower have altered the selective function traditionally carried out by the educational system. Obviously this does not mean that the credentials of education no longer have any value in the labour market, but it does mean that education's 'reproductive' role is now defined in a very different way than it was in the past.

However, change in external conditions will not automatically transform the action and results of schooling, nor produce a transformation, in the short term, of the conditions of access to school. The changes in each of the spheres of the social structure are not governed by the same dynamics and, as already mentioned, the educational system has reached a degree of autonomy not to be underestimated [9].

In recent years, a significant part of the claims and action in favour of popular education has been directed towards pedagogical options other than schooling and largely outside state control. These options are aimed, in preference, at the adult population and evolved from an early priority concern for rural inhabitants, later extending to marginal urban dwellers. The debate concerning these options is at present in full flow. It suffices to say here that it still is necessary to salvage the school and the educational system as a whole, since it is through them that a significant contribution can be made towards the achievement of a democratic society. The factors that prevent the school system from guaranteeing equality in the social distribution of knowledge do not disappear by the mere fact of searching for alternatives other than schooling to reach this objective. In spite of all the limitations pointed out concerning the efficiency of the pedagogical action of schooling, its impact is significant, especially if the point of departure of the school population is taken into consideration. To participate in an institution of secondary socialization and to have access to the basic cultural codes (reading, writing, calculation, etc.) are aspects that must not be underestimated with regard to their effects on individuals and the possibilities that they create to channel more profound social demands.

The democratization of the school cannot be reduced to the problem of access. For access to be effective, it is necessary to guarantee the relevance of the knowledge obtained by the pupils. In this sense, the issue is whether the democratic nature of schooling is guaranteed by offering a homogeneous cultural model (which in a stratified society is the model of the dominant class) or, if instead, it is necessary to respect the cultural models of the various groups benefiting from education. The risk of each of these alternatives are apparent. The imposition of a homogeneous model either tends to fail because of the distance between school socialization and the family environment or, on the contrary, it produces the destruction of the native cultural heritage. Yet respect for the native cultural models can lead, if taken to extremes, to the neutralization of the effects of schooling, leaving the pupils at the same point where they were before gaining access to school.

Viewing the problem in these terms, one of the principal actors in the definition of the democratic character of education is, without doubt, the teacher. Beyond the characteristics of the teacher's social and working conditions, it is necessary to point out the importance of personal characteristics, both in the area of professional competence and in attitudes and expectations. The part played by the teacher in the performance of pupils at school is well known [4]. Authoritarian teaching, especially within the framework of culturally segmented societies, is the way in which cultural domination manifests itself in the sphere of schooling. From this point of view, democratic education should tend to overcome this dissociation between cultural aspects and the technical–pedagogical ones.

Another recent pedagogical proposal for the democratization of schooling is the universalization of pre-primary schooling. This proposal stems from a diagnosis that attributes school failure to the deficit created by early stimulation which is culturally poor. The expansion of schooling for very young children constitutes, without any doubt, a significant objective of democratization. It is even possible to define a type of pre-school educational action that will deal with the special characteristics of a childhood within very limited material conditions of life. But an expansion of such education will not automatically solve the problems existing in the primary school. Research carried out in Latin America shows that the primary school neutralizes some of the effects of pre-schooling preparation [10]. This is because problems concerning the pedagogical action of schooling cannot be solved totally outside the school.

In secondary and higher education, the problem of democratization presents different characteristics. In the first place, the expansion of these levels, particularly secondary education, has been carried out without an organic incorporation of scientific thought, and the old ritualist patterns of memorization and verbalism of traditional pedagogical practice have been maintained. The internal inefficiency and the qualitative deterioration of teaching seem from a specifically pedagogical point of view to neutralize the democratizing effect of quantitative expansion.

In the second place, it is necessary to bear in mind that the internal transformation of post-primary schooling is a necessity that cannot be postponed. Any internal democratization of these levels must include a basic renovation of the curriculum to make it relevant and effective. This implies not only the renovation of content and pedagogical organization, but also the training of teachers and provision of adequate equipment for schools, etc. The democratization of these levels also requires the elimination of the differentiated pedagogical streams mentioned previously.

In recent decades no other social good has had such widespread diffusion in society as education. Through this change great numbers of people gained access to a system of abstract communication and gained the capacity to analyse their personal problems as an effect of the social structure. Fundamentally, education imposed rationality on the mental structure of vast social groups.

This educational change has had an influence on the increase of social conflict. On one hand, the friction between generations has played a dominant part in different types of conflict. Young people are qualitatively different from their elders and have to face the contradiction between their educational attainment (even if it is formal) and the occupations offered to them, which do not always require education and which may have been carried out previously by less qualified persons. Their education prompts them to analyse and to question the pattern of development and the political–social structure, although the opportunities for political participation are limited or are still governed by the 'patronizing' models of the past. In a young Latin America, these contradictions have time and again provoked protests ranging from contestation to youth revolt.

In a period of transition like the one the region is now experiencing, the future is still undefined, and its concretization can hardly be achieved through concensus when traditionalist and modern forces coexist in society. In this necessary conflict, education plays an important part in strengthening the political capacity and participation of the younger generation.

The future tendencies of the democratization of education depend on the democratization of society, and this in turn depends to a great extent on the changes introduced to modify the traditional educational system that still predominates in Latin America. In this perspective, we can indicate some of the social trends that may favourably influence the democratization of education.

Migration trends suggest that towards the year 2000, the rural population will represent only 23.8 per cent of the total Latin American population, of which part will be 'non-farm', another part will be employed in new agro-industrial complexes, and yet another part will enjoy better conditions of viability for their small enterprises. The actual process of destruction and restructurization of the peasantry, with the sequels of social exclusion due to the penetration of capitalist forms, will have run its course to a significant extent, and the relations of power will have been considerably modified. The presently excluded population will have greater negotiating power with respect to social benefits, due to its smaller size and the importance of agriculture, the products of which will have to feed a total population of 625 million in the year 2000, as compared to 373 million in 1980. The parallel interpenetration between urban and rural areas will have accelerated, and modernization will be extended into the latter, with its effects on social mobilization and demand for education.

In the cities, technological change in the production of goods forms part of the basis for the constitution of a new type of proletariat, more educated, employed in more complex organizations, and beginning to express demands that are not limited to individual interests but extend to projects for social change. A qualitatively different demand for education could arise from this new sector.

The so-called marginal urban population already has been settled in cities and has a certain knowledge of the mechanisms of negotiation and the dynamics of conflict with those in power. This knowledge has, at least, secured for certain marginal groups the benefit of some education—to a greater extent than regular employment. Their possibilities for participation are uncertain as regards the future, but the younger generation is better prepared for the analysis of its problems and for political action, and this constitutes a new social element.

Finally, the outstanding feature of the change in the occupational structure is the rapid increase of the communal, social and scientific services, due to the type of development carried out in Latin America. Thus, during the period 1960–70, the number of professionals and semi-professionals increased by 73 per cent. This category includes educators and a large percentage of university graduates. The services sector expanded, along with education, and its constituents live closely related to education, having experienced the meritocratic selection of the educational system.

In those societies in which the model of development is in the process of definition, the intellectual groups can fulfil a significant role, prefiguring images of the future. One of the possible images is that of a society which is neither acquisitive nor stratified, a society in which education is the principal agency of social mobility and the basis for the meritocratic recruitment of élites prepared to work towards a more just, democratic and functioning social order.

The forces that can promote social and educational changes already exist, although it is not possible to predict their orientation nor evaluate the impact of conditions foreign to Latin America that may facilitate or block these changes.

REFERENCES

1. *La enseñanza pública en México a través de los mensajes presidenciales hasta nuestros días.* Mexico City, Secretaría de Educación Pública, 1926.
2. Descripción de las principales tendencias del sistema educativo entre 1950 y 1980. *Desarrollo y educación en América Latina; Síntesis general.* Vol. 2, *El sistema educativo y la situación de la educación básica,* Part IV, pp. 1–63. Buenos Aires, 1981. (Unesco/ECLA/UNDP project 'Desarrollo y Educación en América Latina y el Caribe', Informes finales, 4.)
3. SCHIEFELBEIN, E. Efectos de la educación pre-escolar en el ingreso al sistema formal. In: Comisión Económica para América Latina (CEPAL)/Fondo de las Naciones Unidas para la Infancia (UNICEF), *Pobreza crítica en la niñez.* Santiago de Chile, 1981.
4. DE BRASLAVSKY, Berta P. *La enseñanza de la lectura en la escuela de América Latina.* Buenos Aires, 1981. (Unesco/ECLA/UNDP project 'Desarrollo y Educación en América Latina y el Caribe', Fichas, 17.)
5. TEDESCO, J. C. Elementos para un diagnostico del sistema educativo tradicional en América Latina. *El cambio educativo; situación y condiciones,* pp. 59–82. Buenos Aires, 1981. (Unesco/ECLA/UNDP project 'Desarrollo y Educación en América Latina y el Caribe', Informes finales, 2.)
6. RAMA, G. W. Condiciones sociales de la expansión y segmentación de los sistemas universitarios. In: Ateneo de Caracas/Universidad Central de Venezuela, Centro de Estudios del Desarrollo (CENDES), *Universidad, clases sociales y poder.* Caracas, 1982.
7. PARIAS, Louis-Henri (ed.). *L'histoire générale de l'enseignement et de l'éducation en France.* Vol. IV, *L'école et la famille dans une société en mutation,* by Antoine Prost. Paris, Nouvelle Librairie de France, 1981.
8. TERRA, Juan Pablo. *Alfabetismo y escolarización básica de los jóvenes en América Latina,* diagram 7 et seq. Buenos Aires, 1980. (Unesco/ECLA/UNDP project 'Desarrollo y Educación en América Latina y el Caribe', DEALC/24.)
9. Educacão e marginalidade na América Latina. *Cadernos de Pesquisa* (Fundação Carlos Chagas, San Pablo), No. 42, August 1982. (Special issue.)
10. *Boletín Demográfico* (Centro Latinoamericano de Demografía, Santiago de Chile), Year IX, No. 18, July 1976.

4
The impact of science and technology

Introduction

A science textbook, the classroom television, and the university research laboratory all testify to the close relationship of education to the organized exploration of the universe and systematic accumulation of knowledge, which we call science, and to the purposeful application of that knowledge to solve problems and to meet human needs, which we call technology. Certain indirect aspects of this relationship, although less evident, are especially significant for their mutual development within the total social context. A new technology introduced into production processes, for example, can lead to new socio-economic conditions, such as a shift in the demand for job skills, or a reduction in the work force or in working hours, as well as to new products and services and even to new values and life-styles. These new conditions, in turn, can affect the content of education and teaching methods and may lead to new educational objectives and changes in the structure of the educational system.

Conversely, education is an important factor in scientific and technological progress and economic development. In Chapter 1 (p. 27), Ivan T. Berend affirmed that 'basic mass education and a successful fight against illiteracy were prerequisites of the agricultural and industrial revolutions.... Without education society was not flexible enough, not mobile and not ready to absorb the new technological knowledge....' The on-going experience of the Green Revolution, which originated after the Second World War with the development of new, high-yield varieties of maize, wheat and rice in Mexico and the Philippines, has shown that the success or failure of modern agricultural technology and of the socio-economic reforms which it engenders depends largely on the educational level of the population.

In its assessment of the prospects for the development of education, the International Panel on the Future Development of Education found that

The ongoing transformation of society, due in large part to scientific and technological progress, has important consequences and implications for education, both as a mirror of society and as an agent of social change. Since scientific and technological progress *is not linear, simple extrapolation of trends is an unreliable forecasting tool, and the less foreseeable side-effects of a new technology often prove more significant for educacation than the technology itself* [1, p. 6].

Although some recent forecasts of scientific discoveries and technological breakthroughs have been impressively accurate, it has proved more difficult to foresee their impact on society, and thus their implications for education. Nevertheless, some tentative conclusions might be drawn from an analysis of certain general features of contemporary scientific and technological progress, or what is now commonly referred to as the scientific and technological revolution (STR).

WHAT IS THE SCIENTIFIC AND TECHNOLOGICAL REVOLUTION?

The remarkable expansion of research and development (R&D) activity since the Second World War, particularly in the industrialized countries, is perhaps the most obvious feature of this revolution in science and technology. Research today extends into nearly every imaginable field of human experience, though the specific research agenda varies from country to country. The expansion of science and technology, both in terms of inputs (personnel and funds) and outputs (research findings and inventions), is significant for education in several respects. It is of course the task of the schools and universities to provide basic training for the growing army of scientists, engineers and technicians. Also, in many countries, post-secondary institutions are increasingly called on to provide highly specialized training and refresher courses for personnel at various stages of their professional career. The demand for well-trained personnel to work in science and technology has contributed to a renewed emphasis, reported by countries at various stages of development, on science teaching within general education at secondary and even primary levels.

One clue to the increasing output of R&D activity during the past three decades is the number of scientific publications, which has doubled every five to seven years, a rough indication of the pace of the information explosion. This has confronted educators with a dilemma: how to provide students with a comprehensive and up-to-date basic preparation without overloading the curriculum or extending the basic training period beyond reasonable bounds. The expanding 'knowledge industry' in the industrialized countries also has major implications for the restructuring of the labour force: in certain countries it is now estimated that more people are employed in the collection, processing and diffusion of information than in industrial production or in non-information services. According to the International Panel, 'This significant economic and social transformation poses a number of challenges for education today and tomorrow, which the technology of informatics may help to meet' [1, p. 7]. After noting that some countries are already concerned about the 'new literacy', which is the ability to use computers, the Panel predicted: 'Schooling based on memorization of facts will disappear, and education will shift its emphasis to the development of skills needed to manipulate greatly increased quantities of information in a logical and pluridisciplinary manner. Students will need to learn how to select information and apply it' [1, p. 7]. Some observers attach considerable importance to the generalization of information skills to help prevent the emergence of a new élite with its power based on access to and control of sophisticated information systems.

With the evolution of science and a corresponding trend towards ever greater specialization, there has been a proliferation of new disciplines and sub-disciplines. Although this trend may still be dominant, there is a recent and growing counter-trend towards holistic, systemic, trans-disciplinary and synthetic approaches to problem-solving and even to basic research. Unesco's Second Medium Term Plan notes that

very profound upheavals have reshaped the map of the scientific world and the relations between the various sciences. . . . A new configuration of fields of knowledge could be said to be forming, in which the branches of the future appear to be biology, data processing, systems theory and the communication and information sciences. . . . It is even tending to efface, to some extent at least, the old-established demarcation lines between the natural sciences and the social and human sciences [2, p. 36].

Although this new situation may be due in part to the internal dynamics of scientific inquiry, some observers see it as a consequence of recognizing that global problems require the expertise of many disciplines and the co-operation of many countries for their solutions. Ecological awareness is often cited as a major factor in the rapprochement between the natural and human sciences.

The divergent trends towards greater specialization on the one hand and holism on the other are not necessarily conflicting influences on education. New approaches to science education and technical training are being worked out in several countries with a view to providing a sound general education which emphasizes the unity of the sciences, and can form the basis for specialized training which can be developed throughout one's career. The integrated teaching of the natural sciences will probably be accentuated in the coming years. Some experts feel the trans-disciplinary approach will gradually draw together the methods of the natural and social sciences, making both desirable and necessary some degree of integrated training for specialists in virtually any scientific discipline. Other disciplines, such as philosophy and the arts, are also likely to be affected by holistic and systemic perspectives, much as they have been influenced by the theory of relativity.

Yet another feature of the scientific and technical revolution is the accelerating pace of technological change, evident in the steady reduction of time between the development of a new technique and its application within society. The acceleration of change has far-reaching affects on the economy and on society generally, as well as on the psyche of contemporary man, hence its importance as a factor influencing the evolution of education. For the worker, the STR is rapidly modifying the production process and the conditions of work. Robots of various kinds are becoming common workmates in many countries. Computer-aided design and computer-aided manufacturing are seen by some observers as the harbingers of a new industrial revolution [3]. Labour-saving production and services have made possible a reduction in working hours and physical effort, thereby freeing time, energy and resources for other uses, including education and leisure.

Since application of new technologies has often resulted in the elimination of jobs, it is associated in some countries with growing unemployment. New technologies have also led to the creation of new jobs, often requiring specialized skills, resulting in a continuous transformation of the labour force and working conditions, and thus a growing demand for well trained and versatile workers and a decreasing demand for manual labour. Educational systems in industrialized countries are already responding to this new demand pattern with a shift away from narrow vocational training towards a general, basic vocational preparation which can be supplemented later with specialized training to match specific job requirements. This shift will no doubt contribute to the expansion of lifelong learning structures, such as evening and correspondence courses and in-service training schemes. In some countries there is a growing demand for courses of all kinds to enrich the use of leisure time. Since leisure time is expected to increase significantly in the years ahead, education related to leisure pursuits will probably expand significantly in some countries over the next two decades.

PROBLEMS

Like any revolution, the STR brings with it both promise and problems, some of which have implications for education. In the words of the International Panel 'science and technology are not value-free, and problems arise in the application of new scientific knowledge through technology. Thus the latter appears often to determine the development of society, rather than vice versa; man tends to do what he is able to do. This can and does lead to questionable social development' [1, p. 6]. The Panel noted in particular 'the alarming use of science and technology for military ends, rather than social development' [1, p. 6].

Individual firms and industries, as well as government agencies, are now providing substantial funding for basic and applied research of all kinds which might conceivably contribute to the commercial advantage of the firm or country and to military strength. According to a recent study

Global expenditures on military research and development in 1980 were of the approximate order of $35,000 million or approximately one quarter of the estimated $150,000 million expended for all research and development [4, p. 5].

The Director-General of Unesco, Amadou-Mahtar M'Bow, places this orientation in an ethical context:

the vast human and material resources allocated to arms industries and military research and development are thereby denied to those who are engaged in the world struggle against the poverty which afflicts so many people. The talents and energies of 500,000 engineers and research workers are being used to perfect the technology of death and thousands of millions of dollars are invested every year for that purpose [5, p. 4].

In addition to the reduction of resources available for education resulting from this situation, prospects for the development of education are affected in various other ways. For instance, universities in many countries are obliged to compete for research funding against non-academic institutions which are more amenable to the direct control and the secrecy requirements of industry and the military. As more and more advanced research is contracted outside educational institutions, they may find difficulty in attracting and holding top specialists. Furthermore, universities which obtain research funding from the private sector and even some public agencies are usually bound to pursue research of interest to the funding source, which may be unrelated to important scientific and social concerns of the university.

Concern seems to be growing over the need for a socially controlled decision-making process to govern or orient R&D. Thus, in recent years, a number of countries have adopted procedures requiring studies and public hearings to determine the environmental impact of projects or new technologies before they can be licensed or receive public funding. A number of individual scientists and scientific societies are taking initiatives, such as the Pugwash Conferences on Science and World Affairs, to consider the social and ethical dimensions of R&D and to inform public opinion. (If this kind of concern continues to spread, the training of scientists is likely to be affected, in view of their particular responsibility and influence with respect to the orientation of research and application of its findings.) This may well affect the training of scientists and reinforce both the rapprochement of the natural and the social sciences and the interaction of natural sciences with the humanities. A few university programmes already reflect this new orientation in the training of scientists and engineers.

Closely related to the problem of whether and how to guide R&D in desirable directions is the

common challenge that will have to be faced by most societies—whether industrialized or developing—in the years ahead: to narrow the margin of incomprehension, not to say the cleavage, between the world of technology and the mass of the people, and to ensure the dynamic integration of the achievements of modern technology into the reality of the underlying cultures [2, p. 38].

In addition to improving science education in the schools, there is a need to popularize science and technology, to inform public opinion of major advances in knowledge and their implications for society and for the individual. Socio-economic development is conditioned to a large extent by the understanding and *acceptance of innovations by the general population, or at least by key groups, such as farmers, entrepreneurs, artisans and public officials.*

Probably the most significant problem deriving from STR is the growing scientific and technological gap between the developing countries and the industrialized countries. According to some estimates, nine out of ten scientists work in countries constituting one-third of the world's population. Furthermore, a significant number of these scientists are drawn from the less technologically-advanced countries. It is no surprise, then, that R&D is largely oriented to the needs of interest groups in the industrialized countries and serves to strengthen their advantages in other spheres, notably in armaments and in trade. The developing countries are largely dependent on the industrialized countries to obtain the technologies needed for economic development. Apart from the difficulties involved in negotiating a transfer of technology, the recipient country must have an adequate science and technology infrastructure to assimilate it into its own culture and a relatively stable socio-economic system.

The United Nations Conference on Science and Technology for Development (Vienna, 1979) helped focus attention on the serious ramifications of this situation and the crucial necessity for the developing countries to create and strengthen their own endogenous scientific and technological capacity. It is a major challenge for the educational systems in developing countries to prepare vast numbers of scientists, engineers, technicians, and a more scientifically aware public. Large numbers of teachers would need to be trained to teach science and technical subjects at all levels, and textbooks and other instructional materials relevant to each country would need to be produced. In terms of physical infrastructure, thousands of school and university laboratories and hundreds of research institutes would need to be constructed and equipped. Obviously such a large-scale undertaking could be accomplished only if it were accorded a very high priority by each country concerned and supported by international co-operation. Some developing countries have taken up this challenge and others will no doubt do so. But with the relative advantage of the industrialized countries and their existing momentum it appears highly unlikely that the developing countries can reduce the scientific and technological gap during the next twenty years.

SUPPORT FOR EDUCATION FROM SCIENCE

While the STR generates social changes and problems with an impact on education, new knowledge and inventions are also at the disposal of education to meet its many responsibilities and challenges. However, the International Panel observed 'a considerable gap between research findings in medicine, psychology or genetic epistemology and the science of education, on the one hand, and educational practices, especially teaching methods, on the other' [1, p. 6]. Similarly, the Panel noted 'a marked gap between the introduction of new technologies, with their consequent social transformations, and their recognition in the school curriculum' [1, p. 6].

Government delegates to the 38th Session of Unesco's International Conference on Education (Geneva, November 1981) agreed that research on the teaching–learning process deserves priority attention: 'In particular, the development of intelligence and innate abilities needed to be investigated more thoroughly, with a view to adapting pedagogical methods to specific age-groups and levels of education' [6, p. 19]. Some educators feel that a more efficient application of existing knowledge could improve the quality and cost-effectiveness of education considerably, aspects of particular importance to the developing countries. While recognizing 'a strong need for a thorough, scientific investigation of education itself' [1, p. 7], the International Panel further recognized

the importance for developing countries to undertake research in the fields of psychology and pedagogy within their specific socio-cultural context . . . since the psychological development of an individual is largely conditioned by his or her social environment. Thus, research findings from one country, while of interest to others, need to be verified by researchers in other countries before their implications can be interpreted for education in those countries [1, p. 7].

For some observers, educational technology, if properly exploited, could help overcome certain obstacles and improve the scope and quality of educational services at a reasonable unit cost. A few educators even foresee the advent of 'electronic education', which will exploit the computer and the growing range of electronic media and devices to make education more accessible and individualized.[1] No doubt computer-assisted learning, already common in higher educational institutions in a few countries, will become more widely used in the next twenty years, and the computer will also be used increasingly in the management of educational programmes and institutions. Although there seems to be a broad consensus that the teacher will not and cannot be replaced in the classroom by machines, the growing use of computers and other sophisticated learning aids may affect the learning process and modes of thinking in ways not yet foreseen. This eventuality, however, is unlikely to have any immediate direct impact on education in the developing countries. In general, the International Panel found it doubtful 'that science will provide the developing countries with important new means which could be used on a large scale to resolve their most pressing education problems, particularly at the level of primary education' [1, pp. 6–7].

---

1. See, for example, Peter Wagschal's article 'Colad College: Education ex Machina', *Education Tomorrow* (Washington, D.C.), Vol. 6, No. 2, April 1981.

BROAD IMPLICATIONS
OF THE SCIENTIFIC
AND TECHNOLOGICAL REVOLUTION
FOR EDUCATION IN THE FUTURE

Some research findings and technological developments will no doubt have a direct effect on the content of science teaching and perhaps to some extent on general education, as well as on the teaching–learning process itself. However, education is likely to be far more influenced indirectly by the complex influence of science and technology on society. Because of the uniqueness of each society, generalizations about such indirect influences on education are particularly hazardous to formulate, yet a broad distinction can be made between the industrialized countries and the developing countries. In the former, new technologies have contributed to considerable improvements in the general standard of living over the past several decades, and people have come to expect continuous technological progress and social change. By contrast, the rural majority in most developing countries has benefited relatively little from modern technology. The differences in the condition of these two broad groups of countries suggest that education will have to continue to respond to rather disparate needs and potentials, although one common denominator is the need to prepare people to understand the benefits and risks of new technologies and to cope with a changing social environment.

Unesco's assessment of current world problems finds a promising outlook for the 1980s in certain branches of science in which advances in basic research are linked with technological innovations, some of which may bring about radical changes in people's way of life. 'But in spite of the considerable potential offered by the present-day applications of science for improving the lot of mankind as a whole and the likelihood that this potential will be greatly increased by fresh developments, it must be admitted that the gap between the possible and the actual is still enormous' [2, p. 37]. There is an obvious and vital need to direct the development of science and technology to solve pressing world problems and to increase the well-being of all peoples. In this perspective, education has a three-fold contribution to make: first, education in a very broad sense is needed for the transmission and renewal of culture, thus making possible the incorporation of science and technology into everyday life; secondly, general education, in or out of school, should introduce the student to the basic concepts and methods of science and develop a scientific outlook; thirdly, scientific and technological education at secondary and higher levels must produce the specialized manpower required for research and development. The International Panel identified two specific challenges for educators:

the need to relate science to man's spiritual and humanistic values and the need to develop the critical sense of students so that they become capable of a more objective appreciation of science and technology and can determine the effects and costs of a new technology [1, p. 6].

The impact of science and technology

The five articles which follow in this chapter deal with aspects of the impact of science and technology on education. The first article, by Denis Osborne, discusses the symbiotic relationship between science and technology, then outlines changes in the content, techniques and policies of general education, as well as in the actors in the educational process which are likely to occur in the near future. Mircea Malitza examines probable changes in the content of science education, with particular emphasis on the rapid expansion of scientific knowledge and the persistent gap between this knowledge and what is actually taught in the classroom. In the third article, Harold Shane suggests guidelines for the future development of education, deduced from current thinking in the social sciences. Ivan Obraztsov stresses the growing importance of higher education in the scientific and technological revolution. The final article, exerpted from the report of a recent international congress convened by Unesco, presents a synthesis of current thinking on the significance of science and technology education for national development.

REFERENCES

1. SECOND MEETING OF THE INTERNATIONAL PANEL ON THE FUTURE DEVELOPMENT OF EDUCATION (Paris, 30 November to 4 December 1981). *Final Report.* Paris, Unesco, April 1982. (Unesco doc. ED-81/FUTURED/4.)
2. GENERAL CONFERENCE OF UNESCO (Fourth Extraordinary Session, Paris, 1982). *Second Medium-Term Plan (1984–1989).* Paris, 1983. (Unesco doc. 4XC/4 Approved.)
3. BYLINSKY, Gene. A New Industrial Revolution is on the Way. *Fortune* (New York), 5 October 1981, pp. 106–14.
4. NORMAN, Colin. *Knowledge and Power: The Global Research and Development Budget.* Washington, D.C., Worldwatch Institute, 1979. (Worldwatch paper, 31.)
5. M'BOW, Amadou-Mahtar. A World of Justice, Peace and Progress. *The Unesco Courier* (Paris), March 1982.
6. INTERNATIONAL CONFERENCE ON EDUCATION (38th Session, Geneva, 10–19 November 1981). *Final Report.* Paris, Unesco: International Bureau of Education, February 1982. (Unesco doc. ED/MD/66.)

Science, technology and educational change

Denis G. Osborne

PROGRESS IN SCIENCE AND TECHNOLOGY

Science grows! There are shifts in the focus of interest and revisions of fundamental thinking, such as the introduction of relativity or wave mechanics, but new knowledge builds on past knowledge even when it leads to its re-evaluation. The rate of growth of the sciences has been measured by inputs such as the number of workers engaged in research, and by outputs, for example the number of published papers, but it is not necessary to accept the validity of any particular measures to recognize that scientific knowledge has grown very rapidly in recent years and that it continues to do so. This growth includes the exploration of areas of human experience to which science had not previously been thought applicable. The growth is by no means steady; it changes speed and direction in response to the impetus of original ideas that seem to owe more to individual genius than to the broader historical context. The progress of science depends on who will pay for it, and how much, and hence on its relationship to society and its association with technology.

The word 'technology' could have been chosen to mean the study of techniques, but it is used rather to describe their development and application. Human activity in technology is directed towards an objective and towards the solution of any problems that hinder attainment of that objective. The objective could be putting a man on the moon or improving the flavour of tinned soup: in either case every available technique and scientific concept may be considered and used to help reach the chosen goal. The worker finds the goal clearly defined (though it may need to be modified as the work progresses), but the means by which the goal is to be attained is a matter for choice. Different workers given the same task may choose different approaches, leading to problems when rival manufacturers introduce incompatible technologies (for navigational aids, television or recording systems, for example).

In technology we set clear objectives and choose any available methods to reach the goal; in the basic sciences we explore new territories with less defined goals. It is my contention that most research in the basic sciences is dictated by available technologies. New techniques lead to new science. The engineer's concept of information, derived from work in telecommunications, was fundamental to progress in genetics; other discoveries in the pure sciences have been made possible only by the use of computers or by technologies for achieving very low temperatures. While technology may be considered 'applied science', so may science be 'applied technology'.

If we see technology as the means to reach a given goal, we shall recognize a whole hierarchy of means and ends. The electronic circuitry may be the means, the computer the end result, but at different levels the computer may be the means to execute the programme that diagnoses the disease that suggests the treatment that saves the patient's life. Because of this hierarchical structure, changes in technology at any one level depend on goals set at a higher level. The goals and structure of society as a whole influence the direction of technological change and the rate of progress in technology. Just as there is a reciprocal relationship between science and technology, with each deriving benefit from the other, so there is a reciprocal relationship between technology and society. Technology contributes to economic and social development but also derives its own strength and justification from the social context.

Strong feelings about the place of technology in society are nothing new. However the contemporary examination of technology and its role was given a special impetus by Jacques Ellul, whose book *La technique* [1], published in France in 1954, suggested that technology was not simply produced in response to our efforts to attain our chosen goals but that technology itself determined those goals. Our inability to do something is reason enough for not doing it: but Ellul was concerned that the converse of this is not necessarily true. There may be some things that we win the power to do but which would be better not done.

In a recent analysis of different attitudes to technology, Tom Kitwood [2] proposes a central axiom—that technology, based on the methods and discoveries of science, will bring benefit to all and solve the material problems of human existence—and then considers ways in which this axiom is extended, qualified or rejected. Following Kitwood's analysis, one can see extensions of this axiom by those who believe that the benefits of technology will go beyond the material realm into the social and the spiritual realms. Others put forward qualifications seeking 'limits to growth' (in which technology is to be used to control technology), or advocating the virtue of decentralization ('small is beautiful'), or favouring strict regulation of the use and development of technology, because they see it as the tool of centralized state control. Finally, there is the rejection of technology by those who think it will not bring adequate benefit to humanity to compensate for its power to distort and dehumanize human relationships.

It is not necessary to decide our own attitude to technology in order to make reasonable predictions about its future development and impact, though our predictions will depend on the attitudes we expect others to adopt. However, we need to be aware of the dangers of over-simplification in any generalizations about technology as a whole. There are many technologies: some we may accept in a relatively passive manner, others we will welcome with enthusiasm, others we will reject. We can expect increased experience of technical change, in particular the experience from that of earlier generations, to bring greater discernment. The general debate may focus on finding criteria by which the merits of particular technologies should be assessed. However, it would be foolish to exaggerate the accuracy with which 'technology assessment' can be carried out, and we should expect decisions about the acceptability of technology to depend more on attitudes than on the results of careful argument. Even so we may reasonably expect that the rejection of specific technologies for particular tasks will not be confused with the rejection of technology.

Contemporary research interests

It may help to consider the impact of science and technology on education if we try to analyse contemporary research interests since these are also, of necessity, likely areas of growth in the next twenty years. Three key words serve well as foci for describing some of the pressures of demand for research in the basic sciences and developments in technology: these are energy, environment and information. These categories may not be strictly comparable, but the contrasts between them are important for our purposes.

Energy has been a fundamental concept in the basic sciences for more than a century. Interest in energy arises from its usefulness and the fact that when it is used it is lost or degraded—so that the directed motion of a car, for example, is changed into the random motion of heat, and even the heat in our homes is dissipated through the windows. In consequence, we want more energy. Energy is something we possess. It is locked up in the mineral resources we extract and the food we grow.

The environment, by definition, has always been with us. We become more aware of it because of its deterioration. We do not have more of it, or less. We can have better or worse. We aim to conserve the environment. When the environment is used, we need to sustain and manage it.

Information and its communication is a fashionable concern. The mathematical representation for the communication of information led to new techniques for the generation, analysis, retrieval, and presentation of information. When information is used, it is not lost or conserved; it is multiplied. Information has been in short supply in the past (and still is in short supply in many developing countries), but the problems now are rather of an overwhelming flood of information, of pollution by false or harmful information, and of the need to select useful information from the irrelevancies in which it is embedded.

One further distinction may be drawn between these three categories. Energy is a means of possession, of human dominance over things. The environment raises questions of human interaction with things. Information can be generated by people and can facilitate relationships between people.

The concerns expressed over the last twenty years about the environment and about energy will continue to demand attention, but it seems that the main growth area will be that of information. Developments in communication theory and the mathematical analysis of information will be matched by improved technology, lower costs, wider application and major social impact. The coupling of information technology to production processes can greatly increase productivity. Energy for fertilizers linked with information about their use can lead to increased agricultural production, with prospects of major and rapid improvements as new varieties of crop are introduced—varieties that may themselves be obtained through the use of information science in genetic engineering. The use of computers and word processors can have a similar effect on productivity in office work. Higher productivity is likely to be matched by changing patterns of demand, including the demand for more leisure. We have, perhaps, hardly begun to appreciate the political problems of the leisure society or to consider the opportunities and challenges it presents for education in those countries where it will be an important factor in the near future.

Anticipating the unexpected

It would be foolish to think that we can predict with any certainty the shifts of emphasis in science and technology over the next twenty years. It is safe to assume that we should expect the unexpected. This may come in new fundamental concepts (how valid are our notions of symmetry in physics or our preference for simplicity in explanations?), or in their application. Readiness for unexpected change, preparation for innovation, is one of the demands made on education. However, not all changes need prove unexpected. We should at least try to predict some of the changes in the next two decades.

Over the last twenty years, there has been a tendency towards increased specialization in research and concentration on detail. It is possible to detect in current research trends a reversal of this emphasis, a turning away from efforts to 'know more about less' to a systems approach in which the primary interest lies in 'getting it together'. In chemistry there is more interest in synthesis than on analysis. In biology the frontier is seen as the behaviour of living systems, with more interest, for example, in gathering basic information on flora applicable to conservation and environmental management and rather less on the biochemistry of reactions inside chloroplasts. In astrophysics there is a fascination with the pattern of the universe as a whole and the interrelation of its different components, rather than on any one particular class of object.

In technology, concerns for energy balances, for environmental conservation and for information processing all reflect this same theme of giving more attention to the system as a whole than to its component parts. Somewhat similar concerns are reflected in the fashionable interest in 'science and technology for development' and the task—especially relevant when considering education—of harnessing scientific and technological manpower to work effectively for economic and social development. What other ideas may guide our predictions about future trends in science and technology? I suggest the following.

The general attitude to science and technology will be one of cautious welcome, of acceptance with suspicion.

Suspicion will focus mostly on 'hard' and large-scale technologies, and those with which an identifiable and emotionally disagreeable risk is associated.

There will be relatively greater support for smaller-scale enterprise and for activities that might be considered more humane and safe.

In pure science, much progress will come from the use of recently developed techniques.

In technology, the direction of progress will depend largely on goals selected in response to economic and social pressures.

The quest for political stability within countries will stimulate concern to manage the introduction of new technologies in ways that will be least disruptive (for example, the least creation of unemployment).

International competition will strengthen economic considerations in the selection of new technologies.

War on a global scale will not occur in the next twenty years but the threat of war will remain.

The relative importance of science and technology in developing countries will increase, so that efforts will be made to harness science and technology to the economic and social objectives of development.

IMPACTS ON EDUCATION

Content changes

Continuing progress in science and technology must be matched by continuing change in the content of what is taught at virtually all levels of education. To a large extent the changes to be expected in the secondary school curriculum over the next twenty years will be determined by the need to catch up with developments in the sciences over the last fifty. These will bring to the school curriculum new areas of interest and new methods of thinking and of understanding. Developments in technology may have an even greater impact on what is taught, though much of this will be mediated indirectly through the impact of technology on society as a whole. Where new ideas in the sciences are matched by new methods of doing things in technology the impact on education will be especially marked. These include, I believe, an increased interest in field studies and the 'systems' approach across all the sciences, a shift of emphasis in medicine towards health care and nutrition, and a subject area dealing with information or communications theory.

The renewed interest in field studies in the biological sciences and the concern for science and technology for development, together with an increasing recognition that research frontiers are often on the borders between traditionally accepted disciplines, make it necessary to consider for the secondary school level how best to develop an integrated science syllabus that is more than a superficial summary. When the content of the syllabus is very broad, there is a danger that the subject will be taught in such general terms as to be more a 'science of science' rather than science itself. It seems necessary to include in the syllabus some sections of sufficient detail for this defect to be avoided, even if the choice of sections for this purpose is left somewhat random. Field studies are applicable for physics and chemistry as well as for biology. The field to be studied would include materials and their uses (and the reasons why different materials are best suited for different applications), and this could be linked with increased use of construction kits and mechanical toys. Although this suggestion may be particularly relevant for some developing countries, it is also an important consideration for technologically sophisticated communities, as it offers a foundation both for adaptability to different types of future employment and the more enriching use of leisure.

The assumption of increasing responsibility for medical care by the state and the growing complexity and cost of medical treatment may lead to a recognition of the economic value of a well-taught health component in an integrated science syllabus. The integration could be provided by focusing on the working of the body and the exploration of the environment.

Microprocessors and their use have recently aroused great interest. The basic ideas of information and its communication on which they are based are still, however, much neglected. Ideas about communication channels, binary units (bits) of information, band width and noise, for example, could be introduced into the secondary school curriculum. The need for this is based on the assumption that people mistrust and fear technologies about which they are totally ignorant and that a little knowledge can do much to dispel those fears.

Changes in educational content may be expected also as a result of social changes attributed mainly to the use of new technologies; uncertainty about career expectations will make flexibility and adaptability desirable goals for education and there will be a need to meet the growing challenges of education for leisure. The probability that the worker will have more leisure in the future suggests that sport may play a larger part in people's lives. Sport has received a great boost both directly and indirectly from the applications of technology. Television has given it much wider popularity than it could otherwise have enjoyed. Heated swimming pools, all-weather playing surfaces and the general social setting of increased affluence and better transportation have enabled more people to participate. Physical activity is, in any case, likely to be seen as desirable relaxation by more people as technology reduces the need for physical work.

Flexibility and adaptability in later life will be especially valuable because employment patterns can be expected to change as a result of technological innovation. Flexibility would be fostered by the type of education that is less a training in skills than the development of an ability to set goals and solve problems in order to attain them. There has been much emphasis on problem solving in some educational systems in recent years, and some attention to open ended inquiry or exploration. There seems to have been less attention paid to the setting of goals and this is something to which those concerned with the theory and practice of education may wish to give more attention. The exploratory character of certain contemporary approaches to school science, with ill-defined goals and with an emphasis on open-ended experiments, may be indicative of a pure science rather than a technology orientation.

The evolution of science affects the content of general education through the introduction of new concepts and attitudes, as well as through technology. Thinking in probabilities is one hallmark of the scientist, so the content of general education in an age of science ought to include elementary statistics and probability theory. Moreover this subject, more than any other, may help students to anticipate change that will affect their lives and adapt to it.

Changes in educational techniques

The impact of scientific and technological progress on the means of education comes both directly, through the use of new techniques, and indirectly, through the changed goals and patterns of society. As far as existing educational technologies are concerned—language laboratories, simple computers, systems for programmed learning, for example—it is easy to predict more of the same. Faster information retrieval through computer assisted systems rather than traditional libraries may become available for many in the upper age-groups of secondary schools within twenty years. One consequence of the time saved in seeking information could be an ability to discover contradictory points of view on a given subject and thus to develop powers of discernment, rather than of rote learning. The ready availability of information should, in any case, lead to a continued decrease in the importance attached to memory work in the school curriculum.

Machine assisted learning is obviously suitable, and even fun, for the development of more routine skills of computation, language and perhaps of logic. The use of such machines will enable individuals to progress at different speeds and will free teachers for other tasks. There are, however, a number of different possible consequences in the more general development of the individual pupil that will need to be considered and assessed as new techniques are introduced. For example, will the tendency to assimilate information from the electronic media, including television, rather than from books, lead to a different type of thinking? McLuhan [3] attributes our fascination with sequential ideas to the prevalence of the printed word. Will those who enjoy an audio-visual education from the electronic media be less linear in their reasoning? Again, will a less personal (even if more individual) means of instruction prove damaging to the development of personal relationships and the skills of conversation? It is arguable that the real goals of our educational systems are not so much the attainment of skills and understanding in selected areas but the experience of co-operation and working together to reach a common goal. The use of machine assisted learning for part of the curriculum need not mean losing sight of these broader social objectives. This consideration serves as a reminder that the introduction of any new techniques reinforces the need to examine the goals towards which an activity is directed and to guard against the danger that the availability of the means may determine the choice of the ends.

Progress in science and technology will also have an indirect impact on educational techniques through the changes science and technology bring to society as a whole. Greater productivity could lead to greater affluence and either to problems of unemployment or the liberation of more workers for 'social service', including teaching, because less are needed for agriculture and manufacturing. In practice this could mean smaller class sizes, or more opportunity for less formal teaching in small groups. Such a trend would balance the reduced experience of personal encounter that may be caused by the use at other times of more machine assisted learning methods. Indeed the use of machines for teaching more routine skills would free some teachers for other work, thus facilitating their work with small groups of pupils rather than large classes.

Although progress in science and technology depends upon and fosters increased professionalism and specialization, one consequence of this is a new awareness of the need for balance, of the value of the generalist, and of the necessary interdependence between those whose competence embraces only a small part of the larger whole of human experience. In the school context, this could be reflected in a revived emphasis on structures, giving pupils a sense of belonging to a small group, and less concern to offer a great variety of specialist options for study.

The emphasis on small groups, the problems of finding suitable employment quickly for young school-leavers, and the widely acknowledged, but seldom exploited, evidence that the best way to learn and to understand a subject is to teach it, may lead to greater use of senior pupils as tutors. This could be linked with a recognition that the ability to teach is an asset for all, for parents and managers and salesmen and service engineers, for doctors and paramedical staff, as well as for those employed specifically as teachers. It would follow that basic ideas of education or pedagogy should be included in the secondary school curriculum. If this were done, some understanding of educational methods and techniques would be shared between the teacher and learner to their mutual advantage. In order to hasten the spread of new ideas and new technologies, some societies may link the right to education with a responsibility to help others to learn. In a technological society, we have greater opportunity to be 'teachers all'.

Policy changes

Predictions about the impact of scientific and technological progress on educational techniques and content may lead to educational policies aimed at fostering changes thought to be desirable and mitigating those that are unwelcome. The balance between economic and social factors in the quest for development will influence the character of education and, in particular, help determine the importance attached to science and technology in education. Thus, if there is an emphasis on economic progress and on the role of science and technology in contributing to that progress, the pattern of education will be shaped largely by the demands of technology: to provide a general basic science education for a large part of the population; to stress the importance of mathematics; to give opportunities for highly specialized courses in engineering, science, agriculture, medicine; to create ample facilities (matched by attractive career prospects) for technical education.

However, in a twenty-year time-span, the disillusion now expressed by some people for science and technology may be matched by a disillusion with economic growth and by revised thinking about development goals. If this is so, the policy questions will be less of the type, How can education promote science and technology for the economic benefit of society? than, How can science and technology assist education and promote human welfare generally? Of course both types of question have to be asked, but the weight given to the two will be different in each society at different times in history. Moreover, the appreciation and enjoyment of science and technology is itself an important goal. It is good to know—and to know that we know—more about the world and the whole process of development in which we are engaged. It is possible to enjoy technical competence, seeing things well made and jobs well done. An appreciation of science and technology can contribute much to the quality of life.

Development goals may change as basic needs are better fulfilled. Societies may reach out for more fully human aspirations and for this purpose see science and technology in a different role. How could this be reflected in educational structures and administration? We have considered above the importance of human relationships in education and the role of small groups in supporting them, which will need to be borne in mind when adapting educational structures to make full use of new technologies, especially those technologies related to information.

Needs and opportunities for international collaboration in education

The quantity of international collaboration in any field, and the rate with which ideas are exchanged, structures created or new patterns of behaviour adopted, are consequences of communications technology and transportation. The impact of further progress in science and technology on education will be effected in large part automatically through improved information systems, cheaper telecommunications and easier travel.

This makes it progressively easier for all of us to learn from others. We need to learn more about the impact of education on the growth of science and technology. We need to learn about the success and failure of new educational techniques, including techniques for structuring and administering an educational system. Those concerned with education need the stimulus of new ideas. International meetings and exchanges of staff are proven methods by which this need to learn from others can be met.

However, it is possible that with improved facilities for international collaboration, the technological means will dictate the educational ends. There are several dangers. There is the danger of contamination when false ideas are transmitted, like a disease, through the global village. Although the alternative to the free spread of ideas is abhorred as censorship, some messages—incitement to racial hatred for example—need to be challenged. There is also the danger of gradually reducing the rich cultural diversity of education in different countries to a uniform pattern.

The dangers point to a need for international co-operation based more on a recognition of our ignorance than on an attempt to export our knowledge. Ideas then come as a vision of new goals and new methods, not as a message conveyed by propaganda. The diversity of different national patterns of education becomes something from which we can all learn. The spread of educational fashions, not taken to extremes, can stimulate and encourage. But our attitude as participants in these international endeavours needs to be marked by humility and an earnest desire to lessen our ignorance.

REFERENCES

1. ELLUL, J. *La technique*. Paris, Armand Colin, 1954. (Collection sciences politiques.) (Translated by John Wilkinson, *The Technological Society*. London, Jonathan Cape, 1965.)
2. KITWOOD, T. The World Re-fashioned for Human Use. *The New Universities Quarterly* (London), Vol. 34, No. 4, Autumn 1980, pp. 482–504.
3. McLUHAN, H. M.; FIORE, Q. *The Medium Is the Message*. London, Allen Lane, 1967.

The evolution of science curricula

Mircea Malitza

The factors playing a vital role in the evolution of curricula for science education are socio-economic development, the evolution of the sciences and the evolution of education. The influence coming from within education itself is determined by the evolution of educational policy, as well as by progress in educational research. Nowadays, the concept of lifelong education significantly transforms the aims, the functions and the structures of education; similarly, the concept of integration also calls for new approaches to learning and teaching. Research in education plays a leading role since the evolution of knowledge in psychology may determine the need for educational change.

TOWARDS INTERDISCIPLINARITY: THE EVOLUTION OF THE EXACT SCIENCES

The changes brought about by the scientific and technological revolution have had an impact on all sciences. The emphasis laid on organization and control is highly important. This characteristic is related to the institutionalization and planning of science and to the emergence of large-scale scientific research. However, the scientific discoveries made by large research teams working in huge laboratories coexist with individual discoveries. This characteristic is also related to the integration of science with technology. Most important scientific discoveries need sophisticated technological devices; on the other hand, the research involved in their design also entails advances in science.

An important feature of modern science and technology is their close connection with development, since they are assential factors of economic and social progress. Science education is considered a basic factor for the creation of endogenous scientific and technical capacities and for encouraging the creativity of each country. At the recent United Nations Conference on Science and Technology for Development (Vienna, August 1979), the concerns of different countries, as well as action within the United Nations Development Programme (UNDP), are evidence of this fact. For instance, a main objective for UNDP action is assistance in 'developing a comprehension of science in a given environment, of its possibilities and its limitations and the consequences that may be expected for the human being by the interaction of technological change with the environment'.

One of the characteristic aspects of the evolution of science during recent years has been the development of interdisciplinary fields. The interest aroused by such fields is enormous. Nowadays there is no sharp dividing line between biology, chemistry and physics. The mechanism determining the emergence of new fields is quite simple: a 'discovery' is made (which might be only the statement of an idea) in one field, and its application in other fields is attempted. This is possible since scientific information circulates well and is strongly oriented by the idea of application, not necessarily in the practical sense, but in the sense of an efficient use.

Biology has benefited from achievements in all areas of science, but it also stimulates research in other domains. Dissipative structures and oscillatory chemical reactions are examples of a situation where theories and fields such as differential-equation theory and quantum mechanics are stimulated by the solution of problems posed by biology.

Further studies will be carried out in the experimental field of elementary particles to establish the interaction of high energies, achieved by means of the huge accelerators now under construction. Another experimental direction likely to be continued in the future is the detection of gravitational waves predicted by the general relativity theory. An interesting field of theoretical research is the extension of the relativity theory to phenomena occurring at speeds greater than the speed of light.

In the future laser physics will be a top priority field and one may estimate that developments will occur especially with regard to increasing powers both in continuous and impulse conditions (10^5 W and 10^{16} W respectively). Recent advances in spectroscopy have relied to a great extent on the utilization of the laser as a light source. Apart from saturation spectroscopy, two other techniques utilizing lasers will develop greatly in the future: two-photon spectroscopy and trapped-particle spectroscopy. The most significant applications of these techniques will be in biological and nuclear spectroscopy.

With chemistry, one should first point to the development of technological branches and analytical methods. Because of the world energy crisis, applied chemistry research will be channelled both to more economical use of oil and to the discovery of cheap raw materials to replace it. At the same time more attention will be given to other fields of technological chemistry using natural raw materials. It is likely that there will be a significant boom in wood chemistry. Agricultural fertilizer chemistry will also develop, closely correlated to successes in applied genetic engineering. Attempts are being made to produce artificially micro-organisms able to develop symbiotically, which could fix atmospheric nitrogen to the roots of cereals. Such a solution would eliminate the need for chemical fertilizers, thereby avoiding water pollution and soil exhaustion.

'Traditional' analytical chemistry and all physico-chemical methods that can be adapted to analytical aims will develop, stimulated by two factors: (a) the needs of industry for improved analyses for the characterization and identification of materials; and (b) the environment factor, which has started to play an increasingly decisive role in the rejection or acceptance of some technologies, in relation to their capacity to disturb the ecological balance.

There will be advances in the field of theoretical chemistry, primarily in improved understanding of the relationship between electronic structure and chemical reactivity. The possibility of using high-speed computers and the development of an efficient algorithm for solving the Schrödinger equation for polyatomic systems opens up prospects for predicting the behaviour of a substance in a test tube before preparation.

Mathematizing a field of knowledge means using mathematical models. Mathematical models have already penetrated the most varied domains: management, international relations, medicine, linguistics and even analysis of art. They are used in explaining reality and in forecasting. However, a mathematical model is defined on the basis of assumptions about the object (process) to be modelled. So far, mathematics has not been concerned with the adequacy of these assumptions to the object (process). In the event of results not being satisfactory, the analysis could be started again, under different assumptions. This approach was adequate as far as mechanics or physics were concerned.

Nowadays, as mathematics must increasingly meet the requirements of economic, social and humanistic sciences, the approach is likely to be modified. In the future, mathematics will probably permit 'contradictory systems of axioms and more flexible logic, providing not only for the examination of exact proof but also for verisimilar reasoning' [1]. This presupposes the creating of a logic allowing for the analysis of contradictory axiomatic bases in which deduction will contain an 'authenticity coefficient'. This will also imply a deeper penetration of movement and dialectics into mathematics. Recent research has aimed at building up a dialectic logic and even a dynamic mathematics, based on the notion of the dynamic set [2].

The large-scale use of computers is one of the factors exerting pressures on contemporary mathematics. Innovations will occur in two main directions: telematics, which is the result of connecting huge data-processing centres to the mass-media network (including communication by satellite); and privatique, born from the association of microcomputers with video tapes, eventually branched to the communications networks. Telematics will enable on-the-spot processing of a tremendous amount of data, obtained via satellite from the remotest areas. Terminals will help to connect users to centralized information sources. 'Privatique' will allow for the use of computers in household activities: supervising domestic robots, recording telephone calls, triggering garden-watering devices, obtaining cooking and hygiene advice, gym lessons, and so on.

The impact of computers is also manifest in the development of the new science of informatics, closely correlated with mathematics. As a consequence, branches based on informatics concepts are increasingly studied: algorithm theory, formal languages, numerical analysis, etc. One of the most promising breakthroughs is the brain-computer symbiosis which may give a new dimension to mathematical theory like the one it has already added to applied mathematics. With the increased sophistication of computers, the opportunity to study systems by using computer simulation has been significantly increased. Simulation has become a research tool used in investigating all a system's variants and effects. Important results have been obtained, especially in forecasting.

IMPACT ON SCIENCE CURRICULA

Even if broad trends in the evolution of science are identified, the problem of their impact on curricula is not an easy one, because there is a dichotomy between the exact sciences as disciplines and the exact sciences as subjects to be taught. The difference between scientific knowledge and what is actually being taught is common and will certainly continue. Nevertheless, such differences will probably diminish in the future as science is directed more and more towards application, that is, the needs of socio-economic development; as contemporary culture is increasingly marked by the massive and rapid circulation of information whereby knowledge of discoveries are spread simultaneously all over the world through the mass media; and as a new emphasis on training leads to the allotment of larger sums for research into the design of flexible curricula.

This does not mean that all scientific discoveries will simultaneously be included in the curricula, but dangerous gaps could thus be avoided. In any case there is an admissible lag, as a certain amount of time is needed for knowledge of real permanent value to be sorted out from the mass of scientific discoveries, and on the other hand for scientific knowledge to be translated into a language accessible to children.

A special role in the development of any science curriculum is played by the prevailing epistemological views generally projected in school science—the traditional empiricist–inductivist view is the predominant influence. According to this view, the scientific method proceeds through a number of stages, described by Francis Bacon: (a) observation and experiment; (b) inductive generalization; (c) hypothesis; (d) attempted verification of hypothesis; (e) proof or disproof; and (f) objective knowledge. This positivist view of science and scientific progress relies on the idea of the existence of an objective reality apart from human beings, who can approach its comprehension by the iterated application of the process described above.

New perspectives in the epistemology of science are offered by K. R. Popper's and T. S. Kuhn's theories [3; 4]. Popper's hypothetico-deductive model is based on the idea that there are no discrete stages of objective knowledge, knowledge being at any one time provisional and open to possible refutation. His scientific method goes through the following stages: (a) the problem existing in a theory; (b) the new theory that allows a solution to the problem; (c) deduction of testable propositions from the new theory; (d) tests of the propositions by attempted refutation; and (e) preference established between competing theories. This view makes the critical approach central to scientific progress.

Kuhn's basic view of scientific change consists of paradigms separated by revolutions. Scientists are no longer engaged in research seeking to prove or refute hypotheses. Most of the time they are engaged rather in a puzzle-solving type of activity, having quite explicit expectations for the solution of the problems within the framework of a given paradigm, generally accepted by the scientific community. Only in special revolutionary circumstances are tentative solutions found which violate the current paradigm and surpass the common, routine work of the 'normal' scientist. It is in these moments that a 'gestalt switch' takes place and scientists start looking at things in a new light, as defined by a new paradigm. The process is highly influenced by subjective attitudes and expectations.

These different approaches have an important influence on the way in which science curricula are conceived. A useful approach could be one which goes further than the traditional inductivist–empiricist explanation process: educators should try to develop a critical attitude towards the knowledge being taught (in a dialectic Popperian view) and to foster the relativistic implications of the ways in which human beings view the world.

Discussions on the curriculum have increasingly become objective-oriented. In science teaching, it seems that the general orientation is towards the creation of 'accomplished', broad-minded people who are aware of the fact that science is a leading factor in economic development, yet also aware of its huge destructive potential. The future scientist should be strongly involved in society and be aware of his responsibilities. To quote M. G. Ebison, 'What I propose as a suggestion for you is that science be taught at whatever level, from the lowest to the highest, in the humanistic way' [5].

Until recently, the objectives of mathematics teaching were mainly concerned with logical and formal aspects, aiming at the acquisition of the capacity for rigorous thinking, free from logical contradictions. These aspects proved to be insufficient; the question is not only one of using a clear, rigorous language but also of forming common meanings. And meanings are provided in context, by the application and use of mathematics teaching. Progressive learning, by exposure to various situations, in which the use of mathematics becomes meaningful, should accompany the axiomatic treatment.

A generally acknowledged objective is the development of probabilistic as well as deterministic thought. This process should be introduced from the first elementary grades, the more so as mathematics is increasingly linked with science, where a probabilistic approach is common. Notions related to this approach are relatively easy to teach.

A final objective worth pointing out concerns the development of the capacity not merely to solve problems once they are posed but to perceive them. Along with the usual activities of solving problems and proving theorems, students should have experience in solving their own problems and proving their own theorems. This issue is related to creativity and understanding, and is much too easily overlooked.

Integrated education has been intensely debated. Thus there are discussions on 'global' curriculum integration, the integration of theory and practice, the integration of the natural sciences and the social sciences, vertical and horizontal integration. There has been a recent profusion of valuable works on this theme.

The integration of mathematics with physics and chemistry seems at first sight superfluous, since it is a natural process. However, there is still plenty of room for improvement, all the more so when the material is designed for younger pupils. Mathematical problems, which are often abstract, could be generally dealt with by demonstrating their relevance to physics, particularly in relation to probability theory, the notion of complex numbers, the concept of limits, the introduction and utilization of differential calculus, etc. The laws of mechanics can also be dealt with as elements of algebraic structures and may facilitate the introduction of problems of variational calculus. Although the integration of physics with chemistry is almost inevitable, they are still often taught as though they were separate subjects. There should be a more consistent promotion in the curriculum of the basic ideas of the quantum and relativity theories.

We have previously mentioned the need to make pupils conversant with the concept of the 'model' of physical reality. Almost all contemporary sciences use models as a means of investigating the real world that surrounds them, either physical or social phenomena. The possibility of simulating models with computers has opened up new perspectives in secondary education.

In conclusion one can make the following predictions:
Teaching of science will increasingly be carried out in a more 'contextual' way, pointing out the problems solved by science, in contrast to the axiomatic trends of thought which have prevailed since the beginning

of the century, reaching their peak in the 1950s. This presupposes that more attention will be paid to the history of science.

Teaching will include elements of 'science ethics' and 'technology assessment' appealing to values and a normative approach, in contrast to the positivism that has prevailed so far.

Teaching will cover border areas, where fields with different axioms and methodologies meet, involving unifying 'metatheories'. This will amplify the trends towards integration of sciences, with important consequences for teaching and teacher training.

The system of interdisciplinary work-teams and modular education will develop further.

Computer modelling will have a strong influence on science teaching; it will be practised in all scientific disciplines and will result in a spread of numeric calculus and simulated experiences.

Computers and telematics will shift the emphasis from data, information and memory to process modelling, algorithms and operations.

Scientific organization will thrive, based on decision, systems and game theories and on optimization techniques.

As the immediate future will be dominated by intense research into new energy sources and less energy-consuming technologies, the curriculum will reflect this preoccupation.

REFERENCES

1. BOLTIANSKI, V. G.; DANILOV-DANILIAN, V. I. The Role of Mathematics in Scientific and Technological Progress. In: J. Gvishiani (ed.), *Science, Technology and Global Problems; International Symposium on Trends and Perspectives in Development of Science and Technology and their Impact on the Solution of Contemporary Global Problems, Tallinn, USSR, 1979*, pp. 181–91. Oxford, Pergamon Press, 1979.
2. BRUSILOVSKIJ, B. Ya. *Teoriya sistem i sistema teorij*. Kiev, Vishcha Shkola, 1977.
3. POPPER, K. R. *The Logic of Scientific Discovery*. New York, Basic Books, 1959.
4. KUHN, T. S. *The Structure of Scientific Revolutions*. Chicago, Ill., University of Chicago Press, 1970.
5. EBISON, M. G. The Role of the History and Philosophy of Physics in the Physics Curriculum. In: *Implementation of Curricula in Science Education; Report of an International Seminar on 'The Implementation of Curricula in Science Education with Special Regard to the Teaching of Physics'*, organized by The German Commission for Unesco and the Institute for Science Education at the University of Kiel, Kiel, 16–18 March 1972, pp. 14–30. Cologne/Pullach-Munich, German Commission for Unesco/Verlag Dokumentation, 1974.

What the social sciences suggest for tomorrow's education

Harold G. Shane

The contemporary social sciences draw on appropriate, related disciplines to portray learning experiences that prepare the learner to live with some measure of confidence on a planet which promises to be a troubled one for the foreseeable future.

The implication in current literature relevant to education is that the human race may well become a transient guest on the globe, unless its wisdom more nearly approximates its technological ingenuity. Furthermore, our survival skills of past millennia now threaten to betray us because the conditions necessary to survival are changing! This implies that the many forms of learning, education, and schooling[1] are, now and in the future, called upon to cope with the fact that nature apparently failed to read the French Declaration of the Rights of Man, and hence has allowed billions to be born to an estate neither free nor equal. Life has been and remains competitive and selective. What is more, inequalities in the past twenty or thirty years have grown in proportion to the increasing complexity of human cultures.

Again we infer from the scholars who probe society and culture that one of the important problems of human learning in our era is a deep uncertainty as to where and how to find viable directions in which we and our children might best move. This departure from certainty is for most of the earth's peoples a new phenomenon. Heretofore, in Teilhard de Chardin's words, 'the workers and the disinherited accepted without reflection the lot which

---

1. For purposes of interpreting this article it is important to distinguish between education, schooling and learning. Education refers to experiential input that is derived from many sources, internalized, and thereafter reflected in new or modified ways of behaving. Schooling pertains to formal (or at least planned and organized) instruction to preserve and to extend the ethos—characteristic attitudes, values, and skills plus a spirit of membership in a community—which national, religious, political, economic, and other groups prize and wish their children to acquire. Learning, as identified in *No Limits to Learning: Bridging the Human Gap* (London, Pergamon Press, 1979), transcends both education and schooling in its broader emphasis on skills, methods, knowledge and values throughout life.

kept them in servitude' [1, p. 230]. Now the social sciences teach that civilization is becoming

a co-operative product, that nearly all peoples have contributed to it; it is our common heritage and debt; and that the civilized soul will reveal itself in treating every man and woman, however lowly, as a member of these creative and contributory groups [2, p. 31].

A recent contribution of anthropology, with important educational implications, is the concept that the culture in which individuals share membership appreciably influences what they see or hear and also the nature of their behavioural reactions. Many people assume that everyone exposed to the same set of conditions sees and hears the same things, but the culturally sophisticated individual recognizes that these experiences 'can be handled and perceived out of their systems but *derive their meaning* from the context in which they occur' [3, pp. 9–13]. From the nursery school to the learned symposium, we 'see' and 'hear' with our experiences. Robert Ornstein's observation, 'I'll see it when I believe it,' captures this idea very nicely.

It impresses us, too, that the literature often concludes that new moral bases need to be established on either a metaphysical or secular religion of humanity which differentiates between good and evil and helps good to prevail and to survive the harsh and cruel tests which the 1980s seem to hold. We refer to numerous problems for which our era has found too few solutions.

Economists point to the need for education to lead to the understanding that economic ambition and advantage which fails to serve the general welfare will encourage further the self-fertilizing turbulence which omens of the 1980s portend. Also, while the accumulation of the privileges of wealth are too motivating to exorcize, educational leadership can strive towards greater equity.

The increased use of such terms as microbiology or biophysics, as well as university appointments of professors of geography and history or molecular biology and zoology or psychology and neural sciences, suggest the increased breadth of knowledge which many contemporary scholars are expected to acquire. It also suggests that the increasing specialization of past decades has reversed itself. This cross-disciplinary fertilization, although necessary and desirable, makes it difficult for one to deal with, say, economics or history *per se*. In the process of preparing this article, the writer and his associates became more and more convinced that the social sciences have begun to weave themselves into a seamless web.

EDUCATIONAL GUIDELINES

Educators in the 1980s will more than ever need to remember that learning experiences are, by our definition, a lifelong phenomenon; a continuum reaching from early childhood to old age. Such ongoing education is essential in order to acquaint learners of all ages with the constant appearance of new knowledge and with new interpretations of previously established paradigms in the social sciences. Because change transpires with such unprecedented speed, it is important that not only young learners, but adults as well, be continuously informed. This is especially important since many social decisions cannot be deferred for the leisurely consideration of a younger generation presently in school and hence not yet in a position to exercise leadership in the ranks of government, labour, industry, and so on. Thus, it is in this context of lifelong learning that we present certain premises gleaned from trends in the social sciences.

General premises

Because of the differences existing among learners of all ages, the content of general education must be adapted to their levels of maturity and development. In short, good learning is personalized learning. Furthermore, in view of rapid social and cultural change, children should not be groomed for and locked into life roles which are not in their best interests or for which they have no talent.

Socio-economic trends suggest that a major challenge to education in the 1980s and 1990s will be that of motivating learners of all ages, but adolescents in particular. Many nations now strive to provide basic security through free or inexpensive health and welfare services. At the same time astute young people sense that there is no longer enough European-American affluence to go around as we approach the limits of the earth's carrying capacity. One result is that the potent motivating force of personal gain is reduced. Because many of our young people need neither fear hunger nor anticipate great material improvement in their lives, education must seek new and worthy means of motivating them.

The idea that equal opportunity can and should characterize education needs to be re-examined. The concept of 'equal' opportunity ignores the fact that humans are born neither free nor equal. As a result, in the interest of equity, education needs to be 'unequal' as in the case of the handicapped or the culturally deprived, in childhood and in later life.

In a highly complex world, education, including schooling, should serve to increase rather than to decrease human differences in the ability of learners to contribute to society. Unique minds and rare talents must be encouraged to enable them to lay a track that lesser persons can follow. An exception to this generalization is the need for education to decrease human differences with respect to the ability to communicate more clearly.

Because of contemporary changes in the nature and structure of family life, traditional patterns of home–school and parent–teacher relationships appear to require further study and modification. Both greater parental acceptance of responsibility and more flexible school programmes seem desirable, though both will be mediated by a given culture and its ethos.

Anthropologists point out that in a hunting culture the hunt is the teacher. By the same token, in a highly organized society, the society itself should be the teacher. This concept is one which James Coleman and Alvin Toffler have labelled 'action' and 'service' learning—educational experiences that are sponsored or brokered by the school but extend beyond its walls into the wider community.

In many countries, carefully planned changes in general education are needed to improve the status of women. As the United Nations' representative, Helvi Sipilä, put it, 'unless we take seriously the fate of women . . . I don't think we can solve many other problems: population, food shortage, illiteracy, abandoned children, unemployment, and mass poverty' (4, p. 154].

As a corollary of the point above, the need to improve the status of women suggests that provisions for pre-natal care be improved and that universal early childhood education, as early as age two or three, become an integral segment of the lifelong educational continuum in order to reduce or to prevent problems early in children's lives. Without a suitable foundation in the early years of life, better levels of learning will continue to prove elusive.

Organization of education

At least five generalizations regarding the organization of education are justified, as follows.

First, learning, including all forms of education and formal schooling, can no longer be conceived as a mechanical process or device. It is not something that can be put together as plumbers, carpenters, and masons put a house together. Social change and the prospect of a transitional, and possibly a less energy-intensive society—characterized by dynamic contraction in the use of resources—simply do not lend themselves to the rigidity of traditional approaches to learning.

Second, since the swift flow of events that can be anticipated in the next twenty years promises to foreclose certain options, reasoned educational reforms, both in opportunities to learn and in structure, need to be made rapidly. This is particularly true of changes made in provisions for the continuing education of adults who are already participating in decision-making.

Third, except for some forms of compensatory financial support distributed by central government agencies (support needed to ensure equitable learning opportunities), the organization and control of education should be based on local control and local decisions so that those persons most acquainted with the immediate community's needs have a suitable opportunity to deploy those resources available to meet them.

Fourth, while machines are of proven value in performing certain instructional tasks, the use of such powerful educational agents as television must be made consonant with the best human values and traditions. We reiterate that care must be exercised to reduce the likelihood that unscrupulous political elements will continue to use the media to further their ambitions. Also, learners must be protected from 'junk information' presented by commercial media lest rational attitudes be further undermined.

Fifth, at the transnational level, organizational practices should make more use of educational systems and technologies, as in the United Kingdom's Open University. The media, if kept free of political considerations and of the propaganda of special interest groups, can make significant contributions to the sharing of knowledge and ideas among semi-literate as well as literate populations.

Content and methods

The content of general education and methods of instruction should not indoctrinate the learner with past dogmas, many of which may become untenable, or at best of dubious value, in tomorrow's world. Neither should the past be ignored as a source of information since, as Santayana noted, those who forget the past are condemned to relive it.

In view of human diversity, a good instructional programme should neither turn out programmed pupils nor seek to clone a uniform student product. Valid methods vary from one learner to another throughout life because learners of the same chronological age may differ enormously in developmental age. Those who learn rapidly should encounter instruction that is interesting and intellectually demanding. Slower learners should not be exposed to pressures that are unreasonable for them. The lifelong, seamless, learning continuum concept is again called to the reader's attention as a problem preventing an approach to learning which is designed to reduce and eventually to eliminate the need for compensatory education.[1] In such a continuum special care should be given to defining the policies governing success and failure at any given time since wide differences in performance should be expected from both children and adults.

Because of the need for learners of all ages to anticipate, comprehend, and cope with complex relationships, interdisciplinary learnings need to be incorporated in a general education. This calls to mind the need to develop both an understanding of prevailing threats to the biosphere and the need for a grasp of planetary cultures and what sociologist Robert J. Havighurst has called an understanding of 'human geography'.

1. For an extended discussion of the seamless, lifelong curriculum concept, see Harold G. Shane, *The Educational Significance of the Future*, Chapter IV, Bloomington, Ind., Phi Delta Kappa, 1973.

Trends in the social sciences, with their complexity and their portent of rapid change, make it particularly important for general education to recognize the increased need for basic communication skills, including competence in visual literacy and the spoken word, but also in at least one foreign language, plus the listening and the numeracy skills needed for the communication of ideas. Also, particular attention should be given to helping persons in a wide age range to recognize shoddy advertising, political doubletalk, and propaganda in their various forms.

In the interest of improved learning through general education, the proliferation of elective subjects and options should be re-examined. Discussion–discovery or heuristic methods have certain well-attested values. However, there also are times when learners need to be taught by able persons. The human heritage cannot be acquired exclusively through so-called group processes, heuristic strategies, and interaction!

Because, in a sense, humans create the future, the idea of alternative futures and how to choose among them to serve the world's good should be a component of a general education. The content of instruction should be designed to remedy the presence of the harsh realities of the current era by focusing, when appropriate, on the need for—and peaceful ways of achieving—changes prerequisite to the improvement of the human community.

Innovations in general education often have been little more than the ephemeral mayflies of the educational world. The need for basic changes in our concepts of the learning process has not been taken seriously enough. In the next two decades they must be explored more thoroughly as we seek to improve the quality of general education. Also, changes should be phased in more quickly while time remains, particularly with respect to adult education on a global scale.

Trends in political science suggest continued turmoil, while economists reflect diverse opinion and uncertainty. The field of sociology suggests continued rapid societal transitions and perhaps major transformations in coming decades. Finally, anthropology anticipates the growing importance of cross-cultural insights as a basis for improving the human prospect. In retrospect, then, how can our conclusions be summarized with respect to the consequences for the future of general education as derived from trends in the social sciences? We believe that five broad generalizations can be justified, which when adapted to the learners' developmental level, can have a bearing on improved learning experiences extending from early childhood to the advanced years of senior learners.

First, an effective learning experience should explode myths and focus on realities. This sometimes is a troublesome task in the social sciences because, in the realm of economics for instance, highly diverse opinions exist. But, even here, in the pursuit of truth these conflicting views can be examined as impartially and as fully as possible, if learning is construed to be a process of inquiry which leads to warranted conclusions based on an evaluation of divergent opinion.

Second, the process of learning should emphasize the point that there are alternative solutions to problems. Third, learners should understand that there are consequences of each alternative, consequences with social implications which a suitable educational background will help one to recognize.

This leads us to a fourth generalization, namely that part of the learner's general education consists in acquiring the socially desirable values and intellectual insights on which to base prudent choices among the alternatives that are identified. Patently, this involves a form of moral and values education, but in contemporary, action-oriented settings rather than in abstract, ivy-covered towers.

Our fifth and final point is that general education should motivate the learner to acquire substantive knowledge—the skills and information prerequisite to implementing choices among alternative personal decisions and group policy decisions and practices. Included here are the skills involved in working together, a knowledge of how to organize to accomplish worthy mutual purposes, a respect for expertise in special fields (law, economics, medicine, history, education, biology, etc.), and of course the personal, substantive knowledge commensurate with one's ability to acquire it.

REFERENCES

1. TEILHARD DE CHARDIN, Pierre. *The Phenomenon of Man.* Translated from the French by Bernard Wall. London/New York, Collins/Harper & Row, 1959.
2. DURANT, Will and Ariel. *The Lessons of History.* New York, Simon & Schuster, 1968.
3. HALL, Edward T. *The Silent Language.* Greenwich, Conn., Fawcett Publications, 1959.
4. SHANE, Harold G. *Curriculum Change Toward the Twenty-First Century.* Washington, D.C., The National Education Association, 1977.

Science, technology and higher education

Ivan F. Obraztsov

There is an increased importance of the human factor in the scientific and technological revolution (STR), mainly as a result of a higher level of scientific knowledge and culture. The transformation of human nature through education into a specific and developed productive force is one of the distinctive features of our time and will remain so in the foreseeable future. Education plays an instrumental role in labour reproduction, both quantitatively and qualitatively. Within this context, higher education is important not only to reproduce highly skilled workers and intellectuals for society, but also as a means for society to meet new requirements and satisfy the economic, cultural and intellectual aspirations of more and more individuals.

Contemporary higher education institutions are becoming an instrument of societal development instead of indifferent and inactive storehouses of knowledge, a feature which is closely connected with the concept of the broadening of organizational forms and the content of training. Today many educational institutions continue to emphasize specialization rather than education in a broad sense. On the one hand, the race for credentials that lead to highly specialized jobs, which are relatively new and therefore both prestigious and promising, and, on the other, the interest of employers to obtain such specialized employees, reinforce the tendency towards this kind of specialization.

Experience shows, however, that an individual with only specialized training does not have the proper social and professional mobility necessary to meet the changing conditions of contemporary life. Hence, such training alone is of little use either to society or to the individual. In addition to measures to democratize higher education, steps must be taken to provide a broad general knowledge which will enable graduates to adapt more easily to a wider range of social demands and to continue their studies throughout their lifetime. This requires improving the existing courses, modernizing teaching methods, and developing new educational methods, technologies and organization. The ultimate goal must be to educate a large number of versatile, erudite and highly qualified members of society who can adapt without difficulty to change and make a valuable contribution to the improvement of the existing order. In socialist countries there is a trend in higher education to prepare such graduates by giving them a broader specialization, which emphasizes the fundamental scientific disciplines as a firm basis for later recurrent specialization of a more narrow type.

What are the features of this new orientation in higher education? The major one, connected to the scientific, technical and social changes in society, is that higher education institutions are obliged to satisfy high training standards, expanding and deepening knowledge at a sophisticated level, while providing appropriate training to individuals with different educational and family backgrounds.

Indeed, the STR has fundamentally changed the rate of accumulation of scientific knowledge and has caused an unprecedented intensification in the practical application of scientific ideas and discoveries. The period of renewal of knowledge has declined to between seven and fifteen years; new branches of fundamental and applied science are emerging at a rapid rate. A key indication of scientific and technical progress is the time-lag between the origin of an idea and its broad application. This time-lag has been steadily reduced: e.g. 112 years for photography; 56 years for the telephone; 35 years for radio; 12 years for television; 5 years for transistors; 3 years for integral schemes and only 1 year for the laser.

The renewal of knowledge resulting from accelerating scientific and technological progress affects the form and content of training. It results in a change and renewal of the content of training; in the elimination of gaps between higher education programmes and the development of science, technology, and production. It also influences general education and culture as a whole.

The growth and renovation of knowledge in our era is considered, not without reason, as an information explosion, and it is more and more difficult for mankind to cope with it. Even the individual with exceptional abilities and memory is unable to master available knowledge in any given field; furthermore, even if this mastery were possible, there is a constant need to renew the existing body of information. Obviously, therefore, we should strive not to increase the assimilation of the growing body of knowledge but to organize it so as to facilitate the renewal and deepening of available knowledge and to facilitate the individual's orientation within the broad flow of information.

The main task in organizing a qualitative and productive educational process is to develop a system which gives the student basic knowledge reflecting the contemporary state of science, a sense of logic and a way of thinking, thus providing conditions for productive practical activity and easy access to new achievements in science and technology. What is the core of knowledge required by contemporary specialists?

In spite of the desire to unify basic education, one is forced to admit that the contents of fundamental knowledge should depend on the nature of the particular speciality selected for further study. The main problem is to determine the proper relation between the classical fundamental sciences (of the seventeenth, eighteenth and nineteenth centuries) and the neoclassical sciences which have emerged as an elaboration or generalization of the former. No doubt opinions will vary. Some will maintain that in our times one must favour modern sciences, while others will firmly hold that it is impossible to provide a sound scientific training without considering the whole genealogy of a particular fundamental science.

One should remember that the principle of teaching 'from simple to complex' often becomes one of the main obstacles to reaching a goal effectively. On the other hand, the best results can be achieved by carefully combining the classical sciences with modern, even eccentric disciplines.

Therefore, the transition to broader specialization is a complex and vast process that can be carried out only by institutions strong in science and in pedagogy. Success cannot be achieved merely by introducing new programmes stressing the fundamentals. This broader education needs both a harmonious combination of theoretical and applied education, and a link between specialized training and the broad, scientific, sociohumanistic and cultural development of the individual on the other.

The natural connection of teaching and scientific research is another important aspect of comprehensive higher education. The advantages of this union are obvious. However, one must bear in mind that this union is very sensitive to the quantitative and qualitative characteristics of the scientific component in relation to the essential function of higher education, which is teaching. The quality of instruction in higher education, the stability of pedagogical results and the solidity of the technological and material basis of the educational process have always been inseparable from the level of scientific research. In the past few years, the level of scientific research has improved most rapidly in developed countries where the more effective utilization of the scientific potential of higher education has benefited not only society as a whole but also higher education itself.

It is well known that no matter how brilliant or innovative an idea is, no matter how sophisticated the mechanism implementing it, the effectiveness of innovation depends in the long run on the technology applied. As far as higher education is concerned, effective, high-quality instruction cannot be based on traditional technology determined by cumulative methods (such as merely adding new knowledge to old without proper integration), especially when higher education is being democratized, the scientific and technological revolution is in progress, and resources are strictly limited.

Undoubtedly, such methods must now be replaced by methods and means designed to intensify the process of education, to save both the teacher and the student time and effort. For this purpose the entire process of education must be better provided with a qualitatively new learning environment with new equipment, programmes, methods and technological means that are suitable for teaching both during class and afterward. Already many institutions of higher learning have made numerous innovations in education and research, such as the 'Plato-4' system of the University of Illinois (United States); the system of televised instruction used by the Open University (United Kingdom); and computers and audio-visual educational systems in countries such as the USSR, France, Canada and the Federal Republic of Germany. The use of such systems has had many valuable results. However, the use of new educational technology in higher education institutions has been accompanied by imperfections and difficulties, insufficient capacity and high costs. All this has significantly slowed down the development of new forms of teaching.

We do not doubt that the future of higher education is inseparable from clever, simple, cheap and reliable teaching–learning systems designed so as not to encroach upon the role of man in higher education but to help him in every possible way to learn the joy of creative work and the happiness of discovery.

The growing importance of science and technology education for national development[1]

THE ROLE OF SCIENCE AND TECHNOLOGY IN NATIONAL DEVELOPMENT

Over the last century, countries with a high rate of scientific and technological growth have shown parallel progress in their economic development. This indicates a direct correlation between science and technology, on the one hand, and economic development on the other.

It was unanimously agreed that science and technology, together with the teaching of them through the various types of formal and non-formal education, constituted an essential factor in improving the material and cultural conditions of people's lives and a priority objective of cultural development. It was emphasized that, in the world of today, mastery by a society of scientific and technical knowledge was an essential condition for the assertion of cultural identity and independence and for the promotion of effective participation by the people in determining and implementing collective action for development and thus for ensuring better national control of its results.

More specifically it was felt that the development of science and technology and their promotion through education could and should play a vital role in solving the most urgent problems confronting the world, since these problems threaten the conditions and quality of life of vast sectors of the population and the very survival of mankind. Special emphasis was placed on the role of science and technology for developing the productive potential of society, particularly in the full utilization of human resources and agricultural and industrial activity needed to improve people's material living conditions, especially in the developing countries. With regard to the problem of rapid population growth, the teaching and application of science and technology could make a significant contribution

---

1. Excerpts from the Final Report of the International Congress on Science and Technology Education and National Development, convened by Unesco in Paris from 23 November to 2 December 1981. (Unesco doc. ED-81/CONF.401/COL.10.)

to the development of the resources needed to meet the requirements of an ever-growing population and could also help to ensure more effective control of population growth rates. Lastly, in this connection, there is the mounting urgency of halting the arms race, not only because it places the entire world under the permanent threat of war and destruction, but also because it diverts enormous material, financial and human resources—including highly qualified scientists and technicians—from the loftier aims of economic and cultural development for the whole of mankind.

In this context, there is the need to incorporate science and technology into every part of the life of societies as the ideal means of awakening in the younger generation a scientific perception of reality, by drawing on the full range of educational resources and means available to the community: systematic instruction, information, and popularization methods. Such incorporation should also make it possible to provide young people with the kind of values and attitudes and the powers of rational thought, expression and behaviour that foster the development of both the individual personality and of an intellect that could adapt itself to a rapidly changing environment and find the right answers to the unpredictable challenges the future might bring.

THE CONTRIBUTION OF SCIENCE AND TECHNOLOGY EDUCATION

Developing rational and analytical attitudes and promoting the acquisition of the methods of science were considered of long-lasting value in an area of rapid change, in addition to their value in shaping a mentality well adapted to a world increasingly permeated by science and technology.

Science provides a means whereby the individual can organize his or her own concepts and attitudes, classify experiences and communicate with others. Science can thus claim to make an important contribution to education as a whole, and have a place in the 'core' or central part of the curricula.

Science education was considered to be an indispensable part of general education at all levels and for all target groups, especially for non-scientists such as politicians and administrative decision-makers, whose decisions and actions have direct relevance to the use and misuse of science and technology and its products, especially weapons. All citizens must be exposed to science and its processes in order to learn how to make intelligent decisions, based on informed opinion.

In the industrialized countries, science and technology, like language and arts, has become an integral part of the culture, and thus it has its distinct place for all in the spectrum of education. This does not hold good in the case of developing countries. The development of scientific attitudes on the part of society was considered fundamental for the development and application of science and technology in all countries and especially in developing countries.

SUGGESTED IMPROVEMENTS IN EDUCATION

Care must be taken in developing science and technology education to ensure that modern knowledge is harmoniously combined with the significant contributions of traditional knowledge; partly for the sake of preserving the achievements of the past which hold promise for the future and are essential to the assertion of national cultural identity; partly to enable the least privileged countries to incorporate into their living tradition effective scientific knowledge and techniques for solving their present problems and also to pave the way for the qualitative leap needed to reduce the gap separating them from the industrialized countries. There is a need to emphasize here the part that could be played by computer science and information technology to improve national capacities for the management of development, and by biotechnology to meet the basic needs of the population, especially in nutrition and health.

There is a need to improve the social relevance and effectiveness of education and hence to link science and technology education more closely with the requirements of society. Education should be related to the world of work in such a way that pupils, when faced with specific real-life problems, can more easily grasp the connection between theoretical and practical knowledge, acquire the attitudes and aptitudes essential for productive work (team spirit, sense of responsibility, method, etc.), take their place in society and thus contribute from early life to the collective task of national development. For the same general purpose, science and technology education should be tied in with environmental problems, with a view to fostering individual and collective behaviour patterns that would make for more rational use of natural resources and the long-term preservation of the productive potential of the environment.

The fast pace of scientific and technological change was recognized, and a distinction was made between the need to cope with specific changes already taking place, and the need to prepare the student to cope in adult life with future changes which are of a basically unpredictable nature. With respect to specific changes, two fields were given particular attention: information processing and biotechnology. Information processing was deemed to introduce a true revolution, having an impact not only of a technical nature, but also on the future pattern of social life. This matter was referred to also in connection with the information explosion, which opens up enormous possibilities as to availability and access to knowledge and information. It poses problems to educational systems, forcing them to make choices with respect to subject-matter offerings and to the extent of diversity in their programme. The biosciences were considered important enough for the future of humanity to suggest that the twenty-first century will be the 'biology century'. From the educational point of view, biotechnology is recognized as lending itself to the linking of teaching with research. This provides a remedy to a trend which is considered dangerous, namely the gradual dissociation between teaching and research in many universities in developing countries. In fact, research in some areas within the biosciences does not require very costly equipment and is interesting. Other fields which were considered of importance are alternative energy sources, fibre optics, ecosciences and ocean sciences.

To fulfil the need for a certain degree of specialization, while giving the student a potential flexibility to adapt to change, it is necessary to reconcile two extreme approaches: unification and deep specialization in the sciences. In general, it is recognized that the growing trend towards unification of scientific knowledge appears to simplify matters when it comes to teaching science. However, the scientific community evolves towards an ever deeper specialization. Thus, driving too far an integrated approach to science education might involve the risk of dispersion and superficiality. With regard to technology education, it may be more difficult to talk about unification at the level of basic concepts; but the pursuance of any technological objective requires multi-disciplinarity and collaboration among specialists—a fact that should not be disregarded when designing the educational process.

CO-OPERATION IN STRENGTHENING SCIENCE AND TECHNOLOGY EDUCATION

The whole world is engaged in trying to explore ways and means of moving away from traditional science and technology education to an approach that will more effectively cultivate the intellectual, the behavioural, the social and the psycho-motor attributes of individuals, while giving them the knowledge and awareness required for social and economic development. It is imperative that ideas and experiences be exchanged, new materials and systems be disseminated, studies for evaluating them in different societies be undertaken, and assistance be provided to countries and people for developing their own approaches to new science and technology education.

Areas of commonality of objectives, as mentioned above, should serve as fertile ground for international co-operation at the regional level through the exchange of experiences and expertise in teacher training, development of appropriate educational materials, exchange of personnel and the dissemination of professional information. All international co-operation must be backed by an appropriate national approach to education as a nationwide system involving, not only ministries of education, but also industry, agriculture, etc.

Although international co-operation lends itself to whatever is common to a group of countries, thus implying a certain degree of similarity between them, this does not exclude the possibility that some developed countries can also contribute the experience they have accumulated in relation to certain problems of interest to less-developed countries, thereby narrowing the scientific and technological gap between the two.

Brain drain is normally considered as a negative element in the development of science and technology education in the country suffering from the drain. In addition to whatever international co-operation can do to reduce brain drain, an aspect which could be labelled 'intellectual drain' was considered to be equally important. This refers to the concentration of researchers on problems of international relevance rather than on local or national problems, the aim being publication and the building up of a reputation, disregarding, at times, the context in which they develop their activities. Collecting national experiences of this problem would constitute an important contribution to its solution. These case-studies could help in designing educational processes that sensitize people towards the problems proper to their own national contexts. The information thus collected could be disseminated through technology magazines focusing on development issues of relevance to the countries concerned.

In promoting endogenous development through science and technology education, Unesco's major role should be to seek means of according high priority to raising the capacity and level of performance of local institutions. It was suggested that co-operation should be encouraged through a network of programmes of special concern to the education of the masses and the training of key personnel in various aspects of science and technology education (curriculum design, teacher education, student testing and programme evaluation).

Unesco was also urged to play a special role in facilitating the acquisition, storage, retrieval, analysis and dissemination of ideas and information on science and technology education by strengthening international and regional networking, as well as through meetings, newsletters, etc.

In view of the fundamental role of scientific and technological knowledge in promoting socio-economic and cultural development, and national independence, it was urged that Unesco should continue to promote the access of all countries to the knowledge accumulated by humanity, particularly scientific and technological knowledge. This should be perceived as part of international co-operative action working for the establishment of a world order, founded upon equity and solidarity among peoples.

5
Education and the media

Introduction

The techniques of mass communication,[1] or media, are playing an increasingly significant part in contemporary society, and this gives great importance to their interaction with education, both as an educational support and as a 'parallel school'—a school based on principles different to those upon which traditional education rests. However, although there are many cases in which the media have been used successfully for educational purposes, generally speaking the two institutions of education and the media develop and function in such a way that the co-operation between them that might have been expected has rarely been achieved. Indeed, in many countries the school has often been obliged, in view of the omnipresence of the media, to organize instruction for young people to enable them to make critical and intelligent use of all the information provided for them.

It is admitted nowadays that if the education given in school is to be rationally co-ordinated with the messages conveyed by the media, the relations between the educational and communications systems must be re-examined and their respective roles must be more carefully defined; but it is clear that the foreseeable evolution of the technology of the media, which can be expected to result in more general use, at least in certain industrialized countries, makes the need for such re-examination even more urgent.

PRESENT RELATIONS

In most countries relations between the media and education might be said to be mainly those of mutual indifference or competition, although at an earlier stage it was thought theoretically possible to use the tools of information to facilitate

---

1. The different carriers or bearers of messages (radio, television, the press, the cinema, etc.) some of which can, for example, be grouped together as audio-visual media, or be combined with electronic calculating techniques to form telematics.

the acquisition, transmission and dissemination of knowledge. One wonders whether the school and the media pertain to two types of apparently irreconcilable activity—entertainment and the process of learning—that sum up the essential opposition between two orders of faculties, the school giving priority to reason and logic, while in the media imagination and the senses are supreme. Even when the media try to provide educational material, in the opinion of teachers the knowledge pupils acquire is illusory, because the material has not been integrated into a system of acquiring knowledge that only the school can apply. But beyond this, is it not true that the media reflect society as much as education does, and that education should take full account of their existence and of the influence they exert on young people?

Teachers would say that this lack of co-operation can be explained both by the nature of the media and the way in which they function as an institution and by difficulties that arise in using material, essentially audio-visual material, in the educational process. In connection with the media as an institution, there has been criticism of the commercial interest which, in some socio-economic systems, governs the production and distribution of audio-visual programmes that are intended to reach the largest possible audience, resulting in the impoverishment of the content, which deals mainly with the sensational and ephemeral, and incoherence in the selection of different types of programmes.

The heterogeneous nature of television programmes and their mediocrity may perhaps be due simply to the history of the technology of the media, to which their illogical development, marked by 'too many messages competing for inadequate channel space' (Pierre Schaeffer, p. 178) is to be attributed. If the tape-recorders, lightweight video-recorders, portable videos and small-scale low-cost receivers 'had come before the tall towers and the high kilowattages of the medium and long wavelengths, the face of the world might have been transformed' (Pierre Schaeffer, p. 180). At the level of the teaching establishment, it is the lack of the means of production and, above all, of storage facilities—essential conditions for a real audio-visual education—which no doubt explain the common failure of television for schools.

The educational use of the mass communication media (regional or national television, radio programmes for large numbers of listeners) also has limitations that can be defined as follows: (a) the imbalance between the world of the concrete, which can be shown in images, and that of the abstract; (b) the rigidity of the two systems: rigidity of timetables in the case of schools and rigidity of schedules in the case of media programmes, which do not correspond to school timetables; and (c) the fact that the media dissociate the two functions of education—to pass on information and to mould minds—and perform only the first.

In view of such unfavourable judgements about the ability of the communications system to mould minds, one may ask whether the education system is not reaching a self-defence against the invasion by the media of a domain where, in the past, the school reigned supreme, where it alone possessed knowledge and was alone responsible for preparing young people for life? Might this reaction not be provoked in part by the attitude of the communication organizations, which, while discharging educational functions, as indeed their statutes require, often ignore the educational institutions? Whatever the answers to these questions may be, the very fact that they are asked illustrates the relationship between the two systems. Much remains to be done before education defines its objectives and the world of communicators, in turn, opens its mind to the problems of education.

The observation that such a dialogue is needed should not, however, lead us to underestimate present and previous efforts to bring the world of communication closer to that of education. There have been two principal lines of action to date. The first is to subordinate audio-visual techniques to educational purposes; the second and later one, to teach the use of communication.

There have been many attempts to use the media for educational purposes—examples being the dissemination of educative information and literacy work—drawing on such varied techniques as films, radio, audio-visual packages, records, television and video cassettes, at levels that range widely from nursery school to postgraduate education, and employing a variety of methods, such as groups, conferences and self-teaching. Analysis of these experiments suggests that educators are sometimes too optimistic in their views of what audio-visual aids can do and that they underestimate the difficulties to be overcome, hence their present eagerness to use more lightweight storage and distribution techniques such as local radio, video-recorders, the press or tape-recorders.

Moreover, education is increasingly concerned to teach young people and adults how to make proper use of communication techniques. In some countries many experiments have been undertaken in the training of active, critical and intelligent television viewers. Over the past few years training in visual communication and the arts of the screen, which teaches pupils to appreciate and judge messages, to discern the real and the imaginary, and to choose from the wealth of programmes on offer, has come to figure among the educational activities of schools in certain countries. The major communication media, such as television networks, sometimes take part by consenting to broadcast programmes that match up with school or university curricula. The purpose is to free the individual from the fascination that the media exert over him and to make him more aware of the content of the messages and more demanding in that respect.

So the fragmentary co-operation between the media and education occurs primarily in areas where the barriers are comparatively weak and easy to overcome (Luis Ricarte Soto). There are more far-reaching experiments that aim to harness young people's enthusiasm for television programmes in order to promote general education, to extend pupils' range of interests and to enhance their powers of observation. Generally speaking, however, such experimental co-operation as now exists between the world of education and that of the media is sporadic, albeit admittedly beneficial. It is often organized on a personal or voluntary basis. To make it the rule would require a major *financial effort because of the need to provide every school with audio-visual equipment. Such a decisive change in education as this would represent could only be decided at governmental level.*

PROSPECTS FOR AND PROBLEMS OF CO-OPERATION

The prospects for co-operation between education and communication will be governed both by the evolution of technology, which will bring new opportunities of using the media for educational purposes, and by the future problems of education. These problems will arise from awareness of two major needs: the need to educate a growing number of people and the need to teach more and more new material. Also, in so far as education will be obliged to help formulate adequate solutions to the enormous problems of the developing countries, plus those that arise from large-scale technological change, it will probably be compelled to rely more fully on technology than is now the case.

If the enormous growth of educational needs is compared with the accelerated development of communication techniques that can be used for educational purposes, it might be supposed that the media could help education to meet the challenge of the growing numbers of people to be educated—since the same messages can be transmitted in millions of copies—and that of the growing number of subjects to be taught, by making the best specialists, constantly updated data banks and varied stocks of audio-visual products available for consultation, whatever field of knowledge is involved.

To speak only of television, the improvement of techniques will overcome most of the disadvantages encountered at present. For instance, the replacement of analogous processing of audio-visual signals by digital processing should improve the quality of transmission and enable a single channel to be used for television, radio and telephone signals, reception of teletexts and communication with data banks. Cable television, programme transmission to private receivers by direct broadcasting satellites, the distribution of video-disc recordings, the use of video-recorders programmable several days ahead for recording programmes for screening whenever desired, pay television—all these are ways of putting out messages intended for particular audiences in accordance with their needs. Besides, the more advanced of these systems will be interactive, that is to say the user will be able more and more easily to intervene in the course of the programme. Obviously, the proliferation of communication channels will call for a corresponding increase in programme production, especially in the developing countries, and the introduction of a repertoire of messages suited to the new techniques.

The foreseeable evolution of the use of audio-visual techniques by individuals, and the potential combination of large-scale and small-scale media in more flexible systems, would allow closer co-operation between education and the media. But according to the author of one of the studies which follow (Michel

Souchon) this is possible only under certain conditions. First, the present trend towards using the major communication media solely for the entertainment of the public must be reversed. Second, resources must be distributed more equitably among countries, since they are at present not located where the greatest educational needs are felt. Third, the situation cannot be changed merely by transmitting programmes without studying the educational standards and motivations, the psychology and the particular needs of those for whom the programmes are intended, especially in the developing countries. Fourth, media-assisted education should take into account the demands of modern teaching practice and its two major trends: the tendency towards maximum rationalization of education and the emphasis on the personal motivations of pupils. Lastly, the constraints arising from the professional habits of teaching staff must be borne in mind: the new techniques create a need for technical instruction courses and an often radical rethinking of traditional teaching methods, which could entail changes in the mentality of teachers.

All these considerations, Michel Souchon concludes (p. 172), lead to 'a view of the future in which education and the media are still competitors and rivals, with "tangential encounters" whose impact on educational habits and media operations is slight'. But such views may be valid only for the relatively near future of the next six to ten years. The evolution of ideas and techniques that can be discerned even today—a renewed interest in simpler technology, the establishment and systematic exploitation of cinema and television libraries, for example—suggests that better things may be expected in the more distant future. If these future systems are to be effective, there must be a separation of the publishing, producing, programming, storing and carrying of educational products. This is particularly true of the developing countries, whose dependence in respect of message contents is as great as their dependence in the technical area of carrying.

The prospects for co-operation between the media and education should not, however, be seen as an over-simplified pattern according to which education, with its immutable foundations and purposes, would be the better for a few reforms of method and content, introduced by the new technical potential of the media. It is probable that the trends we have pointed to in the evolution of the technology of communication media and the increased flexibility of use of the latter for educational purposes will in fact be confirmed; but two additional points must also be noted—first, the enormous importance for education of the development of computer technology and, second, the fact that, in Pierre Schaeffer's words (p. 183), telematics and informatics will constitute

a revolution which will affect intellectual work as profoundly as the Industrial Revolution altered the physical nature of work. We can thus reckon on a complete shape-up of the functions of learning ahead of that of the content of knowledge. Education can only be transformed by it, and triply so, in its curricula, its methods and its aims. Even more so than in the case of the mass media ... the influence of computer technology promises to be vital.

In a more general sense, it has been said that the media society will force the school to modify not only its aims and its functions, which would no longer meet the needs of a rapidly changing world, but also its modes of organization and operation.

However realistic these forecasts may be as regards the industrialized countries, it is unlikely that they can be similarly verified in the developing countries, where mass communication media are not so omnipresent and where the main aim is still to set up a formal educational system or strengthen one that already exists. For the most part, however, the use of the media for educational purposes is seen in the context of non-formal education. In this context, Asok Mitra's study on the Indian experiment describes three types of audio-visual education and concludes that, because of the enormous shortage of teachers, the experiment should be continued whatever the educational and technical problems involved. For where there are such shortages the audio-visual media make up for the lack of teachers, just as non-formal education makes up for the inadequate development of formal education.

One of the difficulties of co-operation between education and the media derives from the financial and material aspects of the matter. Even in the developed countries the establishment of the requisite audio-visual infrastructures is relatively onerous, both because of the cost of equipment and because of its upkeep. Luis Ricarte Soto's study indicates that television has not yet become a major medium in the developing countries. In India in 1980, for example, television networks covered only 12 per cent of the country and television programmes were watched by less than 8 per cent of the population. But comparison of the roles played by radio and television in the developing countries shows that radio is, and will on economic and cultural grounds remain, the essential and principal medium, at least in the short term.

More generally, these considerations prompt the thought that the international community will be faced with increasingly pressing problems as the gap widens between developed and developing countries. For disparities in education seem likely to be enlarged by those that already exist in communication media. It is known that in the developing countries the distribution of printed matter reaches only a very small percentage of the public. A large number of developing countries have no television at all (for Africa, the figure is 40 per cent) and even when these countries do possess studios, the service extends solely to the urban centres and generally reaches only the more privileged social classes. Even with radio broadcasts, the developing countries, which have one-quarter of the world's transmitters and receivers, are still at a great disadvantage. Moreover, as pointed out by the International Commission for the Study of Communication Problems [1, p. 129], the higher the level of technology the greater the disparity: it is greater in television than in radio, greater in informatics than in television. The fact that the developing countries now possess only 5 per cent of the world's computer capacity is extremely serious, since the future of the media is linked to the development of computer technology. Further, an alarming qualitative delay can be glimpsed *in addition to the quantitative disparities, since only the industrialized countries will have the new-generation equipment giving access to personalized messages and interactive systems. Other countries will remain at the stage of mass communication, with messages designed for vast audiences and so for the 'average viewer'.*

Such, in short, are the prospects for co-operation between education and the media. With regard to the latter, according to the participants in the Second Meeting of the International Panel on the Future Development of Education,

a distinction should be drawn between radio and television, on the one hand, and other types of apparatus, on the other. The former (radio and television) demand specific control and selection skills, for the speed and intensity of their messages are imposed on the user. In contrast, the 'reproduced' media (cassettes, records, video, newspapers and magazines) can be handled at a pace and in a way which are more compatible with the user's actual needs [2, p. 8].

The Panel also expressed the opinion that, if the further development of sophisticated equipment for flexible use introduces the prospect of 'a possible revolution in education'[1] [2, p. 8] in the industrialized countries, solutions should be sought to

the problems which seem to be associated with the expansion of the media and which may be both general—such as the risks of dehumanization and the disintegration of local cultures—and specifically threatening to the learning process. . . . It was agreed that the fact that the media emerged and developed later than educational institutions must not be used as an excuse for perpetuating a situation in which the former remained autonomous in relation to the latter, and, in view of the far-reaching implications of all the problems considered, it was proposed that the educational communities should be enabled to play a greater role in controlling the media. In that respect, there was reason to think that the future would bring considerable changes in the institutional conditions for exercising this control, on which the educational authorities were consulted only very occasionally. This should enable education to exert a more direct influence on the nature and choice of the messages and programmes intended for the general public [2, p. 9].

As they now stand, therefore, Unesco's new educational strategies for treating education and communication as a single package of problems make it possible to divide current or hypothetical activities into two major groups, depending

---

1. In so far as such equipment, in addition to changing the teacher–pupil relationship, would have the following consequences: it would enable schools 'to advance beyond the rote-learning stage, encourage multidisciplinarity, make it possible for pupils to catch up more readily, provide distance education and enable pupils themselves to monitor their own learning.'—Second Meeting of the International Panel on the Future Development of Education (Paris, 1981), *Final Report*, p. 8, Paris, Unesco, 1982. (Unesco doc. ED-81/FUTURED/4.)

on whether they concern contents and methods, or policies, that is the actual organization of education and communication systems.

Where contents and methods are concerned, the general trend seems to be to make the contents and methods of general education more relevant to scientific and technological progress, and more particularly to the growing role of information and communication in society. Activities to be undertaken for this purpose would be designed to (a) teach the appropriate use of communication at both individual and social levels (communication education); (b) make the necessary changes in educational programmes, grading of material and methods to take account of pupils' everyday cultural world (the parallel school); (c) train educators accordingly; (d) improve young people's reactions to their audio-visual environment, i.e. to forestall or attenuate the effects of the technological explosion in the communication field; and (e) analyse the cultural impact of the development of mass communication media.

With regard to the policies and organization of educational and communication systems, activities should be undertaken whose aim would be to contribute towards a better relationship between education and communication by reviewing their roles and redistributing their functions with a view to the harmonious development of the individual in society. These activities would have the following objectives. First, to encourage public participation in the programming of educational, cultural and communication activities. Second, to bring communication and educational systems together at the level of planning so as to implement a coherent cultural policy. Third, as a contribution towards lifelong education, to bring about a new distribution of educational functions among the social institutions; and to define the tasks and contents that may be assigned to other forces in society besides the school, such as the family, youth organizations, trade union organizations, cultural associations and more especially broadcasting organizations.

Three of the contributions presented here attempt to describe and analyse the present state of relations between education and the media, and then, in the light of the probable evolution of those relations and the challenges that education will have to meet, to suggest possible modes of co-operation between educational systems and the mass communication media. The fourth contribution describes a specific experiment in the use of the media in a developing country, India, within the framework of what the author refers to as 'non-formal' education.

REFERENCES

1. *Many Voices One World: Towards a New More Just and More Efficient World Information and Communication Order.* Paris/London/New York, Unesco/Kogan Page/Unipub, 1980.
2. SECOND MEETING OF THE INTERNATIONAL PANEL ON THE FUTURE DEVELOPMENT OF EDUCATION (Paris, 30 November to 4 December 1981). *Final Report.* Paris, Unesco, April 1982. (Unesco doc. ED-81/FUTURED/4.)

Education and the media: prospects for co-operation

Michel Souchon

EDUCATION AND THE MEDIA: PAST AND PRESENT

The school and the mass media are essentially rival institutions. Teachers everywhere level much the same criticisms against the media. What are these criticisms? The mass media are accused of accentuating the entertainment aspect of their content to such an extent that their message is lost in a flow of meaningless words. Education and the media rest on two irreconcilable principles: the spectacle, with its facility, superficiality, illusion of effortless learning and passivity; and the training process, which implies effort, depth, the solidity of real learning, and activity. Lastly, the most fundamental clash is between two orders of faculties: the school gives priority to reason and logic, while in the media imagination and the senses are supreme. Of course, teachers recognize the benefit to be gained from the efforts of the media men to present educational topics, in popular science programmes for example; but they also point out that such programmes cannot supply the coherent, structured knowledge that only schools can provide, and therefore give the illusion rather than the substance of knowledge. Teachers also condemn what they see as the exaggerated role of fiction in media messages—children today may spend more time engrossed in imaginary adventures seen on films, television or cartoons than in their own doings.

In the developing countries, it is pointed out, there is a discrepancy, and often a conflict, between the ideology or values taught by the school and those expressed by the media: the school is more or less explicitly expected to encourage children to remain in rural areas by instructing them in more efficient farming methods; whereas the media, with their overwhelming power to convince, transmit messages in which towns and urban models predominate. It should be noted, however, that the media exert a fascination over teachers. Whenever a new medium of communication appears, schools are eager to see whether they could use it. In many cases, their efforts have no solid basis of studies relating the various teaching objectives to those of the media, but are prompted by the desire to assimilate the modern media and turn them into teaching means or audio-visual aids. A wide variety of such teaching media is available—radio and television broadcasts for schools, educational films or sets of slides with accompanying sound-track or commentaries, language courses on discs or tapes, more sophisticated uses of the tape-recorder in language laboratories, and so on.

While recognizing the advantages and the many achievements of the media in education, it must be noted that the educational use of the media is limited by three constraints. The first is the imbalance between fields which are very often presented by the media because they are easy to adapt to the screen and have considerable entertainment potential, and fields which are not much dealt with because they are based more on concepts than on images.

A second constraint is that of inflexibility and unwieldiness of the two institutions, which make collaboration between them difficult. The most typical case is that of television broadcasts for schools: it is very difficult to make the timetable of a class fit in with that of the programmes intended for it. Television schedules are just as rigid as school timetables.

The last but not the least constraint is the fact that the use of modern audio-visual techniques tends to separate the two functions of education—to pass on information and to mould minds. But schools have not only tried to integrate media techniques into the school system in the form of audio-visual aids; they have also tackled the problem of teaching young people how to make proper use of the media, which play such an important part in their out-of-school life. Here again, there are many examples of projects aimed at developing a critical approach to the press and an intelligent attitude towards cinema and television.

If we look at the structure of the messages received, the structure of the time spent in viewing or listening, rather than that of the messages transmitted, we shall see that an even smaller proportion of time is spent on broadcasts with an educational and cultural content. The mass media do little to further the cause of education, and the result is that teachers conclude that they should either instruct their pupils in a 'distanced' use of these media or avail themselves of the fascination of the cinema or television, by introducing them into the classroom as audio-visual aids.

THE FUTURE DEVELOPMENT OF EDUCATION: THE MAJOR CHALLENGES

It should be noted at the outset that the situation varies greatly from one region to another. In the industrialized countries the number of children enrolled in primary schools is constant, while in the developing countries the enrolment figures have increased dramatically. Many countries have relatively uniform school systems, whereas in others there are several different types side by side (for example, a traditional sector based on oral transmission, a modern sector for the masses based on literacy education and written work, and a modern élitist sector using new teaching techniques). Of course the greatest variation of all is the enormous disparity of resources between the rich countries and the poor.

Education tomorrow will have to face two major problems—the number of persons to be educated and the number of items to be taught. Many more children and adults will apply to enrol in educational establishments: children in primary and secondary schools in countries with a high rate of population growth, young people kept at school by the extension of compulsory school attendance, and adults for whom the development of lifelong education means re-entry into educational establishments. The problem will of course be most acute in countries where financial and human resources are seriously lacking.

At the same time, the amount of material to be taught is increasing steadily. The pace of technical and scientific advance is such that syllabuses are in constant need of updating. What traditional subjects will have to be dropped? Teachers criticize the media for presenting superficial, incoherent information, but they perhaps run the risk of exposing themselves to similar criticism in the not so distant future.

In my view, the decline in egalitarian ideals is one of the major challenges facing the future development of education. During the nineteenth century and the first half of the twentieth century, school systems were established throughout the world whose ideal was the maximum equality in education and learning: free, compulsory primary education, the extension of universal education in 'common cores' at secondary school level and increased access to higher education. In many countries, however, parallel élitist sectors have sprung up which are run on a commercial independent basis, and whose aim is to differentiate their pupils from the rest of the population.

Another major challenge is that of finding educational solutions to enormous problems such as poverty, hunger, and the technological revolution. Because of such problems there will be more difficulties to cope with over the next few decades. Although technology is advancing rapidly, the unwieldiness of educational institutions hinders the necessary changes.

These observations constitute a brief summary rather than a detailed analysis of the major problems facing educational systems in the coming decades. But what does the future hold for the media?

THE FUTURE DEVELOPMENT OF THE MEDIA

It is not easy to foresee how the media will develop in the future. There is of course no difficulty in enumerating the foreseeable technical innovations. However, what is technically and industrially possible is not always commercially and socially probable. Social probability depends less on existing needs or expectations than on demands made by people who can pay, which in turn depend on market trends and the commercial policies of the audio-visual industry.

Moreover, the media are structured in such a way that a change in the place or function of one of them or the emergence of a new one alters the place and function of all the others. Neither financial nor time budgets are unlimited.

It is unlikely that any substantial technical improvements will be made in the cinema (with the possible exception of the development of the technique of three-dimensional images). Television and video-recording techniques, however, are changing rapidly, in the production, transmission and reception of images. Owing to technical advances and the streamlining of equipment (for example, the conversion, in the case of video-recorders, from 2-inch to 1-inch tapes) one may reasonably hope that manufacturing costs will come down. The use of portable film cameras for electronic news gathering will make it possible to act quickly, so that television will be more like radio as regards the transmission of information. The replacement of analogue methods by digital techniques for processing of television signals should improve the quality of transmission and make it possible to provide links to data banks, thereby ensuring the availability of teletexts either on video screen or on hard copy. The transmission of programmes directly by satellite will encourage countries which are not yet equipped with a ground-based transmission network to save themselves the expense. These satellites will increase frontier overspill and hence the possibility of receiving broadcasts from neighbouring countries. In view of its potential contribution to the field of education, mention should be made of the possible use of 'radiovision' by satellite: the equivalent of one television channel per satellite makes it possible to transmit fifty programmes of still pictures, each with its own soundtrack (the system, still known as Still-Picture Television, was tested in Japan during trials of the experimental satellite).

To reach individual receivers, messages will be transmitted either through individual antennae (different from and more costly than equipment in current use) or through collective antennae and cable networks, a system (known in some countries as 'teledistribution', in others as 'cable-casting') which makes it possible to transmit more programmes to the user—whereas they are limited in number, due to congestion, in the Hertzian system. This system is particularly useful in establishing stations which serve a limited geographical area for the transmission of local news and information. In some cases, which are still few and far between but which could increase in number with the use of optical fibres in years to come, tele-casting or cable-casting distribution makes it possible to install interactive systems, enabling the user to converse with the broadcaster and participate actively in the programme. If optical fibres are used, this system could also be adapted to the single network already mentioned.

The reception of messages on the television screen will also be greatly modified. As already noted, thanks to satellites and cable networks, the user will have access to a greater number of programmes. Moreover, the television set will be incorporated in a system of equipment and services, increasingly referred to as peritelevision. The video-recorder, which is to the audio-visual media and television what the tape-recorder is to soundtrack and radio, makes it possible to record programmes for later viewing. These devices, which are programmable for several days in advance, will operate pre-recorded video cassettes as well as video films produced by the user. It will also be possible to use individual or family television sets, in conjunction with an appropriate reader, to view programmes recorded on video discs (in this case, they cannot be recorded by the user). Finally, the television receiver may be used as a visual display unit for pages of texts transmitted or routed by telephone from data banks (telematics).

These appliances will bring about two major changes in the media system. First, the resultant increase in the number of channels and accessible sources of messages will lead to audience fragmentation and the specialization of content—there will be a transition from large-scale media to small-scale media, from 'broadcasting' to 'narrowcasting'; broadcasters, editors and producers in various fields will appeal more directly to particular audiences; or they will provide a greater quantity of messages to fulfil a single function or demand (sport, information, fiction, etc.). Second, the more advanced systems will be interactive, enabling the user to intervene more and more in the course of the programme. For example, research is now being undertaken on the possibility of producing interactive video discs, in which disc space is made available to the user, and therefore, according to the replies, messages can be recalled, clarified, or renewed.

Such, briefly, are the main audio-visual techniques already in operation or soon to be available, which will be widely used within the next twenty years. It is easy enough to list these devices, but if we are to foresee the future development of the media we also need to know when such equipment will be introduced on a large scale and what part each device will play in the media system.

Moreover, to complicate matters still further, the development of new audio-visual techniques will obviously occur at a very different rate in different countries and regions. In California the public has access to fifty-five television networks (by cable and satellite), and the rate of ownership of video-recorders and video cameras is one of the highest in the world; but several African countries have no television network at all and, even if there is a station in the capital city, broadcasts can only be picked up within a radius of a few kilometres. It seems unlikely that in years to come there will be any narrowing of the gap between countries equipped with extensive networks, able to transmit highly diversified material and specialist programmes in addition to messages for general public consumption, and countries which until the end of the century will have access only to mass media (radio and television in the present sense of the term), and not to peritelevision services. The main difference between the two groups of countries is that only the former group will have the new-generation equipment giving access to personalized messages and interactive systems. The latter group will remain at the stage of mass communication, with messages designed for vast audiences and for the average viewer, without opportunities for genuine feedback.

Many surveys of the media and their future development make no reference to programmes, neglecting the fact that the impressive increase in the number of communication channels will necessitate additional material, if a shortage of programmes or, at any rate, a serious imbalance between hardware and software is to be avoided. It is true that the production of messages is always a step behind the advance of communication technology, and that each new technique begins by transmitting programmes borrowed, for the most part, from earlier techniques—the cinema makes films of stage plays, the radio broadcasts concerts and music-hall shows, and television transmits a lot of films. But technique comes of age when it has established its own repertory of messages.

There will be an increase in international exchanges (buying and selling, coproductions, exchanges in the true sense of the word). This interaction will be as unevenly weighted as it is today, with the same attendant risks: the influence exerted in the first instance by foreign products on national producers, who can only accept these models of international commercial success, is probably at least as great as the influence on users of products which convey—implicitly in fiction or more explicitly in news and documentary items—stereotypes and models as well as standards and values.

Other means will be used to remedy programme shortages, in particular the systematic use of archive documentation, recourse to all existing audio-visual material, the rationalization of production (by re-using 'stock shots', for instance), frequent repeats, etc. It is probable that promoters of new services or new media will want to include educational material in their catalogues.

INTERACTION BETWEEN THE MEDIA AND EDUCATION

The challenge of the growth in the number of persons to be educated can be met by the mass media, since they are able to transmit the same message in millions of copies. The problems arising from the volume of material to be included in syllabuses can be solved because it is possible to have access both to the best specialists in all fields, persons who are familiar with the most recent findings in their particular discipline, and to constantly updated data banks, and also because audio-visual material for use by teachers and students can be produced, stored, catalogued and distributed. Even the problem of economic disparities can be solved: although services such as radio or television broadcasts for schools are costly, so many pupils are reached by them that the cost per pupil is very low. In view of the scale of the problems facing educational systems in the future, there will again be a tendency to hope for too much from both traditional and newly-developed media. It is not very difficult to imagine the illusions that will be entertained. But the statement that future expectations are ill-founded perhaps requires more evidence than the observation that, in the past, the advent of the mass media did more to increase the problems of educators than to solve them. In support of these pessimistic views, it should be said that there are a number of clearly-marked trends which, in all probability, will permanently affect the development of relations between the world of education and the media.

The first of these trends concerns the majority use of the media for entertainment purposes. But there is another factor which does still more to dash our hopes that the media will solve the major problems of education in tomorrow's world, and that is the situation regarding available financial resources. These resources are most unevenly distributed, and are totally lacking in areas where the greatest educational needs are felt. The new media are basically centred more on information, fact-finding, and the transmission of knowledge (even if the unexpected sometimes occurs in this field), whereas the older media (cinema, radio and television) are much more centred on entertainment. The latter will probably be the only media accessible to developing countries, where educational needs are greatest.

The conditions that educational television must meet should be emphasized again, to destroy the illusion that it can provide a cheap solution to the educational problems of developing countries. It is not enough to broadcast programmes, however good they may be, without taking account of the level of instruction of those for whom they are intended, of their attitudes and of their general circumstances, which can consolidate the effect of television—itself merely part of a whole, within which it fulfils its function, and without which it is but a voice crying in the wilderness, or, worse, a factor that serves to widen cultural gaps.

At this point in the argument, mention must be made of the two principal trends in modern teaching practice: first, the trend towards maximum rationalization, the desire to make teaching a technique (teaching by objectives, programmed learning, etc.); second, the trend towards emphasizing the importance of the personal motivation of pupils (non-directive teaching, individualized learning, etc.). Both these trends are opposed to the widespread use of distribution techniques to flood entire areas with educational material, in much the same way as vast tracts of land are sprayed with fertilizers.

Rational teaching methods stress the need for the careful adjustment of teaching aids to clearly-defined objectives and the necessity of monitoring results at every stage of the teaching process. If we look at these prerequisites in relation to the old and the new media, we shall see that traditional radio and television must be discarded in favour of more flexible techniques which make it possible to invervene at classroom level, repeating different stages, slowing the pace or speeding it up, using records or sound cassettes, audio-visual packages, films, video discs, video cassettes, or interactive teletext systems.

Non-directive teaching, for its part, reminds us that nothing in education is assimilated except what the individual's personal interest incites him to seek out and discover on his own initiative. To assist the learner in this process, he must be provided with the necessary documentation and encouraged to reach his own conclusions. The media most used for this purpose will be those which facilitate the storage of audio-visual archives and provide an opportunity to consult them in information centres, for example slides with accompanying soundtrack, films, sound cassettes and discs, video cassettes and video discs.

Whichever trend is followed, it is clear that in education preference will be given to the more recently developed media or techniques of the future, which lend themselves to flexible utilization, decentralized consultation and personalized use—in other words, media whose widespread installation is liable to be slowly achieved in developing countries.

Similarly, in industrialized countries, the most sophisticated new media, those that might be the most valuable if applied to education, are very likely to be used mainly in élitist, privately-run institutions.

Finally, apart from limited financial resources, there is yet another clearly discernible factor which is liable to affect future development—the constraints arising from the habits of teaching staff. The new techniques create a need for technical instruction courses and, above all, an often radical rethinking of traditional teaching methods. The teaching profession may be no more deeply attached to its traditions and practices than any other section of society, but the attachment nevertheless exists, and it would be unrealistic to expect an exceptional adaptability of approach on the part of teachers.

Consideration of these clearly marked trends (arising from the predominance of the entertainment factor in the media, the limitations and disparity of financial resources, and the force of habit in teaching) gives a view of the future in which education and the media are still competitors and rivals, with 'tangential encounters' whose impact on educational habits and media operations is slight. However, such views may be valid only for the relatively near future of the next six to ten years.

ATTEMPTS AT RECONCILIATION AND THE OUTLOOK FOR FUTURE COLLABORATION

The first step towards bringing together the two worlds of school and the media is a renewal of interest in simpler technology. Teachers seem to be fascinated by the most sophisticated techniques, but a more objective assessment shows that excellent educational results can be obtained by using simpler ones, because they are closer to the users and their daily lives. Examples are the school broadcasting projects in Latin America which played a vital part in literacy and 'conscientization' campaigns, and the role of the mobile cinema in India.

The second step, one which opens up new prospects for future collaboration, is the discovery of what can be done by the systematic use of film and television libraries already in existence or now being set up. To take but one example, according to an estimate made by the French National Centre for Educational Documentation (Centre National de Documentation Pédagogique), in France alone 200,000 scientific, technical and industrial films have been produced since the earliest days of the cinema. Archives such as these exist in many countries. Once the various problems involved in making them available to teachers are solved, they will be an almost unlimited source of educational material. Conditions today are more favourable to the solution of these problems than in the past, and they will be more easily dealt with. For instance, once the benefit to be gained from the undertaking is clearly understood, data processing will be of considerable use in solving cataloguing and indexing problems: satellites linked to video-recorders for storing data or the production of video discs may provide a solution to problems of distribution, transmission and reception.

This material will take the form of a series of short notes rather than that of ready-made explanations, which require no intervention on the part of the teacher. This will encourage teachers to look for short items which they can use in their own explanations. If we were talking of written material, we might say that there will be less need for manuals than for dictionary or encyclopaedia entries.

As already mentioned, various systems are possible for the delivery of these documentary elements, among which a choice must be made on the basis of a cost-benefit analysis. One thing is certain: we must eliminate the obstacles and the present confusion between the technical means of delivering messages, the messages themselves (whether these be addressed to the world at large, the 'average' listener or a particular individual), and giant corporations that govern the totality. As such, the concept of the message is now more than merely a dysfunction of the functions of writing, producing, programming, storing and delivering educational products. We are realizing, tardily, how rarely audio-visual means are used in educational establishments and how frequently failure (or partial success) in their use is due to the antagonistic bureaucracy of the bodies which govern the mass media and those which govern educational systems. We must seek a more human level of operation, but this is impossible if we continue to confuse the delivery of messages and the writing of messages, and make these the prerogative of subsidiary bodies for production and manufacture at the same level.

In practice, it is clear that technology is developing in two different directions. First, towards large-scale dimensions—the satellite, which establishes areas of transmission as vast as entire subcontinents; second, towards a more decentralized approach, with individual means of audio-visual recording and storage, or local cable networks. However, these different types of media may become complementary, combining to form more flexible entities than the rigidly structured mass media of today. Such flexibility would certainly enhance their educational value.

Finally, it must be remembered that in the future development of relations between the media and education the dynamism of the major audio-visual and telecommunication firms will be of vital importance. They will see to it that their hardware and software dominate the world market. However, without minimizing their penetration potential, one may say that systems and programmes which are in line with the trends described above will probably have more chance of both educational and commercial success.

The media are the reflection of a world plagued by inequalities—world inequality in the distribution of the means of communication and information inequality of the forces present on the commodity market; plus inequality in the distribution of power in the communication networks between individuals, groups and nations. This situation is fundamentally immoral, and the future holds no hope of improvement; indeed, a widening of the gap is possible, if not probable. In the other field in question—that of education—disparities are no less marked: on the one hand, enormous quantitative and qualitative needs and very limited resources; on the other, needs that are less pressing and mainly qualitative in nature, and no shortage of financial means. It must be repeated that the hope of remedying educational problems through the use of the media is ill-founded, since it overlooks the fact that neither set of inequalities serves to counterbalance the other, but merely to compound it.

The impact of the media on general education

Pierre Schaeffer

HISTORICAL OVERVIEW

Scarcely has the fifty-year-old debate between education and the media drawn inconclusively to a close, than a new partner, informatics, arrives on the scene. Let us try to sum up the earlier stages and examine the media-based society, the computerized society, the place occupied by education in these societies and the new role it is to play.

In the past, there seemed to be an appropriate answer to every educational problem. Severe lag, it was thought, could be corrected by basic education, the effect of which could be multiplied through the immensely powerful vehicles of radio and television broadcasting and perhaps satellites as well. At the other end of the scale, at the very summit of scientific knowledge, inadequate human memory could be supplemented by data banks, with the processing power of computers reinforced by a world-wide data communication network. In this way, the same satellites could carry in their multiple and divergent circuits both the highest and the lowest levels.

Between these extremes, they could also carry a full range of circuits suitable for all cultural gradations, taking into account local needs, population dispersion, and even inadequate teaching personnel. From a distance, then, the multiplier effect of broadcasting appeared to be an ideal answer to an economic and social problem which was crucial in the case of the most underveloped countries. Even if a price had to be paid in terms of greater centralization, ordinary common sense seemed to suggest that an audio-visual programme, carefully prepared by a number of specialists and disseminated via the broadcasting media, would be more efficient and have a greater impact than the long and costly business of training all the teachers required to cover every area.

Pierre Schaeffer

*Parallel flight: the world of learning
and the world of media*

This background made it possible, in theory at any rate, to resolve certain problems of the transmission and distribution of knowledge through the operational tools of the media. More to the point is the fact that this 'best of all possible worlds', utopian though it may be, has been neither suitably approached nor seriously researched. The upshot has been a sort of parallel flight, like the flight of two galaxies, both expanding and simultaneously repelling each other. It is obvious that virtually everywhere, regardless of the disparity of the resources involved, both schools and the media have sought to grow, each institution along its own lines, with its own style, public, personnel, mission and financing. It is striking to observe to what extent the two have remained separate and alien entities in the course of the twentieth century, and to what extent the example of the developed countries has been a determining factor.

As far as the mass media were concerned, information was contemporary, while the schools' area of interest lay in records of the past. Education in the true sense, which the schools appeared to have neglected for some time, was taken up again in the more immediate context of the current scene by way of 'exposure to the world'. With regard to entertainment, as we have repeatedly been told, this could serve a 'cultural' function, provided it was of suitably high quality; indeed, it might be more effective in this sense than many an earnest lecture.

The dominant model

When the time came to provide the developing countries with broadcasting facilities, other options appeared to be available and would have been justified not only by educational factors but also by other factors related to health, agriculture, economic situation, and so on. In the event, while enclaves were organized in the nascent media with a view to serving these needs directly, they were treated as poor relations, preference being given to programmes of the type popular in the industrialized countries. We may add that, in order to be really effective, basic radio broadcasting designed to serve a country's economic and social needs, as well as agriculture and public health, would have had to be supported by a local infrastructure, that is, not only receivers (transistor radios had not yet been invented) but local agents capable of making use of very modest means.

Some comments are required at this point:

With reference to a hierarchy of needs in the developing nations, there is a dominant model favouring the adoption of the most advanced techniques and the most elaborate programming, in imitation of the developed nations.

The reverse may be said of the developed countries with reference to the 'sub-population' in the schools. For want of an adequate supply of suitable receivers, for want of local storage and trained and motivated personnel, these populations are not being reached and the broadcasting media are proving to be ineffectual and irrelevant.

One factor strengthening resistance to change is the development of a 'quarrel between the Ancients and the Moderns'; as depicted by the conflict between McLuhan's 'galaxies'; crudely put, it is a matter of text versus pictures.

In practice, the rivalry comes to be expressed in institutional terms, and through the institutions in question brings professional groups into confrontation.

Lastly, these professionals divide along different lines in accordance with the selection of vehicles which is a predominant element in any educational strategy.

It thus appears that there is a constant confrontation (beyond institutions and functions) between different techniques and budgets, all of which are playing their own game. No one takes the trouble to develop the co-operation that is so essential between ideas and men, between institutions and networks, and even between different kinds of equipment.

Educational television

Thus the two communities which are designated 'the world of learning' and 'the world of the media', while brandishing similar slogans, refuse to treat each other hospitably, although they do borrow from each other, and each is willing to let the other have whatever unappetizing gristly bits it may have left over.

In the opinion of the schools, the mass media were a foreign body, but also a corporate body, and as such presented as competition. Hence the prolonged period of refusal to recognize even the existence of the media, or at any rate to admit that they had any cultural value.

However a forward-looking component of the teaching profession, impelled by a highly original sense of mission, came to stand out from the rest as a sort of commando unit, a hybrid form displaying characteristics of both institutions, inasmuch as it made use of the broadcasting facilities of the one to disseminate the 'content, of the other. This group, the pioneers of educational television, ran the risk of being disowned by those of their colleagues who had remained within the mainstream tradition of either schools or media. It should also be noted that hybridization was only possible by using unfilled 'slots, in the mass broadcasting system. This is what happened in France at any rate, and the experiment will undoubtedly be repeated elsewhere, wherever large-scale distribution is associated with elementary-level education. The same miscalculation, made out of concern for what is in reality a false economy, will recur, the matter of human and material infrastructure will be overlooked again, and all because of the same simplistic assumption about the broadcasting vehicle, which is the predominant element in the system.

Audio-visual diffusion

Audio-visual diffusion—radio and television broadcasting—is slowly emerging from a long period characterized by severe confusion and contradictions, with too many messages competing for inadequate channel space. Yet, in this flood of pictures and sound, what a barrage of recriminations is heard: poverty of contents, confusion of style, monotony of programmes, a frantic search for the average viewer or listener which is not really satisfactory to anyone concerned, the number of viewing or listening hours rising but production declining. While these are generalized phenomena, the same features characterize the audio-visual diffusion sector in the poorer nations, where different causes have produced similar effects.

However, a series of major media have emerged, or will soon do so, which will enlarge the fields hitherto manifestly limited by the Hertzian spectrum—cables and cassettes, for example, trials of which have not as yet proved conclusive. But what is of greater importance in this particular field is the grave dilemma which threatens existing networks and will dramatically change the entire policy of broadcasting systems, their practices, monopolies, legislation and related matters. At both extremes, from ground level to stationary orbits, there is the risk of further pollution from the multiplicity of small transmitters and the plethora of satellites.

Thus, yet again, it looks as if the vehicle of communication will be a determining factor in future systems. Decision-makers will have to choose whether to accept or reject superficial quantitative evaluations and introduce a social or educational dimension; they must not blindly submit to the dictates of the vehicle. In other words, content and vehicle must be suited to each other, and vehicle, production and storage must be correlated.

Getting away from the Middle Ages: the storage of audio-visual material

In view of the difficulty of access to audio-visual material—at least to material considered as the necessary complement to textual documentation—it is clear that the only possible way forward, in the case of audio-visual material, lies in the accumulation and availability of increasingly relevant and selective material, just as it does in the case of textual documentation. In this case, the messages will not be in the form of either broadcasts or film, but will consist of documentary material to be used in local programmes.

Finally, this kind of content, as we know, is bound up with the question of material support, that is, storage facilities such as those whose prototypes today are video-recorders and audio-visual discs in their various forms and presentations, and with their different abilities and selling prices.

Apart from the technological difficulties of producing these various appliances, further advances have been hindered both by the broadcasting networks and by paradoxical failure to voice needs. This is the explanation of another paradox—the lack of quality and emulation in the production of high-quality audio-visual material in the principal spheres of knowledge.

These three points may be summarized as follows.

Existing systems, especially radio and television networks, focus on the superficial and sensational aspects of daily events: they always aim at a mass audience, and any material they produce is unusable except in the context of historical fiction or events relating to contemporary sociology.

Storage units have not as yet been standardized and will need to be introduced with care, particularly as their only sources of material are the cinema and television repertoire.

Finally, there is a need for a special combination of author/producer, serving as both teacher and image-maker, a dual function which is encouraged neither by the institutions concerned (university and television) nor by the market, except in the very few cases of publishing firms with sufficient foresight to sense the still ill-defined possibilities of future development.

Thus storage is barely possible, and the availability of material for it is barely probable. Audio-visual methods are still in the Middle Ages, in the days of *incunabula* and closed monasteries, and the intellectuals have already broken faith.

A historical anachronism

Clearly, then, educational television could have developed differently if the educational institutions of the advanced countries had possessed the means of production or at least of storage. Similarly, if adequate infrastructures for reception had existed in developing countries, it is likely that the media networks might have been able to balance better and more rationally the entertainment of the few with the basic education of the many. It is quite evident that the mass media have imposed a kind of historical anachronism by the very nature of their content, originally based on a newspaper model (broad, one-way distribution of ephemeral, trivial or sensational information).

One would really need to recapitulate the history of technology in order to establish at what point it imposed an illogical development from which the entire world will take decades to recover. If it is to do so, it must reshuffle the conflicting phases of this development. To persuade ourselves of this, it is enough to imagine that transistor radios were invented first, and that the use of wavelengths required only a small amount of energy. In particular, if the tools of production at our disposal such as tape-recorders, lightweight video-recorders, portable video units and small, low-cost transmitters had come before the tall towers and the high kilowattages of the medium and long wavelengths, the face of the world might have been transformed. Not merely the schools but the entire twentieth-century world probably have taken on another appearance.

THE MEDIA SOCIETY

Civilizing the image

This well-worn theme is an instance of the traditional opposition of 'means' and 'content'. In some cases, it serves as an introduction to the question of the mode of culture, in others it leads to an educational debate on the image as a means of conveying content.

Thus, although most teachers are prepared to accept the image, they will argue that the first step must be to teach the child to read images. They have no doubt that this can be done by observing the rules of syntax or even by borrowing from rhetoric, thereby denying two obvious principles: first, children read images very well, if one can talk of 'reading' in this context; second, if children are taught to 'read', they must be taught to write at the same time, a fact which most teachers overlook.

The process of production does not consist in deciphering language, but in using it to communicate. At least the traditions of education do not usually confuse the art of reading and writing with the science of linguistics.

There are two real problems, that of audio-visual equipment and that of audio-visual systems. The term 'audio-visual equipment' means machines that reproduce sound and images, either film or video, the use of which must be paid for at a fair economic and technological price; not only the financial outlay and necessary training, but also the contingencies and complications as well as the mixture of speed and unwieldiness of these devices must be recognized. The term 'audio-visual system' means major units of production and distribution, such as those found in schools, which are imposed from without and are based on the models of the cinema and television.

Material limitations

Even in good working condition, machines finally impose inescapable constraints. Images and sounds cannot be leafed through like books; their length is that of real time. Although they present an unaltered record,

The impact of the media on general education

one must have access to them and organize them by storage and classification methods of which one may be ignorant or suspicious. Finally, unless the user creates his own image, an activity that is a whole new field of experience to be explored, the images are usually obtained from other sources, presented at the same speed as cinema film which, apart from its dramatic impact, has the disadvantage that the user can neither stop nor review it.

All these disadvantages are certainly real and do not emanate from the technology, since, contrary to cinema film which cannot be reversed, video tape can be stopped, rerun, reviewed and corrected. And if one is dissatisfied with the video reels, one can hope for video discs in the near future which will provide instant access to each image and the possibility of unwinding or stopping the sequence.

One of our recommendations is therefore that basic discussion of the image should be replaced by a more careful, less pretentious and realistic approach. The senseless rivalry and fighting to the death between word and image should be avoided (the same could be said of sound) and replaced by a carefully worked out complementary which is subject to constant review and correction. Superficial discussion of the image, if not all semiological ambitions, should be discouraged in favour of a more practical approach, based on learning to 'read and write' the image, and on the application of the skill so acquired to whichever part of the content clearly requires it.

The parallel school

A completely different debate revolves around systems (the machinery of the mass media in contrast to audio-visual equipment). While the latter can be incorporated into educational institutions, as we have just shown, the former exert their influence outside the school and have long enjoyed the prestige of an exclusive novelty. We know that McLuhan went so far as to say that when the child left the television screen to go to school he could only regress. Many educators will reject this with indignation and reply with a claim that television is incapable of disciplining the minds of the young—when it does not actually corrupt them with models of violence, weakness and stupidity—and that school is an antidote. But why should we complain of an avalanche of images and messages which provide an abundance of visual material, the very thing so often lacking in schools?

Several comments are necessary, then, on the 'proper use of the parallel school', in answer to the usual criticisms.

The disparateness of television programmes and the lack of balance between
   fiction and reality, quality and mediocrity, literary and non-scientific
   content, etc. This means, of course, that the school should have supplementary images at its disposal.

The scattering of images in time and the impossibility of inserting them in a curriculum. That is true, but children will remember a programme of several months ago when recall material is available. This leads to the following point, by far the most important.

The flood of unrecoverable images. This is the essential point, which, when coupled with the former, brings out the need for storage in every educational institution. This storage, after some time, will balance the general effect of the messages, and a local film library will serve to complement and counterbalance the daily programmes.

These practical remarks only partly answer the major objection: impregnation by the media leads to the famous 'culture mosaic' defined by Abraham Moles.

We have just shown certain ways of differentiating this flood of images and refashioning it into a more coherent whole. We must admit, however, that there will remain an enormous residue, not only of unusable programmes, but also of undesirable ones. This is where we must adopt a definite position regarding the essential role of the school. The school can very well give advice on good viewing habits, which will not necessarily be heeded any more than that given by the head of family. Why then not make the best of a bad job and incorporate this residue in the teaching scheme?

Our arguments are as follows. Since children generally prefer to watch adult programmes, such viewing cannot be ignored. After all, this viewing, however premature, provides a look a contemporary society, and if programmes are considered bad it is not just the fault of the programme directors, because they are merely providing the public with the diet it wants. In short, whether we like it or not, the media mirror the very society in which the child finds itself. Is it the task of the school to criticize what takes place in reality, or to arrange things so that the child lives artificially in an abstract, aseptic world?

There is no simple answer, so we will not be so presumptuous as to suggest one. It is most probable that the 'critique of values' will henceforth be more important in schools than the discourse on concepts. It is obvious that the existence of schools is based on common sense as much as on knowledge. But perhaps schools should no longer be alone in taking responsibility for such an unfinished and hesitant education. Many children experience elsewhere another educational environment with complementary activities which are freer and less obstructed by the educational bureaucracy. We cannot ask everything of the school, nor bank knowledge alone.

THE COMPUTERIZED SOCIETY

Computer science

At this point we have to define the variety of computer science applications in the educational field. This is clearly a relatively new subject-matter in the field of knowledge, and radically new where its applications are concerned. Even for someone with no knowledge of computer theory, it is sufficient to know how to use a programme to be able to use a computer as a data-processing machine, that is, for storing, classifying and collating data. In other words, the effects of computerization on education are vital and resemble the automation of industry. Finally, it is in fact an ideology, or at least the expression of a trend, which consists in replacing man by a machine that will perform better (for particular tasks), or be more competent (for a given area of knowledge), or heuristic (having an artificial intelligence which is better developed, at least in certain areas).

Telematics, or the interconnection between the means of communication and computers

To summarize, we would venture to predict a revolution which will affect intellectual work as profoundly as the Industrial Revolution altered the physical nature of work. We can thus reckon on a complete shape-up of the functions of learning ahead of that of the content of knowledge. Education can only be transformed by it, and triply so, in its curricula, its methods and its aims.

Even more so than in the case of the mass media, the influence of which on teaching has been minimal, the influence of computer technology promises to be vital. At present, it is willingly used in an auxiliary capacity, but it threatens to become master as well as servant.

What was, in fact, the target of education in our uncomputerized civilization? In theory, it was to provide each individual with knowledge in a given area, where he had a specific task to perform. Beyond this competence, which corresponded in general to a profession or trade, each individual was to receive general cultural training. Every citizen of contemporary civilization received primary education which met the vital economic, political and social daily requirements of being able to read and write—in other words, to communicate.

Having thus roughly summarized the three objectives of any education, let us consider what could become of them in a world of telematics.

At the primary level, while admitting the archaic necessity for reading and writing (but what is the point of arithmetic?), we must include the need to use everyday machines: pocket calculators, automatic devices, terminals, etc. A part of primary education should also be concerned with training the disabled in the skilful use of artificial limbs.

At the secondary level, one will need to become proficient in processing information and interrogating data banks.

Finally, given the exponential growth of knowledge in all areas, the essential thing will be to maintain data banks and to familiarize specialists with their use. We can then see two possibilities, according to whether the task in question is more conceptual or manual. In the first case, intelligent machines will help the specialist and, in the other, robots will carry out tasks better than the worker, who will nevertheless be assigned some sort of supervisory role.

One might thus predict, to the satisfaction of all, an extensive withering away of 'teacher power', a shortening of studies, a lightening of curricula, a reduction of budgets, perhaps even the abolition of universities.

CONTRADICTIONS AND SOLUTIONS

The power of educators: authority or bankruptcy?

In an archaic society (and the early twentieth century seems such to us) communications are sparse and carried out physically, areas are clearly defined and everyone has his place therein, even if it appears unjust to him. Demands are of a rational kind and are negotiated on the basis of social consensus. This consensus recognizes competence and merit, and thus an implicit process of selection and an accepted line of transmission of knowledge and skills. Conflicts due to social injustice are not aimed directly at these values, rather the contrary. The provision of equal cultural opportunity and access to skills are sought for the greatest number in a more democratic recruitment process, which thus comes up against two obstacles. The first is inevitable, since justice done to the greatest number (or less injustice) leads to a harsher selection which will vest educators with increased power. If one fails to recognize the first obstacle, which is alas an objective one, one will discover a second, either subjective or ideological, denying selection and refusing transmission. Accordingly, university authorities who had considered themselves, often in good faith, to be educating for a better, egalitarian world without constraints, found themselves under fire in the name of these very principles.

Internal and external factors which probably accelerated this crisis culminated ten years ago in Europe. Within higher education the greater demand for courses providing more and more extensive and diversified knowledge fitted badly with employment opportunities, since, in contrast to the archaic society which required numerous middle-level skills, the advanced society required a large number of ordinary operatives to perform tasks remotely supervised by decision-makers or technocratic élites.

Towards a new content structure

Thus, our truly surprising conclusion would be that the media society requires schools fundamentally to alter their teaching structure. Since the child is attached to an apparently over-informed world and is threatened by the 'jungle'; since the adolescent is ill at ease in it and rebels with some semblance of justification; since the student stagnates there with an all-consuming sense of futility; how can we maintain these gradations known as primary, secondary and tertiary, as if things had not profoundly changed, as if we still had the time to apply, layer upon layer, the fragile varnish of a knowledge so ill-adapted to its environment?

We consider, for example, that the distinction between primary, secondary and tertiary, while remaining useful for denoting progression in knowledge and ability, reflects outmoded institutions rather than reality. We would suggest rather that the selection or 'proportioning of content' should be effected at each stage according to the same three directions or criteria: (a) the needs of communication (Jules Ferry's introduction of compulsory reading and writing); (b) the development of the mind (in the spirit of the continuing development of the individual); and (c) the adaptation of the student to the contingent requirements of work, taking into account both his talents and environmental factors.

Instead of false problems, or a false relationship between content and media, we will be posing a worthwhile problem and a pertinent question if we consider the correlation between all the media and each of the three directions: communication, intellectual training and competence.

Adaptation of new media to new content

We formulate two working hypotheses which, we are well aware, do not correspond at all to established usage.

One of these hypotheses has been formulated above: for the content of each of the three levels of education, it proposes a functional scheme of which the three main objectives are communication, culture and competence.

The other hypothesis results from our criticism of the media being dominated by institutionalized power, that is, coagulation of content and vehicle with the entity constituting an institution, for example educational television. We thus envisage a complete reworking of the systems. This working hypothesis would have no chance of success if we could not count, over the next ten years, on two powerful trends which will 'put the squeeze on' existing media systems. We are talking about micro- and mega-vehicles: the micro-installations of individual production and distribution and the megasystem of satellites.

The fusion of content and vehicle is therefore likely to be greatly affected by the fragmentation of programmes, channels, slots and networks. Not only will the pretext of the shortage of resources cease to convince, but countless numbers of channels will be in search of material. This opportunity should not be missed by institutional deadlock, and any consequent confusion between vehicle and content must be avoided at all costs. Failure to seize this opportunity to restructure and interrelate will certainly produce renewed technological and institutional conflict, to the considerable detriment of the public, and will at the same time put two ideological tendencies at loggerheads with each other—the anarchy of local stations and the structured system of satellites. An overall solution might be reached if a basic alliance between microcentres and satellites were admitted, at least in the field under discussion (and deliberately setting aside the question of existing radio and television networks). For microcentres are so adaptable to a variety of local needs that they could handle a certain amount of other material in addition to their own.

This project differs considerably from the preceding systems, in that it presupposes (which is perfectly probable and possible) a satellite channel entirely devoted, for a country like France, for example, to the needs of national education. In contrast to educational television, this satellite, even though providing direct transmission, would not be aimed at the consumer as such, but at institutional groups not just those concerned with school, but also those involved with lifelong education, such as local centres and firms. Used in this way, the satellite channel would permit the transmission day and night of such a large volume of messages that it would probably soon outstrip the capacity for production of educational material. We could take advantage of this shortfall to establish stocks of film, or rather of film sequences borrowed from international documentary and feature-film repositories and for which we envisage a supporting role in the cultural field. Eventually the satellite would be used just to transmit educational material.

If it has been clearly understood that we are considering the satellite in its role as carrier, and that it is in no way an educational institution but simply a means of facilitating exchanges between educators, consumers and producers, it will be clear that the essence of the project is to help local groups to regain their initiative and independence on the strength of the service provided by the satellite and, more generally, the developments to be anticipated in telematics.

Naturally, this heaven-sent source of provisions is intended for content classified according to the three criteria already mentioned, and at primary, secondary and higher levels. There is no reason why some documentary material should not be valid for several levels of education and interest, since our hypothesis is centred on an auxiliary audio-visual system and not on the spoken word intercepted by images. These interchangeable multipurpose 'spare parts' could subsequently be recovered and adapted for use in local programmes.

Interaction between educational, cultural and mass-communication policies

Luis Ricarte Soto

A culture, in the broad sense of the term, is the sum of the values, systems of knowledge and exchange, components of learning and artistic expression by which a group asserts its identity. Since education and communication are two aspects of the life and evolution of a culture, these three notions—culture, education and communication—will always be structurally and functionally associated.

On the threshold of the year 2000, many economic beliefs are being overthrown by a series of technological changes, especially in the area of mass communications: the advent, on all sides, of the audio-visual media, the increasing application of data-processing techniques and the ever rapid flow of a constantly increasing volume of information. The development of the tertiary sector confers a growing importance, at the economic level, on the exchange of information. However, these changes have a still greater impact on our cultural environment, calling into question traditional methods of education, upgrading the specialist at the expense of persons possessing what used to be called a 'general education'.

In the next twenty years how will developed and developing countries manage to solve the often disturbing problems posed by this new technological situation? What changes will they have to make in their cultural, educational and communication policies, and how will a balance be achieved among these different policies? And, apart from the problems peculiar to each group, what chances are there of co-operation between these groups of countries?

DEVELOPED COUNTRIES

In some of the developed countries, the laws of free economic competition, and to some extent of profit, exert a direct and sometimes violent influence on the mass media. Educational policies themselves are affected by this state of affairs. The influence of any of the media depends almost exclusively on the size of its audience, the more so because, from an economic point of view, the media are first and foremost a means of advertising. Of course, this is to over-simplify the situation. For example, the position of a private television company cannot be compared to that of a state-controlled one. Yet, even in the latter case, the law of free competition between the various media remains in force, for because of the increasing number of people who watch and listen to the televised and radio news, fears have been voiced that newspapers will eventually disappear.

This special situation of the mass media (mainly television and radio, but also films and the recording industry) gives the youth of the 1980s a character that some people consider disquieting. In news programmes, for example, the need to reach the largest possible public leads to an emphasis on sensationalism at the expense of factual analysis, and the event is seen apart from its significance. The unreal universe that is thrust upon children and adolescents, while it may lead to life-styles that support very real consumption processes, often cuts them off from the world of school and family.

The situation has been thought serious enough for the authorities to adopt a number of measures specifically designed to help young people to divide their time better between the passive watching of the media and reading. The young viewer's interests must be caught in order to persuade him to exercise restraint in watching television.

There are dangers in the mass communication media that ought not to be underestimated, but people seem to be growing aware of the problems. There is a move to establish links between these new communication media and the more traditional world of a culture in which the critical faculties and the ability to make a rational choice were given prominence. This cannot be properly done, however, unless educators play their part.

The uneasy dialogue between the media and the educational world

The relation between the world of the media and that of education has long been one of barely disguised antagonism. The mass media, which are often considered as a parallel and rival school, are said to be guilty of distracting the pupils' power of concentration because of the fascination exerted over them. But, on the other hand, the media convey an enormous quantity of information: during the third Journées Internationales sur l'Éducation Scientifique (February 1981, Chamonix, France) the participants emphasized the role played by children's papers, books, comic strips, science clubs, games, museums, films and television (until the development of telematics) in the transmission of scientific information. Pointing out that children are deluged with information, in an age when scientific knowledge increases a hundredfold every twenty years, one of the organizers defined the respective roles of education and the media by saying that the school should be able to become a centre of coherent thought amid all this information, and should help pupils to be selective, teach them how to learn and enable them to recapture the pleasure of learning.

So the idea of the possibility of collaboration between the media and the school seems to be gaining ground. It will usually be no more than fragmentary collaboration, since its prime sphere is that of subjects that both institutions deal with: art, the theatre and science are discussed both by the media and at school. In these subjects the barriers are comparatively weak, and collaboration is relatively easy.

Other experiments, though still rare, show that more can be done and that the enthusiasm of young people for television programmes can be harnessed in order to promote general education, to extend pupils' range of interests and to enhance their powers of observation. In the long run, the likely result of carrying out more such experiments is the modification of the media as we know them, of the traditional school and of the cultural world of our daily lives.

In developed countries, there is a move to abolish the barriers between the world of education and the media, which appears at present to be gaining approval among educators.

People who can read books critically should be more knowledgeable and more demanding of the media both with respect to the content, because they are better informed, and with respect to the formal qualities of the programmes shown, for reflection on the content must also be reflection on the image. Such people would also be a less easily-manipulated public, more worthy of the media's respect and more respected by the media.

The large-scale entry of audio-visual techniques into the educational domain would drastically modify the teacher–pupil relationship. The teacher would act as a stimulus to thought rather than the repository of knowledge. Relations would be more relaxed.

Yet the difficulties and obstacles inherent in the dialogue between the mass media and the world of education must not be underestimated. Such experimental co-operation as exists is sporadic, albeit admittedly beneficial. It is often organized on a personal or voluntary basis. To make co-operation the rule would require a major financial effort because of the need to provide every school with audio-visual equipment, relatively costly both to purchase and to operate. Such a decisive change in education as this would represent could only be made at government level. Attitudes and achievements in this matter vary quite widely between the developed countries.

The future of mass communication media in lifelong education

The obstacles to establishing educational structures that take full account of the existence in society of the audio-visual media should not hide the very important fact that developed societies are evolving rapidly and that changes in techniques necessitate the training of a growing number of specialists, who must constantly update their knowledge if they are to continue to work efficiently. Hence the need to create lifelong education structures. Programmes to meet their needs could be organized at all levels, but they will always have common characteristics similar to those required for the introduction of audio-visual methods in education: the use of more flexible methods than those of the traditional school, the development of initiative and the capacity for independent study on the part of pupils and students, and more practical teaching which is closer to the real interests of the learners. And, above all, in most instances such programmes will largely rely on the use of the media and more generally of audio-visual methods.

For instance, at the higher education level, the Open University of the United Kingdom offers a second chance to those who have failed to get into a university in the traditional system, or who for various reasons were prevented from attending.

Anyone over 21 years of age can study at the Open University, and it confers degrees of BA and BA Honours which are equivalent to the degrees of other universities. Teaching is by correspondence, radio and television, and students who possess the technical apparatus (video tapes) enabling them to view previously broadcast programmes have increased opportunities. In 260 centres throughout the country, tutors counsel the students and guide them in their work. There are similar schemes in other countries, for example Diff in the Federal Republic of Germany, Ofrateme in France, Teleac in the Netherlands, Tru in Sweden and Télé Kolleg in Switzerland.

It has been pointed out that the media, in addition to providing the technical means of organizing a lifelong education system, speed up the process once it has been started. It is therefore to be expected that such flexible teaching structures will play an important part in education in the future.

The computerization of society and its effects on the educational and cultural environment

Computer technology and telematics will bring about major changes of various kinds in the daily life of tomorrow's citizens. Even before the potential implications of computers for everyone have been clearly perceived, extensive studies have been made on the conditions in which computers should be introduced in schools and universities and the possibility of doing so. These studies emphasize the changes in education entailed in the introduction of computers. The computer-assisted teaching method is seen as an extremely versatile tool, a most effective method for the self-testing of acquired knowledge and one which, when used in certain ways, can stimulate the pupil's creativity and inventive powers.

The cultural environment will certainly be profoundly modified by the computer and telematics revolution. New problems will arise. In future illiteracy will not necessarily mean the inability to read, write and count, but probably the inability to use an electronic information service in order to find a job, housing or cultural facilities.

The novel communication medium of telematics therefore relates to a new cultural universe—a universe in which, more optimistic observers believe, everyone will be able to have access to all sorts of information, and the quality of communication between people will be enhanced. Pessimists, on the contrary, insist that there is a danger of impoverishing both language and, in the long run, human relations, a kind of desocializing of the individual, inasmuch as communication with others would tend to become anonymous. It has been said that the use of computers would mean that the world as a whole would grow closer but the individual would no longer have neighbours.

In market-economy countries, the most acute problems are those associated with the massive introduction of audio-visual and television techniques in the cultural sphere, since they themselves are governed by the rules of free competition. The laws of the market economy make it difficult to harmonize cultural, communication and educational policies.

To some extent, developed countries with planned economies avoid the difficulties of harmonizing the media and education. Generally speaking, the conflicts between the media and education are less acute than in market-economy countries, for a large proportion of television time is occupied by plays and concerts. The radio, which reaches a large public, also broadcasts musical and literary programmes. Similarly, the opposition between reading and television 'consumption' is less marked.

Such countries are striving to democratize education and to give pupils equal opportunities to enter the different levels of education. The policy of narrowing the gap between urban and rural areas—if there is one—will probably be pursued, for city people are considered to have easier access than rural dwellers to training that raises their cultural level. This policy is implemented through cultural education given in rural teaching centres and through out-of-school activities.

DEVELOPING COUNTRIES

The conflict between Western cultural models and indigenous culture

For almost twenty years most developing countries have been marked by cultural dualism. This phenomenon, sometimes called 'heteroculture', is characterized by the coexistence of two cultural matrices, both considered vital, yet antagonistic—first, the traditional model, the return to the old values, a model to which people are still deeply attached; and second, what may be called the 'Western' model, which, at least for the moment, is the principal basis of development technology. In many countries, the return to traditional values is acquiring greater importance in the choice of educational and training programmes.

Certain governments, even if their development models are strongly influenced by Western ones, are increasingly inclined to consider the aspirations of their people who wish their own cultural values to be emphasized. This trend towards promoting indigenous cultural values will no doubt become more and more marked. These facts will have to be taken into account in future international cultural relations.

Co-operation between educational, cultural and communication policies in the assertion of political independence

In the decolonization process which took place in Asia and Africa in recent decades, cultural, educational and communication policies have tended to promote both the development of indigenous culture and the consolidation of political independence.

For many years most developing countries, in working out their educational systems, followed Western models, in which the idea of economic growth predominates. As a sub-system of society, therefore, the function of education was to train children to be producers. Most of these countries have also given priority to the training of an élite, concentrating on higher and university education at the expense of primary and technical education. Since the Western development model, apart from being a production model, implies different attitudes and cultural aspirations, this sort of education is not suited to the cultural values of the countries concerned.

Another problem is that of the language of instruction. The adoption by certain countries of a Western language as a vehicle of culture may have two different connotations. It may simply confer prestige upon the lifestyles of the former colonial power at the expense of traditional ones. On the other hand, as is the case in Africa south of the Sahara, it may be a means of finding a common language in a region where linguistic diversity hampers communication.

Interaction between educational, cultural and mass-communication policies

The contribution of the media to educational and cultural action

In a study of future prospects, the opportunities offered to education by the development of the media must be taken into account. Such opportunities must be considered from both the qualitative and the quantitative point of view. Generally speaking, television is not at present a significant factor. In India, in 1980, television networks covered only 12 per cent of the country and television programmes were watched by less than 8 per cent of the population. In Kenya, television reaches a mere 500,000 viewers, which is not many compared with the 5 million people who regularly listen to the radio. Since purchasing power is low in developing countries, to be able to acquire a television set is exceptional good fortune. If we compare radio and television in developing countries, it is evident that radio is the principal medium of mass communication. In Asia (excluding Japan) for instance, the number of radio receivers totalled 69,764,000 in 1976, against 15,651,000 television sets. The situation is similar in Africa and Latin America. But the principal value of this means of communication lies in its cultural dimension: in a number of countries it reaches the rural population, including illiterates. Consequently, in countries where the state controls communications, the radio broadcasts educational programmes for all levels. For economic and cultural reasons, radio broadcasts will continue to be the principal communication medium, at least in the short term.

As regards the press, the developing countries, in which three-quarters of the world's population live, possess only half of the world's newspapers and receive a quarter of the copies printed. Most influential newspapers are based in major cities. Moreover, the press, which is largely dependent on advertising for its finance, conveys a model of Western consumption proportional to the strength of the ties between the economy of developing countries and that of Western developed countries. In developing countries, of course, the major obstacle to the growth of the press is still illiteracy and the low rate of school attendance.

The media and literacy teaching

The problem of illiteracy is far from being solved. An estimated 940 million people will be illiterate at the beginning of the twenty-first century. Every effort must therefore be made to eradicate illiteracy. But only a few countries have organized and co-ordinated their educational, cultural and communication policies with a view to achieving this goal. Reading material for the newly literate is rarely printed in newspapers. Literacy projects are not often part of an ambitious cultural policy. A developing country, however, can use the broadcasting facilities it possesses, small though they may be, to good effect for the promotion of education and culture, but the state must determine the general lines along which culture should develop. Measures of this kind, which would enable the media to promote literacy campaigns more actively, do not appear to have been taken.

Prospects

In the future, the media will probably play a major role in the dynamics of the interaction of cultural and educational policies. Some achievements, for example, experiments in the broadcasting of educational programmes by satellite in countries such as India and Indonesia, provide real evidence of this trend. Speaking of the microprocessor and of telecommunications, Jean Tinbergen, winner of the Nobel Prize for economics, said that as a result of the technological revolution, plans could be made for a single educational network with common data centres and common telecommunications infrastructures, based on structures common to the entire system. It will therefore be preferable to set up a satellite-based educational system rather than to use existing networks. This would mean that there would be two systems within the satellite telecommunication network—one for broadcasting programmes for the general public on television stations, whether private, semi-private or state-controlled (with financial aid from advertising); and the other a televised educational system. In both cases the importance of the 'cultural environment' in which modern technologies arise must be borne in mind.

In the not too distant future, audio-visual media may therefore occupy a position equal if not superior to that occupied by the radio in developing countries. However, developing countries whose educational, cultural and communication policies are essentially state-controlled will probably adopt a more critical and reserved attitude towards the massive introduction of technology in education. In other developing countries, 'mass culture' broadcasts (produced and distributed by cultural industries) will probably increase at the expense of private groups and individuals who will gain no special benefits from this modernization of communication techniques.

On the other hand, the press, instead of expanding, might remain embryonic, as is now the case in most developing countries. Such a situation would have a bad effect on education at all levels, especially on literacy work, in which the reading of books and newspapers plays an important role.

Constantly increasing and ever-changing demands will be made on international co-operation, as each country's cultural characteristics, including those of developing countries, will not cease to assert themselves. They will have to be considered in connection with co-operation in education and mass communication if we are to avoid producing standard projects, whose execution very often yields results that are disappointing in relation to the effort made.

Interaction between educational, cultural and mass-communication policies

In the sphere of communication, special attention ought to be paid to the press in developing countries if it is not to be the first victim of the harmful effects of modernization.

The new educational opportunities offered by satellites have given rise to projects that may even bring about cultural integration. That prospect would be contrary to the very spirit of international co-operation, since it is a denial of individual cultures. It would be likely to give rise, in developing countries, to a tendency to refuse co-operation that takes the form of integration rather than that of participation.

The mass media: partners for development

Asok Mitra

The aim of this discussion is not to see formal schooling and the media in adversary or substitution roles; rather to examine an intimate and continuing partnership between the two in which each complements and enriches the orther in a national effort towards the best and most economical solution for bringing equal opportunity within the reach of all in the next twenty years. There are strengths and weaknesses both in the formal school system and in the mass media. The national task will be to emphasize strengths and limit weaknesses. Intimate collaboration between the two systems and approaches is essential, but is by no means easy to achieve. A number of political, social, cultural, administrative, organizational and investment priorities will have to accompany or even precede a change in orientation of education to bring it about.

THE MEDIA IN FORMAL SCHOOLING

Around 28 per cent of the total population in the Indian subcontinent is under 10 years old. The 10–14 age-group make up about 12–14 per cent of the population. Illiterate, semiliterate and functionally illiterate adults make up about 30–35 per cent of the total population. This poses the problem of training several kinds of teachers. First, an increasing number of primary- and secondary-school teachers are needed in rural areas where there is not even a minimum of teaching aids, experimental materials and instruments. Second, a new category of teachers is needed for non-formal education, for informal education and adult literacy, and what may be called informal schooling. There is also a need for training another category of teachers to disseminate the technological, economic and social lessons which can assist social transformation and an improvement in the quality of life and the environment.

For the first category of teachers, structured and consecutive courses for both teachers and advanced students through radio, television and satellite, aided by short instructional films or film strips have proved useful in the physical, chemical and biological sciences and even in mathematics. They have effectively contributed to raising the efficiency of formal schooling, particularly in rural areas where qualified teachers and essential equipment are not always available. Nevertheless, there are some problems: (a) inflexibility of scheduling on the radio, television, etc.; (b) the predetermined and immutable presentation of the message, ruling out the possibility of revision or correction; (c) lack of instant interaction between the person delivering the lesson and the learner; (d) one-shot lessons and a corresponding absence of elucidation and elaboration; (e) frequent lack of graduated structuring from easy to difficult stages; (f) absence of optimum mix of the various media, chiefly instructional and methodological films, radio, television lessons, and traditional media such as theatre and puppetry; and (g) the disaggregation of target audiences into homogeneous age groups.

The mass media in India, particularly All India Radio (AIR), Doordarshan (the television authority), Satellite Instructional Television Experiment (SITE), the forthcoming INSAT, and the Films Division have conducted an impressive array of experiments all over the country in many languages, followed by programmes which now have a set form, content and perspective. There are three main types. The first aims at upgrading the capability and knowledge of teachers, mainly at the primary and secondary school level, chiefly through AIR and Doordarshan with the help of instructional films and printed guidebooks. Teachers thus can become acquainted with teaching equipment, tools and methods that are too expensive to be acquired for individual schools, particularly in the natural sciences. The second consists of teaching special language courses, primarily to teachers and advanced students. The third is supplementary teaching by reputed teachers on television. The classroom teacher is expected to explain the details of the programme to the students at the end of each lesson and in the process learn himself.

The experiments would have been far more effective, both from the point of view of cost and quality, had there been universal availability of radio and television receivers all over the country. Television is still too expensive for a receiver to be owned by all schools; there are also problems of operation and maintenance of radio and television sets in the classroom, which reduce their effectiveness.

The positive aspects of the use of mass media in education have been appreciated inasmuch as each lesson dispenses a single theme and is delivered over a large linguistic region. It has the psychological advantage of a 'direct' message. The accomplished radio/television 'teacher' often injects a personalized, intimate character to the message. The listeners feel they belong to a community of 'receivers' and are participating in an activity of national importance.

Asok Mitra

THE MEDIA IN NON-FORMAL AND INFORMAL EDUCATION

The media have been used extensively in India for the National Adult Education Programme (NAEP) which includes adult and functional literacy, with special reference to adult women; the Experimental Non-formal Education Programme (ENEP) for the 9-14 age-group together with a scheme of assistance to voluntary agencies for non-formal education for the same age-group and various programmes which, to distinguish from informal education (learning by doing), I would like to call informal schooling.

The adult education and functional literacy programmes in India are well known and literature on them is readily available; it is therefore unnecessary to discuss them again here. The Experimental Non-formal Education Programme (9-14 age-group) and the schemes of assistance to relevant voluntary agencies deserve attention. If successful, they will fulfil a vital need in India where a substantial proportion of children aged around 9 are compelled to work, and often do not attend school or drop out of it in order to earn a living for themselves or supplement the earnings of their parents. Nor is it easy to envisage that in the next twenty years this juvenile workforce will disappear. The programme, introduced in nine educationally-backward states to start with, began with an extensive experiment in 21 blocks and 200 centres in clusters of 10 villages each in July 1978. The aim is to bring about universalization of elementary education through non-formal channels, with a view to enabling willing children to gain entry into the formal school system at multiple points and improving the quality of life of children through non-formal education. Part of the course is tailored to formal elementary education, mainly literacy and numeracy, while the other part is an adaptation of the non-formal adult education curriculum to the needs and capabilities of young minds, mainly addressed to problems of health, vocation, social awareness and the environment. Interesting and wide-ranging experiments are in progress to work out suitable approaches. An appropriate mix of the media to be used still remains to be satisfactorily worked out.

The media in India have achieved notable success in what could be aptly described as informal schooling. It is unfortunate that these efforts have not won their deserved acclaim. The essential ingredients have been the ability to draw large homogeneous groups together, and to offer graduated and structured courses on problems of agricultural production and vocational learning. There have also been regular school subjects like geography, history and the cultural traditions of India symbolizing unity in diversity. There are, of course, the unavoidable handicaps of lack of feedback, of personal interaction between teacher and learner, and of inability to confine the audience to a fixed age-group.

AREAS OF POSSIBLE CONFLICT IN GOALS

Because the media developed as a vehicle of commerce and salesmanship, the qualities of brilliance, virtuosity, slickness, technical excellence, economy of time and material, stylishness and sophistication are at a premium in the largely literate developed world. Media professionals in the developing world tend to feel inferior and frustrated if they do not keep up with their counterparts in the developed world, particularly in the area of sophistication and even slick gimmicks. They need constantly to be reminded that the illiterate or semiliterate, particularly the adolescents and adults among them, learn new things more slowly and forget them more easily. On the other hand, these people probably know a good deal more about many topics than is imagined, are quiet and unforthcoming, are far too nervous or selfconscious to concentrate for long, may get depressed, absentminded or tired after a day's work, and will leave the programme if it does not meet their learning needs. In short, television or radio entertainment, or for that matter cinema, stage or puppetry, which media men are professionally trained to consider primarily as 'show', are very different from 'education'. This is particularly so for illiterate and semiliterate audiences in the underdeveloped world, where a viewer often finds it difficult to make the connection between a three-dimensional real-life event and its projection on a flat screen. In such circumstances, one must forget the idea that the medium is the message and reinstate the supremacy of the message itself.

Feature producers engaged in 'schooling' have to combine some of the major qualities of a classroom adult education teacher with those of a media presenter. The presenter has to be encouraging and friendly; ask and anticipate a series of questions by getting to the root of the problem; take firm control of his unseen student and get him back to basics, start off with a few small exercises which he knows the student could do; explain to the student exactly what he is going to do; which methods he is going to use and so on; and remember to recapitulate. He has to be sympathetic, empathetic, objective, patient, flexible and able to 'listen' to his unseen student. These qualities are difficult to come by in a presenter.

Furthermore, media programmes often are expected to achieve too much in too little time, much like sales advertising. Many programmes in the India media, particularly those of AIR, Doordarshan and SITE, have failed to succeed because they have been insufficiently graduated from easy to difficult and inadequately structured. They have often tried to include more than one message at a time, faltered between serious lessons and trivail, and failed to explain difficult concepts clearly. There is no place for the 'subliminal message' in these lessons. Nor must the television or radio teacher presume superiority over the classroom teacher, who should feel that he is receiving no more than friendly help. Quite often, moreover, the programmes are put out without being pretested on a live audience.

The sales lobby for the production of cinema, radio and television hardware, together with that for the supporting hardware of studios, of distribution outlets and receivers, spurred by the astonishing rate of growth of electronics in the last thirty years, have often made more claims for the modern mass media than are justified by results. Media are merely tools and can often produce results opposite to what are outwardly professed or promised. Like all means of production, the nature of their ownership often determines the social values and the results they produce.

RESULTS OF MEDIA INSTRUCTION: AN ASSESSMENT

In spite of claims that educational television would serve as a catalytic agent for overall educational reform, upgrading of the quality of instruction, reforming curricula, reaching large numbers of students, equalizing educational opportunities, and reducing unit cost of instruction, various evaluation reports on SITE, for instance, prepared under government and academic research auspices, do not readily support these claims.

It is held that satellite and television have not been very successful in (a) increasing awareness, knowledge and practice of various agricultural innovations; (b) bringing about significant changes in attitudes or practice related to birth control; (c) bringing about desirable changes in social behaviour and political participation, organizational activities or leadership; or (d) substantially increasing self-help capabilities. SITE did, however, increase the occupational and economic aspirations of child viewers 'even to unrealistic limits'.

Some of the aspects of satellite and television education that are not systematically appraised are (a) who has access to educational programmes; (b) what groups systematically benefit from them; (c) whose values are transmitted; (d) what language is used; (e) what skills are developed and in which groups; and (f) what opportunities are provided for the majority to employ their skills and participate effectively in decision making. Even SITE did not succeed in reaching the most disadvantaged—the rural poor and the urban unemployed and their children—even when it aimed at doing so. Doordarshan and SITE, even when they strive to reach their audiences, often end up with inappropriate programme content which represents language, behaviour and values reflecting those of the dominant groups in society, particularly the urban and 'cosmopolitan' élite.

Researches undertaken under the auspices of the National Council of

Educational Research and Training (NCERT) have shown that educational television and SITE may have served to accelerate rural–urban migration in some regions, put a strain on existing school resources, exacerbated the problems of unemployed schoolteachers and even given them a sense of inferiority. NCERT does not know whether or not the cost of this type of schooling is higher per pupil than in classroom teacher schools; or whether pupil performance is significantly or consistently better when television has been used than when teachers were simply retrained to use more effective curricula. What is more, teacher retraining costs are often lower than the cost of operating an educational television system. In any case, even the most persuasive argument in favour of educational television or SITE—the need for reducing the shortage of qualified teachers—demands that a programme should run for at least ten years to make it effective and bring it up to operational capacity.

EXPECTATIONS AND REALITIES

Finally, it is important to bear in mind that radical changes in education cannot be expected without transformations first taking place in the whole of society; that the media cannot achieve all that is claimed for them if the national school system and educational opportunities remain the same with only incremental expansion and reform; and if there are few fundamental changes in the philosophy, structure, content and outcome of the national schooling system.

There are a number of other issues crucial to the question of partnership between schooling and the media in India. First, can educational television reform a country's educational system to the same extent that an expanding school system can improve the quality of instruction? Second, deeper thought is needed as to how the basic educational problems of a country are related to overall development and exactly how the media, together with other educational resources, can help meet specific educational needs. Finally, what are the long-term consequences of using the media in trying to solve problems likely to arise from expanded schooling: do they threaten the utility of the classroom teacher, and are educational improvements through use of the media as long-lasting as they are so readily, but often uncritically, assumed to be?

In conclusion, I should like to return to the vital need to train communicators and media teachers properly both for non-formal teaching in particular disciplines and in the wider problems of social and economic development. The communicator needs professional training in his complex task of combining instruction with information and entertainment.

The main reason why most features fail to be sufficiently analytical and thought-provoking, and therefore remain insufficiently informative, instructive and entertaining, is the lack of adequate training among feature writers and mass communicators. Training should cover three distinct areas: first, the art and technique of producing informative and entertaining features, particularly in the vernacular languages; second, intensive education in development problems; and third, training in self-evaluation. This kind of training alone can help features to attain an acceptable analytical and penetrating quality and to ensure that the products are self-contained and comprehensive as well as entertaining.

6
Interaction between educational policy and cultural policy

Introduction

The analytical techniques and standards applied to the relations between education and culture depend, in the first place, on the definition of culture we adopt. We may consider, for instance, that 'the field it embraces extends in fact to cover all the experiences and events of the life of a community. The need to distinguish this field from those, for example, of education or communication, and to discuss cultural activity separately from economic activity, is the result of a very recent development in the history of mankind—that of industrial society. This breaks with the longest period in man's history, a period in which culture could not be assigned to any specific area, since it was present everywhere' [1, Paragraph 246]. This kind of overall definition of culture, however, while rich in potentialities—in so far as it implies taking into consideration the interrelations between culture and all that makes up social life, and ultimately reflecting on the cultural dimension of development—can hardly be applied to the analysis of the dialectical relation between the cultural content of education, especially its relevancy to the values of a particular community, and the cultural role of education as a system for transmitting knowledge and values.

The result is a tendency, particularly in the industrialized countries, to adopt a functional and/or institutional definition of culture since the aim is to detect its links with education seen as everything relating to the activity of educational systems (including lifelong education)—an approach which by its very nature has less point in many of the developing countries, for two reasons. First, the essential nature of an industrial society, which explains why the field of culture is distinguished from others, is not characteristic of most developing countries. Second, for historical reasons the educational systems in such countries are marked by the adoption and perpetuation of foreign models, which knew nothing of the languages, aspirations and deepest cultural values of these societies, if they did not deny their very existence.

Then again, as Andrzej Sicinski stresses in the introductory remarks to his study, it is open to question whether there is really any point in discussing the interrelations between educational and cultural policies in general terms and without any specific reference to a particular society, in view of the importance, among other factors, of (a) the nature of the economic and political system, because of the role it assigns, particularly in the cultural domain, to planning and the importance it gives to private initiative; (b) the level of material development reached and its more or less egalitarian distribution, which determines the cultural level of the population; (c) the propensity or the resistance to change of a particular culture and its sensitivity to values originating in other cultures; and (d) the place that education occupies within the system of values of a given society.

Finally, it is relatively easy to see what may constitute an educational policy, even by implication, for in all countries the educational system has only limited means (budget, teachers, etc.) of meeting the demand for education, and this inevitably gives rise to judgements, to specific choices, and to programmes, if not in all cases to the elaboration of principles; but the meaning of the term 'cultural policy' varies considerably from country to country. Since there is, more or less, no such thing as a measurable social demand for culture addressed to an institution capable of meeting it, cultural policy is really nothing more than all the various activities undertaken by the authorities in the field of culture, the value of which it is difficult to assess by using general criteria and without taking account of their own terms and inspiration. So whether we are thinking of institutions and budgets, administrative and personnel structures, or the domains covered by cultural policies, the differences between countries are not only a matter of the resources available for culture, but also of the authorities' conception of their own role, of culture and artistic creation, of cultural practices and participation in cultural life.

Therefore we must at least distinguish between industrialized and developing countries: the former, especially the market-economy countries, are characterized by the dominance of the mass media in the functional and structural combination of the ideas of culture, education and communication; whereas for many developing countries the main problem resides in the more or less implicit choice, in a context of rapid adaptation to change, between adopting the models of Western societies or 'their own cultural elements' (Luis Ricarte Soto).

THE INDUSTRIALIZED COUNTRIES

Much has been said about the cultural impoverishment that results from the emergence, to the detriment of folk cultures and cultural plurality, of a 'mass culture' associated with the mode of development of the industrialized countries, and more particularly with that of the media, its hallmark being the standardization of cultural products designed for the widest possible public, the homogeneity of which products too often means that they are substandard. At the same time, instances of cultural alienation have been observed, either through the suppression of cultural minorities and especially of their language in some countries, or through the influence that certain countries exert on others through the media—an influence that is sometimes called aggression. So, according to Claude Fabrizio

The coming of the industrial era has altered considerably the dimension of the problem and consequently, no doubt, its nature. Traditional cultures are always cultures of the villages, of small communities, even if belonging to particular ethnic groups gives broader scope to their cultural testimony. The massive arrival on the market of technological products, especially after the Second World War, their powerful impact on cultural demands, the unprecedented uniformization of cultural models which followed, have upset all former situations. The problem of the industries of cultural products and services is henceforth at the centre of discussion on cultural development. This is particularly true of the advance of mass communications which, if they represent one of the most important cultural realities of today, are also one of the most ambiguous and the most open to controversy [2, p. 375].

The growing importance of audio-visual media, the increasing application of data-processing techniques, and the rising volume and pace of information flows that have accompanied the mode of development of the industrialized countries have a profound effect on the cultural environment. And indeed, such high levels of television 'consumption' as are now prevalent in these countries as a whole—the consumption of mediocre and standardized programmes with little cultural content—cannot but impinge on cultural life, whether because of the amount of time given to them or because of the attitude, generally a passive one, of the 'average' television viewer which keeps him away from other possible forms of cultural activity. Some countries have found this situation so alarming that action has been taken to teach young viewers to use television properly and to develop their faculties of criticism and discernment.

Apart from the risks of manipulating public opinion for commercial or political ends, the cultural dangers that accompany the expansion of mass communication techniques are apparently more and more clearly perceived today, especially in the market-economy countries, where the underlying logic of their dynamism—competition and the search for the largest possible audience—is not always compatible with cultural activities based on other principles. Of course, the media have many beneficial uses, and their potential is enormous, but attempts to use them for the implementation of cultural policies cannot fully succeed 'without the intervention and co-operation of educational circles' (Luis Ricarte Soto). The use of the media for teaching cultural subjects would alleviate some of the drawbacks and deficiencies of both institutions in respect of cultural education.

Another phenomenon with major implications for education and culture is the development of data-processing and telematics, whose impact on education requires further study. For if the new communication medium of telematics relates to a 'new cultural universe', the relations that it will establish with education must certainly be defined, since 'in future illiteracy will not necessarily mean the inability to read, write and count, but probably the inability to use an electronic information service' (Luis Ricarte Soto, p. 191). Of course, the *problem of relations between education and culture cannot be reduced to that of the impact of the media on both these areas, however powerful it may be.*

Additionally, according to Oleg K. Dreier, the nature of relations between education and culture is dominated by the change in that concept of knowledge: the scientific and technological revolution has opened up a gap between humanist culture and the new culture associated with increasingly specialized scientific and technological knowledge. That gap has been reflected in education through its content and syllabuses, despite the strong wish for interdisciplinarity. The new element that has appeared in the last decade is the emergence of the global problems concept,[1] which has made it possible for questions previously regarded as closely related to the scientific and technological domains to begin to be examined in a broader context (sometimes at world level) as part of a move towards synthetization. Two trends are therefore discernible—a trend towards the integration of knowledge and a trend towards merging the two types of culture, due particularly to the impact of the ecological situation. Also, according to Dreier, one of the conditions that promote these two trends is the transformation of education itself, since its underlying principles and present division into disciplines permit neither genuine assimilation of overall scientific concepts and recently attained scientific knowledge nor the integration of knowledge, which presupposes the organization of teaching based on 'problem-solving'.

But education, whatever adaptations may be called for in its ends or in its means, will continue to play a considerable role in cultural development because its general function is to transmit values and also because of the training it provides and the influence it exerts on the production and consumption of cultural goods. The school, therefore, is the very basis of cultural development (Andrzej Sicinski): indirectly because education is an important factor in economic development, which largely determines the opportunities for cultural development; and because the influence of school education is commensurate with its enormous role in the process of socialization of the individual, in shaping personality and attitudes and, lastly, in passing on cultural values. This means that education determines people's ability to communicate and to understand the symbols of culture, and contributes to shaping the life-style of individuals and groups. The school also plays an important part in moulding creative minds and more generally in shaping 'cultural needs'. The reasons are, first, that the standard of education contributes to an increase of people's interest in and aptitude for culture; and second, that the school plays an important role in shaping people's attitude to education itself and therefore, in the final analysis, to culture.

1. In this article on 'Education and Cultural Policy in the Developing Countries' (see pages 217–22), Oleg K. Dreier discerns three groups of global problems: (a) those pertaining to basic socio-economic phenomena (development, peace, etc.); (b) those concerning mankind's long-term resources, the protection of the environment, etc.; and (c) those relating to the links between man, society, and modern social processes (scientific and technological progress, education, etc.).

Interaction between educational policy and cultural policy

THE DEVELOPING COUNTRIES

While the preceding remarks are general in scope and apply to the developing countries as well as to industrialized countries, the problem of the interrelation between education and culture is particularly acute in the former group of countries, whose educational systems have in the past developed without regard for the cultural needs and values of the societies for which they were designed. So the effort that these countries had subsequently to make in order to achieve development—a concept that is meaningless except in terms of the goals that lie behind material and social changes—was to engender serious problems in the relation between education and culture.

Nissanka Wijeyeratne (p. 225) observes that although the developing countries are at different levels in the transition from traditional to modern societies, 'they are united in their desire to become modern industrial societies but at the same time to preserve the most valued elements of their traditional culture'. In his view, the real problem in the interrelation between education and culture lies in the relevance of education to what should be its twofold function: identifying and sustaining the historical, cultural and religious traditions of the country, and fulfilling its needs as a modern, changing entity. He goes on to observe that educational systems have paid no heed to cultural development, since education is in reality controlled by the dominant groups of society to suit their definition of social priorities. And if, he writes, curriculum reforms are in the hands of specialists not influenced by national philosophies, their innovations may not produce the desired changes. For those reasons, while acknowledging that the school is the best institution for developing co-ordinated educational and cultural programmes, he notes that it cannot be expected to be fully equipped to tackle the problem of interrelating educational and cultural policies, particularly since moral, ethical and religious education is best imparted outside the school.

With regard to Africa, Jean Pliya argues that the colonial school formed part of the colonial strategy of cultural domination, and was a device to alienate the child from his family, social environment and ancestral faith. Although political nationalism originally fed on reactions hostile to cultural alienation, the pull of the values of Western civilization is still strong today, despite a sustained demand that the cultural identity of African communities be safeguarded. In Pliya's view the chief contradiction stems from the attempt to integrate African cultural values into educational systems derived from the colonial era, and the use of 'ministerial instructions, decrees and decisions' for this purpose. However, regardless of the evident delays, he considers 'the more clearly these countries realize the need to assert their cultural identity in order to escape foreign domination, the more vigorously they can set about self-centred, self-managed development' (Jean Pliya, p. 230). This in no way means that their identity must be asserted to the detriment of their scientific links with the world at large or must imply the rejection of other cultures, since cultural identity can only be asserted in a universal perspective.

*Interaction between educational policy
and cultural policy*

Hence the crucial question is education's place and potential role in the problems of cultural identity, for while it draws its substance from the traditions and values of society, it also helps to create and advance new values and attitudes. Thus the International Panel on the Future Development of Education concluded that

the essential difficulty for the future of education would seem to be that of asserting cultural identity in the face of the emerging 'universal' culture being created by the expansion of the mass media, which were alleged to be imposing the life-style, behaviour and consumption patterns of the industrialized countries. This 'world culture', which offers certain advantages such as that of bringing peoples closer together, might also—by homogenizing the products of culture—lower their quality and thereby lead to certain phenomena of cultural alienation, for which education could be held largely responsible [3, p. 10].

In this context, one of the major concerns for many developing countries is that of the language of instruction, since language is the medium through which the essential content and values of a culture can be brought into the realm of the school. This question touches on our basic ways of thinking and of seeing things, and this explains the inadequacy of would-be reforms that merely bring a national language together with a set of values that have been imported ready-made or with very superficial adaptations, or that are designed at most to modernize language-teaching so as to make pupils bilingual, without tackling the problem of content and intellectual techniques in its entirety. This is why the policy of promoting national languages is fraught with difficulties that are not wholly educational in kind. Jean Pliya considers that one of the main obstacles to the assertion of cultural identity in Africa consists both in the weakness of the national languages, due to the very real difficulties encountered in using them in education or even in functional literacy teaching, and in the prestige which still attaches to the language of colonization.

The foreseeable development of interrelations between educational policies and cultural policies should be marked by the primacy given to culture in the broadest sense of the term; thus education should meet the principal priorities established by the African countries—to safeguard at all costs the cultural identity which will serve as a dynamic basis for a new type of school and to educate pupils for development. A new kind of education, seen as part of a 'combined network' (Jean Pliya, p. 233) organized by the local community, would make it possible for the links that should exist between the school and the population to be forged anew and for the problems of economic, social and cultural development facing those communities to be tackled in a practical manner. But this means, first, that this new type of school would have to be established on a larger scale than the national framework, in order to benefit from regional solidarity; and second, that care must be taken to ensure that the implications for the training of teachers, teaching methods and the African-

Interaction between educational policy and cultural policy

ization of educational content do not lead to the marginalization of the school with regard to the international educational system.

The same idea is developed by Andrzej Sicinski, who believes that the 'habitat school', well integrated into its social milieu and the community for which it plays the role of a cultural centre, is the only type of school that could decrease the present gap between education and social reality, and also make it possible to integrate educational and cultural policies in the developed countries. The prospects for interaction between educational and cultural policy in industrialized countries appear to be dominated by the role of the media, whose effectiveness, unless harnessed to cultural and educational policies designed to take advantage of them, might well become an obstacle to the goals they pursue. The foreseeable development of techniques would make it possible to use the media in that way and in conditions such that the major traditional handicaps of such methods (standardized, cumbersome and inflexible messages) can be overcome. Be that as it may, and regardless of institutional and financial problems, educational policies should, if they are to make use of the media while safeguarding their essential functions in education and pursuing the goal of raising the standards of public education, draw as completely as possible on cultural elements that correspond to cultural policies defined elsewhere. But while it is relatively easy for schools in countries with planned economies, where the authorities determine the principles and modes of action in the cultural domain, to take cultural policies into consideration, it seems to be less so in other countries. There, cultural policies, often fragmentary and partial in scope, are based on a combination of direct intervention and incentives on the part of the state, a great deal being left to be determined by the market, which tends to satisfy only people likely to make cultural demands for things they can pay for.

These observations apply also to the developing countries, where they are accentuated, first because of the extroverted manner in which educational and audio-visual institutions were established and developed, and second because of the profound cultural alienation from which society in these countries usually suffered. Therefore the main question, in the developing countries, will be how education can face up to objective and immediate constraints of an economic and social order, while at the same time striving both to transmit what is alive in the cultural heritage and to foster the emergence of innovative aspirations and methods in matters concerning development.

The following four studies, two of which deal with relations between education and culture in developing countries, analyse from different angles the relation between educational policies and cultural policies, and attempt to predict their future evolution in a time of potentially greater cultural development and better integration of school and society.

REFERENCES

1. GENERAL CONFERENCE OF UNESCO (21st Session, Belgrade, 1980). *Preliminary Report of the Director-General on the Medium-Term Plan for 1984–1989*, Part I. Paris, Unesco, 1980. (Unesco doc. 21C/4.)
2. FABRIZIO, Claude. Cultural Development in Europe. *Cultural Development: Some Regional Experiences*, pp. 371–463. Paris, Unesco, 1981.
3. SECOND MEETING OF THE INTERNATIONAL PANEL ON THE FUTURE DEVELOPMENT OF EDUCATION (Paris, 30 November to 4 December 1981). *Final Report*. Paris, Unesco, April 1982. (Unesco doc. ED-81/FUTURED/4.)

Educational objectives and cultural values

Andrzej Sicinski

One may distinguish three main objectives of education: first, education of the worker; second, education of the citizen; and third, education of the human being. Each of these is related to culture in a specific way, the term 'culture' being used in this context to mean a system of values, norms, ideas, patterns of conduct, and so on.

In the education of the worker, the person is seen as an object. In fact, what is needed for such an object is not so much education but rather instruction or training in some useful skills. In this perspective, insufficient education may often be evaluated less negatively than an 'excess' of education. In such a situation, contacts with culture should be rather restricted.

The education of the citizen implies adoption of a different perspective, within which the individual is a subject, but with rather restricted interests and capabilities. The main life-role of an individual is assumed to be that of a member of society or of a community. Education, as well as culture, then has an instrumental value: it must be assessed from the point of view of the interests of a given society, state or community. Cultural policy should select cultural values according to the interests of the state or community, as seen by those responsible for social policy. It should also stimulate people to an effective performance in their role of citizen.

Finally, in education of the human being the person is both a unique individual and a multi-functional, developing subject, playing different roles during his or her lifetime. In this case, education is a value in itself, and its results must be evaluated both from a collective and an individual perspective. Education of the human being should train people to make choices; cultural policy should also contribute. Its aim must be to provide opportunities for contacts with as many cultural values, ideas and products as possible, without any restriction of access to achievements of human thought and activity.

These three kinds of education are obviously theoretical types. Usually in reality we find a mixture of them, with one type being dominant.

Andrzej Sicinski

THE 'LEARNING SOCIETY'

This discussion of interrelations between education and culture, and between educational and cultural policies, is based on the assumption that a knowledge of their nature could be useful for improving the effectiveness of these policies. This objective can be considered in the broader perspective of a concept sometimes referred to as the 'learning society'.[1] The main idea of this concept is obvious: the aims of education are so complex and its process so complicated in the contemporary world that no particular educational institution is able to cope effectively with them; the only solution is to restructure society to enable it to engage all its segments and institutions in the process of education.

It is quite evident that such restructuring would not be an easy task. Nevertheless, in spite of all the possible difficulties to develop a learning society, it may be useful to take it into account, at least as one possible approach, in discussions concerning contemporary educational needs, means, and policies. The concept of a learning society implies, among other things, that strong interrelations exist between different domains of social life. Hence all policies and plans for action should take into consideration those interrelations and try to make use of them. This is the case for educational and cultural policies, as well as for their connections with economic policy or social policy, for example. Within this perspective we shall focus our attention on the role of education in cultural development, then on culture as an element of the educational process, and finally, on some educational problems in cultural activities.

EDUCATION AS A BASIS FOR CULTURAL DEVELOPMENT

Education is an important factor in economic development, and the level of the economy plays a major role as far as opportunities for cultural development are concerned. However, the immense importance of education from the cultural point of view, both in the family and at school, lies in its role in the socialization process and in shaping the personality, system of values and attitudes of the individual. Education determines the possibilities of communicating with other people and the understanding of the symbols of a culture. It also shapes the so-called 'higher needs' of the human being, which unlike primary needs, do not develop fully in a spontaneous way. Finally, education contributes to shaping the life-style of individuals and groups.

---

1. In December 1979, for example, the 'Poland 2000' Committee of the Polish Academy of Sciences organized a conference entitled 'The Learning Society: Reality and Prospects'.

These features of education are decisive for people's interest in cultural values and for their ability to participate in culture. One of the effects of its functioning in contemporary societies is the rapid increase of what could be called a 'cultural public' (book readers, cinema goers, etc.) and the attraction to cultural values of new segments of the population. The school plays a particularly important role in this respect. School education is the main factor in shaping cultural needs, since the family is usually unable to produce such cultural 'newcomers'.

Two aspects of school education are particularly important in this connection. First, general education at every level of schooling contributes to increased interest and aptitude for culture. Second, the school plays an important role in shaping people's attitudes to education itself. In discussing the three types of objectives of education, we stressed a distinction between education having an 'instrumental' value or a value in itself.

Nowadays, many societies are facing a tremendous increase of candidates at each level of schooling. Decision-makers are in many cases opposed to a rapid increase in enrolments, arguing that the national economy does not need so many people with university (or with secondary) education. On the other hand, some people, particularly those representing an interest in cultural development, criticize this approach, recalling that similar arguments were formulated in Europe a century or so ago against peasants' aspirations to primary education and, later, against workers' aspirations to secondary education. History has shown in any case that popular movements or trends towards an increase in the level of education cannot be reversed by arbitrary decisions. We believe that it is necessary that both educational and cultural policies prescribe measures to dissociate education and jobs in people's thinking and attitudes, so that education will be viewed as a cultural value, a value in itself.

CULTURE
AND THE EDUCATIONAL PROCESS

Most of the contents and means in cultural activity play an important role in education. In fact, one may say that education is based on them: thus classes dealing with literature, history, philosophy or aesthetic problems, for example, present in a direct way certain elements of culture. In this respect, two factors seem to be of particular importance in many societies: the role of the mass media and the idea of a 'habitat school'.

In many countries the main problem lies in the lack of relation between the school and the mass media. Primary and secondary schools often act as if they were the only source of information for their pupils. They neither try to make use of knowledge conveyed by the mass media, nor do they include in their curricula any interpretation of what comes through the mass media. Educators do not seem to understand that in the modern world, with its powerful mass media, computers, calculators, etc., school programmes should stress not so much the acquisition of facts, but the ability to search effectively for needed information and to make appropriate use of it.

At the same time, as a rule, the mass media do not bother too much about educational effects. Depending on the system of ownership, they accept either economic or political criteria of effectiveness, not educational or cultural values. It is clear, however, that such mutual ignorance decreases the potential of the mass media and of the school as a means of education and is in direct opposition to the idea of a 'learning society'.

One of the most important institutions of a learning society could be a 'habitat school', for example a primary or secondary school well integrated with its social milieu and its neighbourhood, serving as a cultural centre for the community. Only such a school could decrease, or overcome completely, the present gap between education on the one hand and social reality on the other. This type of school would also make possible the integration of educational and cultural policies at the local level.

EDUCATIONAL PROBLEMS
IN CULTURAL ACTIVITY

According to one view, the mass media (or, strictly speaking, educational radio and television), not the school, should be the main source of information. According to this view, the role of the school should be to systematize acquired knowledge and to equip pupils with a methodology for ordering that knowledge rather than merely to transmit substantive knowledge alone.

We think that this opinion overemphasizes the potential of the mass media and underestimates the functions of the school. At the same time, however, we believe that the present use of the mass media for educational purposes at all levels is just beginning. The present limited use of the mass media in education is not due to a lack of ideas or will on the part of mass media professionals, but rather to a reluctance on the part of the schools. The mass media constitute a 'cultural institution' which may, and should, participate purposefully in the process of education.

Cultural clubs and centres (at factories or in residential areas) are particularly important for the education of adults, for example in the teaching of languages and humanities and for popularizing science. Like the school, they may also help systematize the flood of information coming from the mass media. They have, clearly, some important advantages over the mass media: first, they have a direct, personal contact with people, which makes it easier to influence effectively interests and attitudes; second, they provide opportunities for participants not only to 'consume' cultural values in a passive way, but also to be active in the field of culture. Such activity clearly plays an immense role in the process of education. Special schools for developing artistic abilities and skills, such as schools for the visual arts, theatre or music, have an important role to play.

THE WORLD CONTEXT

In most cases educational and cultural policies have had exclusively national scope and aims. They differ in that respect from economic policy, which more and more often goes beyond national boundaries. The situation must change eventually, as economic and political co-operation will be impossible without understanding and co-operation in the fields of culture and education.

A need for international policies concerning education and culture is important for international co-operation, but no less so for national policies. One of the most discussed and even fashionable problems of at least the last two decades is that of 'identity'. Particularly in wealthy West European and North American countries, questions of personal identity are of great importance. In other regions, particularly Africa and Asia, problems of cultural identity of some sections of the population have arisen.

Problems with identity, that is difficulties in seeing one's self or a population group as a defined system and a part of a larger super-system, occur as a result of rapid changes in the contemporary world, particularly changes in social and economic structures, as well as in people's social and geographical mobility. A 'lost' identity is re-established when individuals or groups are able to find a new 'locus', a new frame of reference for their values, feeling, and sense of solidarity. It is clear that in spite of all discussion concerning the world tendency towards a 'global village', a new 'locus' could be a nation, a state or a religious community, but not humanity or the human species.

Solidarity with contemporaries, with past and with future generations, although not common, is dramatically needed. In fact it is a main condition for the successful development of the contemporary world. To create such solidarity, some general changes in culture and in education and new approaches to educational and cultural policies are required. The following comments suggest some possible practical actions to bring about such changes.

A set of systematic educational actions could increase people's knowledge of other cultures, their histories and their particular values; it could highlight the similarities and common interests, in spite of all differences, between people living in different countries and cultures and make clear an increasing interdependence between them. This would help to increase (or to create) people's awareness of humanity and people's feelings of solidarity on a global scale. Such actions could possibly be based on the best anthropological and sociological studies,[1] not only on superficial impressions.

There is a need for a series of television and radio programmes spreading such knowledge and attitudes about the interdependence of cultures among people of different levels of education. These programmes should be prepared and periodically renewed by an international body composed of sociologists, anthropologists, psychologists, educators, artists and journalists.

Ideas concerning the diversity of cultures and the unity of humanity should be introduced into textbooks at all levels of education.

Special, regular, international programmes for teachers along similar lines could also play an important role.

A special 'translation policy' should promote the best literary works (novels, short stories, poems, essays, plays, etc.) from less well-known languages.

Finally, some touristic and cultural programmes could be proposed and supported by transnational, international and national, educational and cultural organizations.

To sum up this discussion, one can stress a few main points. An integration of educational and cultural policies is much needed in the fast-changing contemporary world, in which we see the daily emergence of new challenges for the individual, for entire societies, and for humanity. Successful integration of these policies and their integration with economic and social policies would be possible in a 'learning society'. Now and in the near future, stress should be laid on 'education of the human being' and on the 'world context' of education. Necessary changes and innovations must be introduced in educational policies at different levels: local, national, international and transnational.

---

1. There is a need for systematic studies on the probable 'functionality' of the basic values of different cultures in the world of tomorrow.

Education and cultural policy in the developing countries

Oleg K. Dreier

The dynamics of modern social progress have considerably influenced the formation of the socio-cultural policy of the developing countries. The modernization of contemporary culture is a long-term problem of historic significance. However, modernization does not exclude the preservation of cultural traditions and originality. Moreover, the assertion of national culture is a major element in the developing countries' struggle for independence.

Scientific and technical progress has contributed to the emergence of a new concept of cultural progress connected with a combination of endogenous and integrated development. It should be noted that the most widespread form of the modernization of culture in the developing countries is the Westernization of the traditional mode of life (for example, striving for greater incomes, unrestricted consumption, an urban way of life), which leads to a state of profound crisis—a crisis of traditional culture under the impact of haphazard modernization, and a crisis of modern culture introduced and rapidly disseminated in an unprepared cultural-historical medium. For if a society as a system is unable to freely and easily 'digest' a too great portion of modern culture (mode of life), then culture as a system is also unable organically to infiltrate society: some elements become hypertrophically developed and others are minimized.

FROM THE SCIENTIFIC AND TECHNOLOGICAL REVOLUTION TO THE EPOCH OF GLOBAL PROBLEMS

By the middle of the twentieth century, the achievements of science and technology, coupled with serious socio-economic changes particularly in the developing countries, gave rise to the thesis that the present should be regarded as the epoch of the scientific and technological revolution (STR). Thus, attention was drawn to the revolutionary character of the changes occurring in science and technology and in social processes.

In the late 1960s and early 1970s the emergence of the 'global problems' concept contributed to a partial removal of some of the STR problems from the agenda. In other words, problems formerly related to the STR began to be examined in a broader context, with the dominating significance now being ascribed to their global status. Global problems are those bearing on the interests of all mankind, requiring constructive co-operation between all countries for their solution.

Global problems can be structured. The first group includes those connected with the realization of the basic socio-economic processes of our time (the problem of war and peace, the problem of economic development, etc.). The second group of global problems includes those establishing the connections of man and society with the social processes of modern time (the realization of the achievements of scientific and technical progress, the problem of education, etc.).

Naturally, these groups of global problems are dialectically interconnected with subproblems in each group (for example, the environment cannot be protected without an efficient system for the rational use of nature). On the other hand, these groups of global problems are closely interconnected. For instance, an effective solution to the educational problem is a function of a whole number of global problems, including those of war and peace, scientific and technical progress, economic development, and so on.

The problem of education is high in the hierarchy of the global problems of our epoch, and has often been underestimated. What then is the link between the global problems of today and the problem of education? First, education, with its essential economic function, has a direct impact on production. Moreover, by improvement education can become more efficient. The development of education exerts a considerable influence on all aspects of the activity and existence of modern social structures.

Second, the development of education is directly connected with the entire system of modern scientific knowledge. The higher the scientific potential, the higher the level of education. On the one hand, modern scientific knowledge, by broadening our ideas about the objective picture of the world, enlarges the potential of education; on the other hand, the rising quality of education contributes to raising the level of scientific knowledge.

Third, education possesses important social functions in its contribution to the advancement of the self-consciousness of the individual and his adequate evaluation of socio-economic and politico-ideological processes.

THE 'CULTURAL GAP'

The problem of education touches not only on the practical questions of economic development, but also on problems of a philosophical character. One of these problems is that of removing contradictions between 'two cultures'. This refers to the 'cultural gap' that was noted in the mid-1950s between natural scientific and humanitarian cultures. Participants in the discussion on the subject voiced apprehensions that the preservation of the modern trends of scientific development could lead to greater antagonism between natural-technical and socio-economic knowledge and would be related to the loss of interconnections between different spheres of science.

The significance of these views have persisted into the 1980s: the gap between natural scientific and humanitarian cultures is still discussed. However, new aspects have emerged and at present a growing tendency towards their synthesis can be seen.

Scientific knowledge is now faced with problems requiring greater integration, while preserving differentiation, in the structure of interconnections between natural, technical and social sciences. It should be emphasized that the trend towards the integration of knowledge is not an element of only the present stage of scientific development. Marxist works of the nineteenth century and the attempts of representatives of logical positivism in the first half of the twentieth century expressed the desire to achieve 'unified science'. But not until about 1980, in the process of the emergence and development of global problems, did these trends begin to emerge, particularly under the impact of the present ecological situation.

Education not only reflects new trends in the structure of modern scientific knowledge—for any fruitful field in science should find an adequate expression in a corresponding course of studies—but also galvanizes these new trends. It is widely believed that the improvement and advancement of education is a major element in preventing and eliminating the gap between cultures, and in removing discrepancies between individual fields of modern scientific knowledge or its allied branches.

FROM CRISIS TO REVOLUTION IN EDUCATION

There is evidently a tangible connection between the crisis of education and the structural changes in modern scientific knowledge. On the one hand, there is the growing trend to differentiation in science: new scientific disciplines come into being faster than they can be assimilated in the structure of education. On the other hand, the possibilities of integrating science are expanding, demanding intensified links between all fields of modern scientific knowledge and all spheres of education. In other words, the modern structure of education is unable to cope with assimilating scientific achievements and synthetic concepts.

Thus, to date, education both lags behind science and lacks efficient levers to integrate knowledge. The content of the educational process does not correspond to the status of knowledge. This process does not presuppose the study of individual subjects, although this will remain its basic element, but that of individual problems which concentrate a whole range of subjects around them. We have in mind the orientation of education to studying subjects in a generalized context. These trends have certain specific features in the developing countries.

EDUCATIONAL CHANGE IN THE DEVELOPING COUNTRIES

School in the developing countries is going through noticeable changes. Most important, in our view, are the departure from an early differentiation, immediately after the primary school, and attempts to create uniform curricula and a uniform type of educational establishment—up to the sixth, eighth and tenth year of education in both town and country (for example, in Sri Lanka, India, Pakistan, Algeria or Mali). Serious changes are made in the curricula—courses of languages, history, culture and art of the country concerned, and the fundamentals of political knowledge, are introduced. New textbooks have been written in many countries of Asia and Africa. In African states, the aim of elementary, 'basic' education is clearly formulated: it should reflect the culture, traditions, knowledge and customs of society as a whole, and be carried out with the active participation of the entire population.

The future of the systems of national education in Asian and African countries undoubtedly depends on the training and retraining of teachers, with due account of the achievements of the scientific and technological revolution, all the more so since the functions of teachers in Afro-Asian countries are not confined to the educational process as such; they are also entrusted with a responsible task of conducting cultural and educational work among the adult population.

SOME TRENDS FOR THE FUTURE

The availability of higher education in the developing countries began to increase only after independence. Several universities that had been opened during the colonial period mainly served the needs of the colonial administration. The annual growth rate of higher education in Asian and African countries is much greater than that of elementary and secondary education.

This rapid growth has not always been accompanied by the creation of improved material conditions, which has given rise to unemployment among people with a higher education. The problem is connected with both the general economic situation of these countries and lack of adequate planning. As a result, many countries have to restrict enrolment in institutions of higher learning.

We consider it expedient to study the proposal advanced by the noted

African scholar, Joseph Ki-Zerbo, on creating in West Africa 'common markets' of specialists for moving personnel from one country to another. An analysis of the distribution of students by departments shows that the share of students at the engineering, agricultural and natural science departments is lower than that at the humanities faculties, which is true of a majority of countries in Asia and Africa (except the Islamic Republic of Iran, Zambia, Kenya and Sierra Leone), and constitutes less than a third of the total number of students.

Recently independent countries now face the acute problem of regional integration, both in the training of middle-level personnel and in the field of science, industry and infrastructure. This involves great political and economic difficulties. However, one thing is certain: many countries need a pooling of effort in order to carry out their principal economic tasks.

A major problem facing the developing countries in the field of school education for the coming decade is to create such a combination of school subjects that will give the necessary practical training to those who will not continue this education. The experience of the socialist countries in combining school studies with labour is attracting more interest.

The campaign for eradicating illiteracy among women is to proceed more rapidly. It should be noted that women themselves are more energetically demanding the development of female education and want to take a worthy place in the social life of their respective countries.

The emergence of new forms of teaching complementing school studies will be a major event for many developing countries. These will include rural centres for adolescents, short-term courses of occupational training, and special educational programmes regularly broadcast on radio and television. More subjects meant to prepare people for practical activity will be incorporated into the curricula, networks of technical education centres will be expanded, and more specialists will be trained to tackle important global issues, such as the ecological problem.

EDUCATION AND SOCIAL PROGRESS

The improvement of the system and structure of education is one of the elements in the moulding of a harmoniously-developed personality, a major component of social progress. Social development has an impact on achieving educational plans in different socio-economic systems.

Contradictions in the systems of education in advanced capitalist countries have been caused by economic, political, ideological, ecological and other difficulties experienced by Western civilization. Many of these contradictions and difficulties are also characteristic of Afro-Asian and Latin American countries, especially those inheriting Western development principles and culture.

The epoch of global problems also engenders numerous difficulties in the educational system in the USSR and in the socialist community countries. Many of their problems are of an objective character, determined by the rapid development of science and the differentiation and integration of modern scientific knowledge. The structure and system of education should be adapted to new trends connected with scientific and technical progress. The point is to improve not only the system of education as such, but to change social conditions. Marxists constantly emphasize that an adequate application of man's inner forces is only possible in corresponding social conditions which contribute to a manifestation of man's individuality.

The close connection between economic development and the educational level of the population, on the one hand, and an enormous discrepancy between the financial and technico-organizational possibilities of the developing countries and their requirements in the field of education, on the other, make the problem of cultural transformation insoluble unless there are profound socio-economic changes.

The moves towards democracy in the developing countries are many and varied, determined by a variety of adopted reforms and methods of implementation. The search for and choice of the way of national renaissance take place in a most difficult struggle against the forces of external and internal reaction.

A study of the relation of cultural policy to education shows that despite considerable difficulties and contradictions, the developing countries, on the eve of the twenty-first century, are on the right road to solving the problem of education.

Education and cultural identity

Nissanka Wijeyeratne

The last two decades have seen hitherto unimagined achievements by mankind, which are rapidly changing both the interrelations between cultures and individuals' views of their own cultures. It is from such a state of cultural flux that one has to look forward and plan a cultural policy for the next two decades.

Culture represents the total of human activity and cannot be considered in isolation. It is closely and totally linked with the modes of production, social organization and infrastructure, with the values and norms of a given society of which it forms an inalienable component.

The meaning attributed to culture today is changing. The élitist culture of a few decades ago has given place to a mass culture with full participation of the community. Phenomena such as the mass media, communication systems and fast modes of travel have helped to bring about mass culture. Some see it as a homogenized influence which has submerged man's identity; others see it as a trend towards a universal culture which will be a panacea for all ills. Whether this trend has been to the improvement of man's condition or not is a controversial issue, but for the cultural policy-maker it is important to recognize that the trend towards a mass culture exists and must be taken into account in planning for the future.

The emergence of free and independent nations during the last few decades has resulted in a renewed growth of the indigenous cultures of hitherto colonized and dominated peoples. Colonialism brought in the culture of the colonialist within which indigenous cultures were kept submerged. With the welcome re-emergence of diverse cultures, there is a simultaneous emphasis on the search for a unity within the cultural diversity which can reflect the ethos of the whole community. But one must remember that there are some prerequisites to be taken into account in renewed cultural growth. No culture can flower to its full in an environment of illiteracy and abject poverty and the resulting moral and spiritual degradation.

Nissanka Wijeyeratne

A LOOK AT EDUCATIONAL DEVELOPMENT

Since the level of general education in the more economically advanced countries has for a long time been so high that any further advance will not have immediate or greater effect, we shall confine our attention to the developing countries, which have achieved substantial progress in education during the last two decades. Although enrolment in secondary education has expanded faster than enrolment in primary education, emphasis has been on democratization in the distribution of education, especially at lower levels. Educational development plans have usually given some importance to social equity, to improving the relevance of education to national needs, and to other qualitative objectives such as the development of science teaching. Serious attempts have also been made to improve educational systems to make them more relevant to national life, culture and to the needs of regional populations within a country.

There have also been insurmountable problems in educational development. About a third of the children of primary-school age are not enrolled in school, and about a third of the adult population is illiterate. The drop-out rate is high and the quality of learning, as determined by student attainment, is low. There is no harmonious relation between education and work; the quantitative expansion of education has often sacrificed quality; and there is a serious lack of adequate finance. All of these factors strongly influence the interrelations between cultural and educational policies.

FUTURE NEEDS

Unesco's twenty-first General Conference reaffirmed that culture forms the basis of the values through which each individual recognizes his identity, as does the human community. The conference emphasized that realization by a society of its cultural identity as an essential factor in development and at the same time as the basis of relations, dialogue and fruitful exchanges between cultures, may contribute to international understanding and peace. Therefore future national cultural policies will have to foster the harmonious development of all cultures in mutual respect and appreciation of their own specific values. This development must be based both on aid to artistic creation and active participation by all who so wish in the enrichment of cultural life, and on the preservation of the cultural heritage. Cultural policies will also have to promote the formulation and application of development strategies in which culture is both a factor in development and one of its results.

The general policy for education in the future will be to eradicate illiteracy, to eliminate all forms of inequality and discrimination, and to improve the quality and relevance of education to meet the requirements of multi-dimensional, endogenous development.

Education and cultural identity

The concept of 'relevance' of education is its function in identifying and sustaining the historical, cultural, and religious traditions of a country and fulfilling its needs as a modern, changing entity.

TOWARDS EDUCATIONAL AND CULTURAL UNITY

The need for fresh thinking in educational planning is widely accepted. The development of culture, including character development, has been an inbuilt aim of educational systems for so long that it is almost taken for granted as a main concern of every community. In fact, the content of education is identical with culture and its utilitarian, moral and aesthetic elements. Since education plays a major role in the socialization process—the transmission of culture whereby people learn the rules and practices of social groups—newly-independent nations and developing countries are very conscious of the pitfalls of blindly adopting alien systems of education. Developing countries are united in their desire to become modern industrial societies but at the same time to preserve the most valued elements of their traditional culture.

Interrelation of education and cultural policies is necessary for all development plans concerned with the quality of life. Each country will have to evolve a technology suitable for its own needs, adapted to its particular labour and capital market. This is important, since in practice all cultural and educational policies are to a great extent shaped by an overall economic plan. An organized educational system is often not geared to achieve these aims and objectives. In reality, education is controlled by the dominant groups of society and tends to meet their definitions of social priorities.

There is a growing belief that moral, ethical or religious education is better imparted outside the school, and that generally speaking the school cannot assume responsibility for every aspect of a child's development. Consequently we cannot expect schools to be fully equipped to tackle the problem of harmonizing cultural and educational policies. For example, a brief survey of education for moral values in New Delhi has indicated that existing school curricula do not specify the position of moral education in study schemes, nor was a conceptual framework provided for developing values in pupils. Nevertheless, most of the schools in the survey considered the moral development of pupils to be one of their responsibilities and a large number preferred to introduce moral education as a separate subject.

Even as regards cultural heritage there are disagreements. Some people argue that the wish to identify oneself with one's cultural heritage is not universal; some sustain a passive curiosity about their own cultural heritage and feel that to insist that everyone identify with his cultural heritage is authoritarian. Thus one must look at the role of non-formal education in considering the prospects for interrelations between cultural and educational policies.

The school nevertheless remains the best-equipped institution to carry out planned education and cultural programmes. Experience has shown that students are overburdened with school work even at home and that they have hardly any time left for sports, music, dancing and other artistic pursuits. Aesthetic education, instead of becoming a part of the school curriculum, is becoming a field of specialization. Very little use is made of the mass media, especially television, in education. Universities, the 'seats of excellence', are becoming teaching institutions instead of places of educational and cultural innovation and research.

CULTURE AND THE MASS MEDIA

Modern communication systems and the mass media are undoubtedly the most powerful influences shaping mass culture today. The mass media, especially television, have had an impact on Western culture for more than two decades. Though there have been many benefits, the ill effects have also led to serious concern, as expressed by one author: 'This sort of common culture does not unite people; it only depersonalizes them—turns them into so much material for receiving impressions. A herd or mass is a very different thing from a community. It dilutes and does not enhance personal relations. It is the malignant social growth which threatens personal values in the world today' [1, p. 20]. Although this may seem an extreme view, it can serve as a worthwhile warning to newly-emergent nations where the mass media are rapidly expanding.

One must also take into account the positive aspects of utilizing the new media in educational and cultural activity.

It is also evident that the mass communication media are particularly useful tools for the development of education, especially for the benefit of the most disadvantaged strata of the population, and far-reaching instruments for the spread of science. In so far as culture is concerned, they may, depending upon the use made of them, either contribute to the strengthening of cultural identity or, on the contrary, accentuate the phenomenon of deculturation, not to say cultural domination [2, p. 54].

Many Third World countries are now adapting the mass media as a powerful tool for both education and entertainment. However, much vigilance is needed in order that these same tools do not become another form of the cultural domination of the less-developed by the more-developed societies. Future cultural policies will have to set down guidelines for the beneficial utilization of the mass media for the cultural development of young nations.

The need for a conscious attempt to overcome the ill effects of the domination of news agencies in information dissemination and shaping public opinion has been strongly emphasized and action on this has begun. The uneven division of economic power has led to an uneven distribution of 'media power' in favour of the industrialized countries, which hold a monopoly on the international media network and control international opinion. The less economically-developed nations' voices have often not even been heard. A growing awareness of this situation, especially during the last decade, has led to a call for a new international information order. Unesco has already started action in this field. The Non-aligned Movement decided to establish an information centre at Colombo at its Conference of Foreign Ministers in New Delhi in February 1981. The role of a new international information order in shaping the culture of both developing and developed countries must also be seriously considered.

The above comments point to some directions in which a cultural policy should move. Culture must be considered as a component of development as a whole. Planning in the cultural domain should marry quality and democracy, while avoiding the snare of a culture which is either 'state oriented' or simply esoteric and removed from real life. The development of a mass culture which truly reflects the aspirations of all peoples should result in a new humanism enveloping the unity of all cultures, while fostering the identity of each.

At a national level, recording all valuable cultural elements can put each citizen more closely or more genuinely in touch with the culture and heritage of his country. There is a need for concerted, conscious action on an international basis if the new tools of communication and mass media are to be used to foster such development.

Above all it is necessary at all times to remind ourselves that those entrusted with guiding a cultural efflorescence should enjoy a considerable measure of non-interference. André Malraux said, eloquently, that 'speaking of aesthetics exclusively we have only one way of ensuring freedom, namely to choose the right men for particular tasks and, once appointed, to leave them in peace' [3].

REFERENCES

1. JEFFREYS, M. V. C. *Personal Values in the Modern World*. Harmondsworth, Penguin, 1962.
2. M'BOW, Amadou-Mahtar. *Unesco and the Solidarity of Nations: The Spirit of Nairobi*. Paris, Unesco, 1977.
3. *Journal officiel de la République française*, Year 1965–66, No. 78 A.N., 15 October 1965. (Debates of the Assemblée Nationale, First Sitting, Thursday 14 October 1965.)

The evolution of the notion of education and of its functions in African society

Jean Pliya

Faced with the colonial strategy of cultural domination, which was aimed at upsetting and shattering the social coherence of traditional Africa and destroying the bases of social integration such as history and the mother tongue, the subjugated peoples, in particular their tribal chiefs, were at first overtly hostile. Their hostility was directed at the white man's school, which they considered a factor leading to alienation, a subtle way of turning the child away not only from agricultural work but also from his family and sociological environment and from his ancestral or Islamic religion. The conflict was particularly bitter in countries where resistance to colonization was strongest. However, in the context of a market economy where 'social work is transformed into "economic" work' [1, p. 12]; where the school gives rise to social classes which often have conflicting interests; the sons of slaves or of tenant farmers, who had filled the places in the school system left vacant by the sons of chiefs or of other distinguished people, rapidly became the zealous assistants of the colonial administration and were seen as the privileged class in the new society, as educated people close to the white man and separate from the rest of the population, who had no power and no recognized culture.

This conflict between traditional education and colonial school-based education has subsided, and most people are now aware that the school is closely related to occupational, social, economic and even political success. This explains the increased demand for relevant and efficient education. However, the ensuing increase in cost to these countries at a time of rapid demographic growth and hard-won economic development, aggravated by the failure of the 'development decades', has had an effect on the quality and relevance of education, all the more so as in Africa today education must fulfil several requirements for the future: it must give pupils knowledge and skills, and it must teach them how to take action and how to live. This means that existing systems must be radically reviewed, aims must be reappraised, and new educational plans must be examined to ensure that they serve the case of genuine development.

Traditional African education is essentially a community function fulfilled by and within the community, be it the family, the clan or the

*The evolution of the notion of education and
of its functions in African society*

tribe. It formerly prepared the child to embark smoothly upon his moral, occupational, economic and political life, without agitation or risk of failure. But with colonization came the closed school, which was seen as the best way of obtaining a socio-vocational education; the community's role was diminished as the child was cut off from it and handed over to professional educators. This kind of school generated conflicts due to the need for adaptation, introduced the notion of failure through competition and selection, thus creating antagonistic social classes, and impaired both the unifying nature of education and the comprehensive nature of the educational environment. Above all, by dividing, separating and alienating, it encouraged the cultural extroversion of African children.

The prestige retained by the colonizing country's language plus the difficulty of mastering national languages, which have not been sufficiently studied, and of using them in teaching or even in basic functional literacy work, are factors hindering the assertion of cultural identity, which in the past was negated, destroyed, indeed obliterated by the formal ban on speaking African languages at school. Today it is far from easy to smooth out this distortion.

Although cultural and scientific co-operation at an international level is still a necessity that African countries appreciate and pursue, it seems to synthesize all the aspects of this subtle dependence. Foreign teachers, administrators and other experts or research workers inevitably transmit an alien model of civilization through their mentalities, the content of their teaching and the technical equipment which countries sending aid provide to back up their technicians.

Colonialism has had an enduring effect on the African cultural and educational environment. Feelings of failure and insecurity, reinforced by the fact that selection is based on school marks and examinations, are widespread and are helping to swell the ranks of the unemployed and socially maladjusted. The new social divisions are of two kinds—first, divisions between those who can read and write and those who are illiterate, shut out of society and little affected by acculturation; and second, divisions within the category of those who have attended school, between lower- and middle-level employees or poorly-paid producers of goods and university-educated managerial staff, who are considered highly cultured and exceptionally gifted.

Although regulations precluding the study of African languages, history and culture were annulled after 1958, when independence was achieved in various countries after nationalist struggles, the values of Western civilization still have great attraction. Prejudices against manual and productive work remain firmly entrenched.

To a large extent, political sovereignty led to control of educational policy, for political nationalism had initially relied for support on a reaction against cultural alienation and against the negation of the black man's dignity, through Negritude and authenticity movements. Once political power had been won it became possible to reject the cultural bases of colonialism and to initiate reforms designed to 'Africanize' education.

In countries where the fundamental reforms were based on socialist ideologies, such as the United Republic of Tanzania, Guinea, Congo and Benin, changes were intentionally revolutionary, and teaching methods and requirements for obtaining certificates were altered to ensure that both child and worker were more aware of the nature of their own problems and how to solve them.

But these changes, brought about as they were by ministerial instructions, decrees and decisions, have done little towards achieving the desired development. Still, the more clearly States realize the need to assert their cultural identity in order to escape foreign domination, the more vigorously they can set about self-centred, self-managed development. Their realization of this need took place in a period full of vicissitudes—the neo-colonial period which began in the 1960s. After twenty years of exercising this new sovereignty, of the Africanization of educational systems and of more or less radical reforms, it would appear that neither the influence of dominant foreign socio-cultural systems, nor the consequences of economic domination, have yet been counteracted.

EVOLUTION OF MENTALITIES

The mentality of African schoolchildren is marked by these inconsistencies in their education, as well as by their parents' attitudes and society's new values.

African schoolchildren look for the easy way out and are unwilling to deny themselves anything in a society characterized by bitter rivalry. They want a lot of money, as fast as possible. Children today do not readily accept school or family discipline, without which they cannot learn how to use their freedom or acquire a balanced personality. They claim many rights, while recognizing few duties. Being confined within a selective school system in which ruthless competition holds sway, they cram, refuse to help each other, and resort to even the most selfish means to achieve success.

Parents, anxious for their children to succeed in the competitive life of school and university, are prepared to make heavy financial commitments, regarding the education of the younger generation as an investment. If there is no road to success in their own country, parents who can afford it send their children to other African countries or to Europe, a step they are all the more likely to take because they reject national educational reforms which, in the final analysis, only lead to badly-remunerated careers or training on the cheap for jobs that are not competitive on an international level. Wealthy parents—merchants or civil servants—who give their children such advantages are well aware that they are building up tomorrow's ruling class, for the most eagerly sought-after diplomas are always the gateway to promotion. Many parents are also nostalgic about a 'good' education along European lines.

Middle-class and poor families also make great sacrifices to attain the same objectives. They invest a large proportion of their income in their children's schooling, for education is hardly ever really free in any African country. Admittedly, countries with substantial resources, yet a low percentage of children attending school, have a policy of promoting education on a non-paying basis by providing grants for all pupils and students. None the less, parents always pay something—quite a lot in cases where the state refuses to meet the heavy costs of education, for which it does not possess sufficient resources. The state may officially say that education is free, but the facts are always harsher, and it is money that determines which schoolchildren will have the best chance to get a good education, thereby reinforcing the arbitrary nature of neo-Malthusian selection.

As even well-educated parents do very little to help their children assimilate what they are taught at school, it is usual to engage a tutor or someone to supervise their studies—an experienced teacher, a student or a pupil, depending on the parents' financial means—which obviously increases educational expenses.

EDUCATION AND CULTURAL IDENTITY

African cultural values are not being integrated into educational systems derived from the colonial era as rapidly as they should be, and many difficulties are being encountered. In some countries emphasis is placed on national languages, as in Nigeria, Guinea and the United Republic of Tanzania; in others the traditional pharmacopoeia and medicine, oral literature (tales, proverbs legends), history and African literature are successfully integrated into the syllabuses. But care should be taken to ensure that a false Africanization does not in fact contribute towards the further marginalization of African schools and turn African research workers into 'learned providers of information, people who are particularly good at piling up knowledge which has its centre ... elsewhere' [2, p. 31]. Emphasis should not be placed on the assertion of the cultural identity of African countries in such a way that they close their doors to scientific knowledge. In any case the trend towards Africanization will certainly increase in the next two decades, for Africans, whether educated or not, are taking a growing interest in African music, and much is being done towards the local publication of schoolbooks, works of African literature, scientific journals and so on.

EDUCATION AND DEVELOPMENT

Development is one of the priorities for education in the years ahead, if not the main one. In what circumstances will the school find a long-term solution to development problems, and what will be the implications of such a solution for the status of education as such?

First, schools will have to be encouraged to provide more information about the nature and requirements of endogenous development (i.e. human, geographical and political factors); new teachers must be educated accordingly; and those already employed must be retrained so that they can preserve and revitalize their country's cultural identity and meet the needs of the population. Such teachers will become efficient educators for development. The content of education will then have to be adapted to these aims, and a judicious balance will have to be struck between such adaptation and the link that must be established with the international educational system. In this way a school education will give all pupils a better understanding of the requirements of endogenous development.

However, the isolated endeavours of a few countries will probably be of no avail unless the regional, continental and intercontinental solidarity of developing countries is strengthened. Just as the introduction of productive work in educational systems, which all African States have decided upon, has to a large extent remained a dead letter, despite the encouragement given by Unesco, the Network of Educational Innovation for Development in Africa (NEIDA) and the African Bureau of Educational Studies (BASE—Bureau Africain des Sciences de l'Éducation), so education for development will not succeed unless a concerted, overall strategy, co-ordinated with the educational systems of the developed countries, is progressively and resolutely implemented within the framework of realistic solidarity contracts in which each partner's cultural identity is recognized; for 'since domination implies the negation of the dominated person's identity and of his culture as the foundation of his identity, solidarity is possible only between two poles which are not identical but identified' [1, p. 15].

An education of the kind we have indicated should therefore be polyvalent and specialized, so that it can transform a complex environment; it must be shorn of all useless knowledge; it must aim at responsible action and development on the part of the individual and the community; it must be focused on the socio-cultural environment, to meet both personal and national needs based on the educated individual's participation in community efforts for development; it must accept that productive work, whether rural or industrial, plays its part in the school and that pupils in their turn play a part in the real world of work and culture.

NEW RELATIONS BETWEEN THE SCHOOL AND THE COMMUNITY

In future, the purpose of the school will not be to provide instruction or even an education which develops the minds of young people within a closed system and then turns them out into an environment that is not their own and in which they behave and react as foreigners. This is why it is preferable for education to be dispensed within a combined network, to promote endogenous development as organized by the various sectors of the local community—the labour force, those engaged in various kinds of development work, political authorities, teachers, pupils, and students—whose business it will be to find practical answers to the problems of economic, social and cultural development.

The discovery of these new relations between school and community depends on an explicit national decision, a definite choice made by society as regards the type of economic and human development to be promoted in order to give genuine satisfaction to people's needs. It also depends on the definition of a community education in whose syllabus the values of modern civilization and those of traditional civilization are integrated, and which uses appropriate educational facilities and qualified educators, whether professional or not; for in traditional African society 'the educator's functions do not and cannot fall into the category of socio-professional work' [1, p. 11].

Educational power should be wielded not only by the usual bodies—ministries of education and centralized, hierarchical institutions, administrative staff who draft texts, inspectors and heads of schools who put them into effect, teachers obliged to teach syllabuses that are based on tests and competitive examinations—but also by the child's or worker's families and local community.

In the 1980s we should analyse the evolution of the concept of education, in order to devise a strategy for implementing a new educational policy for African countries. It should however be remembered that it is difficult to effect radical changes, for changes are costly and do not always prove successful. The most urgent problems must of course be tackled, but we must strive to see what are the crucial factors in an educational strategy for the year 2000. The form our action will take will be determined by the following major aims: to consolidate cultural identity and to define, accurately and realistically, the essential educational requirements for the endogenous development of the community and of people united on a national level but co-operating with other peoples in building a new future for mankind.

REFERENCES

1. COLIN, R. Heurs et malheurs de l'éducation solidaire. *Recherche, pédagogie et culture* (Paris), No. 49, September–October 1980, pp. 9–15.
2. HOUNTONDJI, P.-J. Distances. *Recherche, pédagogie et culture* (Paris), No. 49, September–October 1980, pp. 27–33.

7
Material, financial and human resources

Introduction

RECENT EVOLUTION OF EDUCATIONAL RESOURCES

As a social institution and an important sub-sector within the service sector of the national economy, education consumes for its operation considerable material, human and financial resources, which, according to the approach that is adopted, are seen either as expenditure or as investments. The availability of these resources depends on the level of development and on the degree of priority which the authorities accord to education, which in turn depends on the tasks that a society seeks to accomplish by means of education.

The guiding principle for the international community in determining the volume of resources to be assigned to education is based on the assertion that education is a fundamental need and a human right. It is, however, a need that is far from being met in a world where hundreds of millions of children are not enrolled in schools or give up school attendance before they have learned to read and write. It therefore seems essential to mobilize the maximum resources in order to remedy the situation. This is especially true if one considers the fact that in many countries the demand for education has already acquired proportions greatly in excess of the capacity of the educational systems to meet it; that the population explosion is all too likely to accentuate the existing imbalance between the demand for education and available internal resources; and that the world today, which is undergoing all sorts of changes, is making new demands on education.

The past two decades have seen a considerable growth in aggregate Public Expenditure on Education (PEE) which, at current costs, has risen from a world figure of $51,600 million in 1960 to $474,000 million in 1978, i.e. an increase of a factor of about 9.2. Another development of the past few decades has been the diversification of sources for the financing of education, largely due to the launching of qualitatively new types of formal and non-formal education and to the will to apply a policy of lifelong education. In addition to

TABLE 6. Evolution of public expenditure on education

	1960			1978		
	PEE (billions of dollars)	PEE as percentage of GNP	PEE per inhabitant (dollars)	PEE (billions of dollars)	PEE as percentage of GNP	PEE per inhabitant (dollars)
World total[1]	51.6	3.7	23	474.0	5.6	146
Industrialized countries	47.1	4.0	49	418.9	5.9	366
Developing countries[1]	4.5	2.3	3	55.1	4.1	26

1. Not including China, Democratic Kampuchea, the Democratic People's Republic of Korea, the Lao People's Democratic Republic and the Socialist Republic of Viet Nam.
Source: International Conference on Education (38th Session, Geneva, 1981), *A Summary Statistical Review/ of Education in the World, 1960–1980*, p. 68, Paris, Unesco, 1981. (Unesco doc. ED/BIE/CONFINTED/38 Ref. 1.)

ministries and bodies which are responsible for education at national and local level other services, organizations, foundations and enterprises now play an important part in the financing of education.

The increase can be seen very clearly if one compares it with the increase in Gross National Product (GNP), since, as a percentage of GNP, the PEE went up from 3.7 in 1960 to 5.6 in 1978.

A few special features should be noted, however. First, there is a clear tendency towards a declining growth rate, which is borne out by a study of the trend in the GNP elasticity of PEE. Thus there seems to be a widespread reduction in educational investment due both to the economic crisis and to a change in the attitude of the public authorities towards education (Jean-Claude Eicher).

A second point to be noted is that a substantial proportion of the growth in PEE is not related to the increase in real resources, because of a 'relatively faster growth of prices in the educational sector, which alone accounted for over 50 per cent of the increased share (in GDP)' [1, p. 75].

A third point, which is related to the second, is that the growth in PEE is

TABLE 7. Evolution of PEE growth rate and of its elasticity in relation to GNP

	1960–65	1965–70	1970–74	1974–76
PEE percentage growth rate	10.90	6.40	6.60	3.30
Elasticity coefficient of PEE in relation to GNP	2.10	1.36	1.27	1.38

Source: J.-C. Eicher and F. Orivel, *The Allocation of Resources to Education throughout the World: A Statistical Study*, Paris, Unesco, 1980. (Current Surveys and Research in Statistics, CSR-E-35.)

accompanied by a rise in expenditure per pupil, and the cause of that is not necessarily simply price rises. Between 1960 and 1978 PEE per pupil increased by a factor of 4.7 in the developing countries and 6.8 in the developed countries [2, p. 71].

A fourth point is that the slowing down in the rate of growth of PEE in relation to GNP in the 1970s is attributed to a fairly marked decrease in the rate of growth of expenditure on equipment, which in the West has levelled off at 20 per cent of total educational expenditure [1, pp. 75–6].

The fifth point is that the gap between the groups of countries remains wide. Although the resources that the developing countries assigned to education throughout this period grew more quickly (8.5 per cent per annum) than did those in the developed countries (6.5 per cent per annum), the latter spent a larger proportion of their GNP on education. The developing countries have nearly two-thirds of the world school population, yet they benefit by only one-eighth of world spending on education. In respect of per capita PEE, the gap between the two groups of countries is of the order of 1:13 and if one compares the developed countries with the LDC group, the ratio rises to 1 : 75 (Malcolm Adiseshiah).

The sixth and last point concerns the efficiency with which available resources are used, which varies according to their distribution among the different levels of education. In recent years, their distribution has given rise to criticism in several countries. Between the early 1960s and mid-1970s, the growth rate for public expenditure in secondary and higher education in several developing countries was four to ten times higher than in the primary sector. Admittedly, that trend reflected certain views and beliefs that were inherent in educational policy at the time—now called into question—which gave priority to the higher levels, overlooking the fact that in the developing countries those levels of education were very costly because of the lack of coherent educational systems, the impossibility of attaining optimal dimensions in the training of certain categories of specialists, and the involuntary recourse to foreign teaching personnel (who sometimes made up 80 per cent of the staff) and to imported equipment. Today, it seems, these views have been reconsidered, and some figures even show that primary and non-formal education have a higher rate of efficiency than secondary and higher education.

In conclusion, it should be noted that the International Panel on the Future Development of Education has stated on a number of occasions that the availability of resources for education is becoming a major problem of our time. The problem arises because of budgetary decisions to satisfy the needs which are regarded as more urgent in conditions of penury (for example, food), and also because of political decisions—some of which are open to question—based on other priorities (for example, expenditure on armaments). It has been also emphasized that the inadequacy of resources sometimes gives rise to a regrettable distortion of the pattern of educational expenditure, in which the relative amount of teachers' salaries, which are the main item of recurrent expenditure, continues to increase, while the resources for other current expenses (main-

tenance of buildings, renewable equipment and teaching aids of all kinds) are in increasingly short supply. This impairs the quality of education, the effectiveness of teachers' work and of the educational process as a whole. The problem of resources is not always a matter of the lack of finance; staff and equipment may be inadequate.

The effects of the growing inadequacy of resources are obvious because the majority of countries devote very little of their PEE (less than 5 per cent) to school building. In many countries the 'model school' is still an isolated teacher working in a decrepit, unsuitable building, often rented and therefore difficult to convert into a proper classroom, without any back-up teaching materials. Too many schools in the developing countries, at both secondary and higher levels, are using substandard teaching materials (including those needed to overcome the language barrier) and in many rural schools even the most elementary materials, such as books and school supplies, are completely lacking. Generally speaking, very few countries have devised an overall strategy for the development of school equipment industries, and it should be emphasized that this situation must be taken into account in any serious consideration of the future development of education.

As regards the problem of mobilizing and using human resources, the first point to note is that the problem of providing training in some subjects at the secondary and higher levels is far from being solved, and that several Arab and African countries have to use foreign teachers, who in many cases will naturally apply their own teaching methods. In respect of teacher recruitment most countries come up against budgetary restraints, which is why recruitment lags behind the growth of the school population, especially in primary education in the developing countries, where overcrowded classes of fifty to sixty pupils per teacher are still the rule rather than the exception. Furthermore, most countries are faced with serious problems concerning teachers: their geographical distribution (urban areas being definitely favoured over rural areas); their use (not very intensive, too often part time); and their quality (lack of organized systems of lifelong or further training). There is therefore room for a real manpower development strategy for educational systems (Jean-Pierre Jallade).

RESOURCES FOR EDUCATION:
PROSPECTS

The outlook for resources depends above all on the future trend in PEE. Some writers say that, in the past, the chief reason for the rise in spending was the increased enrolment at all levels and the priority given to the higher levels of the educational system. In coming decades, quantitative expansion will play a greater part, especially in the developing countries. However, a less costly model for educational growth could be found by adopting a new educational policy to broaden the base of the educational pyramid to the benefit of the primary sector, adult education and vocational training.

It might be possible to exert some influence on another factor which determines the resource needs of education (and the efficiency with which they are used, which will be examined below) by reducing the number of pupil years required to complete each level. At primary level, for example, it is 60 per cent above the normal, because of the large number of repeats and drop-outs. A policy based on an in-depth analysis of the real social and educational causes of this phenomenon, designed to reduce repeat rates to the bare minimum, would in theory enable 10 to 15 per cent more children to be enrolled without increasing the intake capacity and therefore the cost (Jean-Pierre Jallade).

On the other hand, the third factor in the rise in PEE—action to improve the quality of education—although a lesser cause than the rise in school population, will be more important in the near future. It will be particularly difficult to effect substantial economies in that respect at the level of primary education, which in many countries is still of poor quality.

There is yet another factor to take into account, although its importance from this point of view is open to question: the introduction of new teaching facilities. Until now, wherever new educational technology has been introduced into the educational process it has entailed increased expenditure and the recruitment of extra staff, without any appreciable improvement in the cost-effectiveness ratio, for which, it is true, satisfactory methods of measurement have not yet been worked out. Many specialists believe that education in the future will be inseparable from sophisticated technology. G. Psacharopoulos has this to say on the subject:

It is perhaps easier to see the teacher of the future as a computer programmer rather than someone standing in front of a blackboard, with chalk in his hand. Recent developments in silicon-chip technology might make the blackboard itself a thing of the past, and replace it by individual television-screen monitors. Rapid cost reductions of the associated hardware make this a highly probable prediction for the near future [3, p. 460].

In the absence of sufficiently representative data on the implications of the new technologies for PEE, let us accept the conclusion arrived at by Unesco on the basis of expert estimates: if the use of these new techniques remains marginal they will result in additional costs of the order of 15–30 per cent. Conversely, the widespread introduction of this type of innovation within the framework of a radical reform of the educational system, its aims and methods, could bring about a reduction of costs in certain conditions [4, p. 11].

So the growing demand for education, the need to improve its quality, and the advent of educational technology all lead one to believe that the resource needs of education are going to increase more rapidly than the means available. In that event there are really only two ways of making up for the discrepancy: the mobilization of extra resources and the more efficient use of available resources.

Of the factors to be taken into account in mobilizing extra resources for

education, the International Panel on the Future Development of Education highlighted the following points.
Additional taxes levied regularly or exceptionally on certain activities or sources of income.
Financial participation by those within the higher income categories who benefit from secondary and higher education, so that free education in countries where costs are particularly high shall cease to encourage élitism.
Participation by business undertakings and employers, especially as regards vocational training, the development of which has often contributed to an increase in business productivity without employers having to bear the costs.
At least partial self-financing of educational establishments, especially at the secondary and higher levels, through their activities for the production of goods and services and their research work.
Direct contributions from communities, groups and firms in the form of materials and labour placed at the disposal of educators.
Civic service to be performed by young people over a limited number of years.
Various suggestions have been made on how to obtain resources from extra taxation, among them a special one per cent tax on industry's wage bill (already levied by certain countries to help finance vocational training), a special tax on agricultural exports, the taxation of luxury goods, or tax reforms to make the middle and higher income groups pay more (since they now receive more in educational subsidies for their children than they pay in taxes).[1] But if we remember that in the developing countries, as a rule, taxation can mobilize resources to only a small extent and that the burden of taxation is in the end borne by the disadvantaged, we shall see that the opportunities for mobilizing extra resources by fiscal means are not as great as one might suppose.

The financial involvement of those receiving an education is increasingly attracting the attention of experts. Jean-Claude Eicher writes that at first sight it may seem anti-democratic to ask families to provide a large proportion of the finance for education. That is certainly true of primary education and the entire field of compulsory education, but it is not necessarily true of higher education, since most of those who go to universities in the developing countries, where education is extremely costly for communities, come from privileged backgrounds.[2]

In Africa, for example, public expenditure per pupil expressed as a percentage of per capita GNP was of the order of 18 per cent for primary education

---

1. The World Bank has this to say on the matter: 'Public expenditure on secondary and higher education tends to redistribute income from poor to rich. . . .'—*World Development Report, 1980*, p. 49, Washington, D.C., World Bank, 1980.
2. M. Blaug writes, with reference to G. Psacharopoulos: 'Free higher education is a form of regressive taxation which makes a mockery of the policy of egalitarianism to which most Third World governments are dedicated.'—M. Blaug, 'Economics of Education in Developing Countries: Current Trends and New Priorities', *Third World Quarterly* (London), Vol. 1, No. 1, 1979, p. 77.

in 1978, as against 68.2 per cent for higher education. In other words, the amount spent on one year's study for one young person whose parents could usually afford to pay at least part of the cost was enough to send almost forty more children to primary school. Jean-Claude Eicher feels that thought should be given to raising the enrolment fees for higher education and altering the grants system to provide more substantial scholarships for the least well off.[1]

The involvement of business undertakings seems to offer good prospects, especially in the matter of vocational training, and is all the more desirable in that vocational and technical education is very costly and not always adapted to the technology used in a particular country. Vocational training may be either ad hoc or continuous, full time training or alternating periods of work and study. Many writers on the subject think that, since there is a risk that those being taught will be subordinated to the interests of the firm, the responsible authorities at the highest level should maintain supervision of training content, especially as far as the general and cultural aspects of education are concerned.

The self-financing of educational establishments can play only a limited role in reducing educational expenditure. The experience of countries such as the United Republic of Tanzania, Benin, Burkina Faso and Panama shows how schools can help in different ways to improve the material conditions of their own existence, for example, by forming brigades or production units so that pupils can manufacture goods for sale, the revenue from which goes some way towards meeting the schools' expenditure. Provided that neither educational standards nor the children's free time is affected, such a scheme may be used to a reasonable extent to make up for the lack of resources from which the educational systems of a number of countries suffer, especially since productive work is of undoubted educational value.

As regards community involvement, it is interesting to see how in several countries certain items, such as teachers' salaries, school building projects, and equipment, are charged to the community. For example, there are many instances in the socialist countries of collective farms and industrial enterprises that maintain kindergartens and schools. Several countries in Africa rely on community action for school building. The people always make their contribution in kind—a direct contribution to the enrichment of the nation, the effects of which on educational resources are often not fully appreciated. This system may be of particular interest to those developing countries whose

---

1. In view of the evidence that the problem of PEE is becoming more acute, and the interest being aroused by the idea that those who receive an education should contribute to its cost, some specialists go further in their interpretation of this trend. For example, G. Psacharopoulos predicts 'a gradual shift of the finance structure of education from public to private funds'; a loan thus being an appropriate way for the individual to provide private finance. 'A loan scheme is fairer in the sense that it is the person who benefits who ultimately pays the costs of his or her education,' he writes.—G. Psacharopoulos, 'Towards an Atomistic Model of Education', *Prospects: Quarterly Review of Education* (Paris, Unesco), Vol. X, No. 4, 1980, p. 458.

economies are not yet full market economies, that is those in which the channels of distribution do not necessarily coincide with the market and in which the market is not the only or even the main regulator of manpower resources, consumer goods or equipment.

Other ways of mobilizing human resources for education are the public or national educational service, voluntary service schemes and welfare organizations, all of which are aimed at using the energy, enthusiasm and knowledge of educated young people who desire to participate in the revitalization of education, to carry out educational projects such as literacy teaching. Countries such as Cuba, Nicaragua and Ethiopia provide interesting examples of this.

All these methods of mobilizing additional resources are mentioned here not as substitutes for the normal procedure of providing finance out of the state budget but as complements to it, which in some circumstances can help to overcome difficulties encountered in the financing of education.

Although in some years external aid represents almost 10 per cent of the total PEE of the developing countries, it is still of only marginal value and is no more than a supplement to the proper financing of their educational systems, which cannot always be depended upon. Even if one agrees that it can act as a catalyst, a boost or an indicator of what should be done, it cannot replace the efforts and resources which these countries must themselves devote to the development of their education, especially when one considers that external aid is always fortuitous and is often hedged about with conditions set by the donor. The International Panel on the Future Development of Education has emphasized that, even if future external aid offered appreciable opportunities, it should not produce paternalistic attitudes on the one side and 'wait and see' policies on the other. However, if the international climate were to lead to a curbing of the arms race, the opportunities for external aid could be substantially increased. Recent studies show that in 1980 military expenditure worldwide reached $500,000 million, or 6 per cent of world production, a figure comparable with that of educational expenditure. The developing countries spend more for military purposes than they do for education. About 50 million people now work directly or indirectly to satisfy the demand for military production and services, and in the 1970s nearly 20 per cent of the world's scientists and engineers were working on military research. If one includes both regular and paramilitary forces, there are many more military people in the world than teachers. All this goes to show that progress in the field of disarmament, by unblocking resources destined for military purposes, could contribute towards solving the problem of resources for education. The international community could play a greater role in the solution of problems which are of such dimensions that it is beyond the power of certain countries to tackle them independently. The International Panel, for example, proposed that the general extension of primary education should be regarded as a worldwide responsibility and that an international funding system should be worked out and put into operation in order to attain that objective by the year 2000.

The problem of resources for education is not only a question of mobilizing *financial resources, it is bigger and more complex than that. Educational industries should therefore be established either at the national level—as for example in Nigeria, where centres for manufacturing and distributing school equipment have been set up in many regions—or based on groups of neighbouring countries, which would be a better arrangement in the case of smaller countries.*

The production [of the various kinds of teaching materials] in the developing countries themselves would enhance their collective self-reliance in respect of manufacturing industries, replacing the present world distribution of labour by arrangements more favourable to the developing countries. The new production capacities should be divided among the developing countries, thus providing each with a market covering several States [5, para. 92].

It was stated above that a more efficient use of available resources has an appreciable effect on the deficits to be expected. Although it is very unlikely that innovations in education can produce a rise in productivity comparable, for example, to that achieved by the industrial sector in recent decades, the importance of this factor should be very widely recognized, especially as far as the secondary and higher levels of education in the developing countries are concerned. For while the unit cost in higher education in European countries is roughly half the per capita GNP, in the African countries it is nearly seven times the per capita GNP.

The clearest indication that an educational system is not efficient enough is unquestionably the number of repeaters and the drop-out rate. It is a serious problem at all levels, but especially in primary education, where it exacerbates the inequality of educational opportunity. It is estimated that between 12 and 14 per cent of pupils enrolled in primary schools in the developing countries repeat their courses, and that on average the wastage must be considerable: according to a study made in one country, the additional cost for primary education was of the order of 50 per cent.

Is there any way of improving the efficiency of the use of resources? Many countries are considering taking steps to provide in-service training for teachers and to improve their pre-service training; they are trying to solve the problems of wastage and poor school results by improving the efficiency of teaching. A systematic and persistent effort to use the teachers available more effectively would also mean that one would have a reserve of available finance which could amount to between 25 and 30 per cent of the operating budget [4, p. 10].

Considerable improvements could be made in the building, upkeep and use of educational premises. One of the best ways of economizing on resources is to use premises intensively, no matter what the cost. There is no reason why most buildings cannot be occupied throughout the year if school timetables and out-of-school teaching programmes for young people and adults are carefully planned, as has been done in many countries. If premises were used in this way there would be much less need for new buildings, although of course some additional premises will be required because of the increase in the school population. Some countries seek to reduce the cost of new building projects by opting for local architecture based on the use of materials and skills available on the spot, and this enables communities to play an active part in the design and construction of school buildings.

The future evolution of educational systems is likely to be marked by more frequent use of specialist administrators to run the larger educational establishments and take charge of central and regional administration, while educators will be trained to manage educational establishments. Many countries are hoping to make savings and improve the efficiency of their educational system through measures they have recently taken to achieve a better balance between different levels of the administration, greater decentralization of decision-making, and to induce communities to participate in the planning and running of schools. Restoring the credit balance between the various levels of education, as we have seen, reducing non-teaching costs, reducing an unjustified diversity of courses, and eliminating duplication in programmes are all measures which education officials can consider with a view to making the resources at their disposal more effective. That is a task primarily for high-level officials. Finally, the measures to be taken will be effective to the extent that they derive from a new, more tangible and realistic notion of the nature of PEE and of educational resources in general, which is in line with the profoundly-changed view we now have of development and with the political will to guarantee the effective exercise of the right to education, while at the same time creating the conditions that favour its development. Voices are being raised more and more often in favour of an interdisciplinary approach to the problems of socio-economic development, industrial or agricultural revival being regarded as a broader process than mere investment in equipment and one which must be accompanied by a redistribution of resources in favour of education, since it is education which turns these investments to account and on which their effective use depends.

In the two studies that follow, Jean-Claude Eicher and Jean-Pierre Jallade analyse in depth some aspects of the problem of educational resources; their points of view and sometimes their interpretations of facts may differ, but the solutions they suggest seem in general to be closely related.

REFERENCES

1. *Future Educational Policies in the Changing Economic and Social Context.* Paris, Organisation for Economic Co-operation and Development, 1979.
2. WORLD BANK. *Education: Sector Policy Paper.* Washington, D.C., World Bank, 1980.
3. PSACHAROPOULOS, G. Towards an Atomistic Model of Education. *Prospects: Quarterly Review of Education* (Unesco, Paris), Vol. X, No. 4, 1980, pp. 456–61.
4. UNESCO SEMINAR FOR NATIONAL SPECIALISTS AND UNESCO EXPERTS IN EDUCATIONAL PLANNING (Paris, 19–28 June 1978). *The Mobilization of Domestic Resources for Formal and Non-formal Education. Annotated Agenda—Working Paper Prepared by the Secretariat.* Paris, Unesco, 1978. (Unesco doc. ED-78/CONF.734/Ref. 1.)
5. MEETING OF EXPERTS ON MAJOR PROBLEM AREAS OF EDUCATIONAL REFORMS IN THE 1970S AND 1980S (EXPERIENCES AND PROSPECTS) (Paris, Unesco, 24–28 October 1977). *Annotated Agenda—Working Paper Prepared by the Secretariat.* Paris, Unesco, 1977. (Unesco doc. ED-77/CONF.628/Ref. 1.)

The material, financial and human resources of education

Jean-Claude Eicher

THE EVOLUTION OF PUBLIC EXPENDITURE ON EDUCATION IN THE WORLD SINCE 1960

Aggregate public expenditure on education throughout the world rose, at current market prices from $51,600 million to $474,000 million between 1960 and 1980—an increase of 920 per cent.

However, the rate at which it is rising has declined markedly during the period, the mean annual rate of increase of real Public Expenditure on Education (PEE) reaching 10.9 per cent between 1960 and 1965 but dropping to 6.4 per cent between 1965 and 1970, levelling off at 6.6 per cent between 1970 and 1974 and dropping to 3.3 per cent between 1974 and 1976. This decline in the growth rate is confirmed and made clearer by an examination of the Gross National Product (GNP) elasticity of PEE (see Table 8).

Slowing down of investment in education is, therefore, extremely widespread. It is due both to the economic crisis and to the change in the attitude of public authorities towards education. Does this mean that a

TABLE 8. Elasticity of public expenditure on education in relation to GNP by region, 1960–76

Regions	1960–65	1965–70	1970–74	1974–76
World	2.10	1.36	1.27	1.38
Industrialized countries	2.06	1.33	1.41	1.28
Developing countries	2.16	1.66	0.92	2.45
Africa	2.30	1.60	1.49	2.81
Latin America and the Caribbean	2.57	1.11	1.22	0.60
Asia	1.45	1.14	1.34	2.12

Source: J.-C. Eicher and F. Orivel, *The Allocation of Resources to Education throughout the World: Statistical Study*, p. 38, Paris, Unesco, 1980. (Current Surveys and Research in Statistics, CSR-E-35.)

TABLE 9. Trend in net enrolment ratios in primary education in a cross-section of developing countries, by region, 1970–78

Region	Countries whose rate attained or exceeded 75 per cent in 1970 — Countries with nearly 100 per cent by 1978	Countries whose rate attained or exceeded 75 per cent in 1970 — Countries whose rate progressed little or none	Countries whose rate was between 30 and 75 per cent in 1970 — Countries which made significant progress (20 points or more)	Countries whose rate was between 30 and 75 per cent in 1970 — Countries which made little or no progress (less than 10 points)	Countries whose rate was below 30 per cent in 1970 — Countries which made significant progress (more than 15 points)	Countries whose rate was below 30 per cent in 1970 — Countries which made little or no progress (less than 10 points)
Africa	2	2	4	7	3	6
Latin America	3	6	–	2	–	–
Asia	2	4	2	2	1	1

Source: *Unesco Statistical Yearbook, 1980*, Table 3.2, Paris, Unesco, 1980.

lower priority is given to education because needs appear to be broadly satisfied, thanks to ten to fifteen years of intensive public investment? The data concerning school enrolment rates and staffing levels and their recent evolution in the developing countries provide us with the beginnings of a reply. At this stage we shall merely note the level to which it is unanimously considered that everyone should have access, that of primary education. If we group together by major regions those Third World countries for which continuous data are regularly available regarding net enrolment ratios (ratio of primary-school pupils in age-groups that come within the period of primary schooling to the population in the same age-groups), we observe the trend set out in Table 9.

These results are relatively discouraging, showing as they do that of the 54 countries surveyed (28 in Africa, 15 in Asia and 11 in Latin America), 30 have failed to achieve any significant increase in the proportion of children who have completed their primary schooling recently, and that this is true both of countries that have already reached a high school enrolment level and of countries that are lagging far behind. The data also confirm that a great deal remains to be done in Asia and above all in Africa, since 15 countries out of 28 still provide primary schooling for less than 50 per cent of the school-age population.

Can it be said, despite all this, that the quality of the educational services provided for those who do attend school has improved? As Table 10 shows, not even that claim is justified, if we take the pupil–teacher ratio as our criterion.

In Latin America and Asia, the pupil–teacher ratio has remained fairly stable, whereas the situation is clearly more serious in Africa, where the vast majority of countries have experienced a setback, in some cases a major one.

The material, financial and human resources of education

TABLE 10. Trend in the pupil–teacher ratio in primary education, by region, 1970–77

Region	Number of countries in which the ratio has improved (by 2 or more points)	Number of countries in which the ratio has remained virtually constant	Number of countries in which the ratio had declined (by 2 or more points)
Africa (27 countries)	5	5	17
Latin America (11 countries)	3	4	4
Asia (14 countries)	5	5	4

To sum up it can be seen that, despite the considerable investment which has been made in education throughout the world during the past twenty years, there has been a marked decline in the growth rate of public expenditure on education since 1965. If we examine probable future trends we shall get a better idea of the scale of the problems and constraints created by this situation.

MEDIUM-TERM TRENDS AND PROBLEMS

The estimates given here are based on school enrolment projections carried out by Unesco and also on a hypothesis concerning the evolution of educational costs, by educational level, in relation to the GNP.

In the developing countries we observe that the gross enrolment rate in primary education is not expected to exceed 95 per cent by the year 2000, which means that there is still some way to go before universal schooling at that level is achieved.

A comparison of the major regions reveals significant disparities and, what is most important, an uneven rate of progression (Table 11). Latin

TABLE 11. Percentage trend in the gross enrolment ratio in primary education in the Third World, 1980–2000

Region	Year 1980	Year 2000
All developing countries[1]	86	96
Africa[2]	78	93
Latin America and the Caribbean	104	109
South Asia	83	93

1. Not including China, the Democratic People's Republic of Korea or Namibia.
2. Not including Namibia.
Source: Unesco, *Trends and Projections of Enrolment by Level of Education and by Age, 1960–2000*, p. 35, Paris, Unesco, 1983. (Current Studies and Research in Statistics.) (Unesco doc. CSR-E-46.)

America, for example, which was already fairly close to attaining universal schooling in 1980, will have fully attained it by 2000. By contrast, the other two continents are far from achieving a fully literate child population.

Costs per pupil have increased considerably in the past, at all educational levels. This is due to two factors: the increase in the production cost of educational services the quality of which remains constant, and the improvement in the quality of educational services.

In the first section of this chapter, it was noted that certain indices pointed to a levelling off of quality and even sometimes its decline. If, in addition, we take account of the observations on the decline of economic growth, it is reasonable to assume that the quality of educational services will remain constant in the coming years.

On the other hand, production costs are bound to increase, not only because of price rises but also in real terms, because salaries represent the major part of the costs, and it may be supposed that teachers' living standards will rise, as they have generally done in the past, more or less in step with the GNP.

TABLE 12. Trend in enrolment and enrolment ratios by level and by region in the Third World, 1975–2000

	1975			2000		
	Africa	Latin America	Asia	Africa	Latin America	Asia
Number of pupils in primary education[1]	44 243	57 213	136 077	127 483	118 449	260 145
Number of pupils in secondary education[1]	7 811	12 151	47 128	32 884	35 474	119 570
Number of students in higher education[1]	865	3 451	4 581	3 967	13 228	13 434
Actual enrolment rate	32.6	54.8	38.0	48.6	69.0	44.5
Number of pupil equivalents[2] in primary education[1]	103 089	111 539	262 675	460 188	304 481	594 129
School-age population	135 715	104 403	358 097	262 311	171 665	584 596
Hypothetical enrolment rate	76.0	106.8	73.4	175.4	177.4	101.6

1. All these figures are in thousands.
2. This figure is obtained by multiplying enrolment figures for secondary and higher education by a coefficient equal to the ratio of their unit cost to that of a first-level pupil.

The material, financial and human resources of education

The hypothesis of a rate of growth of costs per pupil equal to the per capita GNP therefore appears to be realistic, but it does not reflect a determination to promote educational development, inasmuch as it presupposes that most countries will be impelled to abandon the attempt to improve the conditions in which schools are run and the standard of school building.

If the cost per pupil were the same at all levels and/or if the projections reflected the same increase in enrolments at all levels, one would only need to apply the coefficient of growth in enrolment ratios to the percentage of GNP spent on education for the last year for which figures were available in order to obtain this same percentage for the end of the period.

However, these hypotheses have not been confirmed. Costs per pupil are rising significantly with the level of education, and anticipated enrolments are increasing at a relatively greater rate at the secondary and, above all, the higher levels. Enrolment figures for the higher levels must therefore be converted into enrolment figures for the first level, since in terms of costs the enrolment of one pupil at the secondary level is equivalent to enrolling x pupils at the primary level ($x>1$), and the enrolment of a student in higher education to enrolling y pupils ($y>x$).

In the case of the developing countries, this simulation yields the results presented in Table 12.

The hypothetical enrolment ratio will be seen to have increased between 1975 and 2000 by 130 per cent for Africa, by 66 per cent for Latin America and by 38 per cent for Asia. It may therefore be said that, were these hypotheses to be confirmed, the percentage of GNP accounted for by public expenditure on education would rise as shown in Table 13.

Here, too, the situation in Africa must be regarded as disturbing. For if the region is to reach targets which, once again, may appear modest in relation to the legitimate ambitions of the different African countries, it will need to earmark almost 11 per cent of its GNP for public expenditure on education. Because of the very size of this percentage, because no country has yet reached it, because there seems to be a ceiling of about 8 per cent, and because of the urgency of other community needs, it would be unrealistic to suppose that the target could be reached if new resources are not made available and if the educational system is not radically reformed in order to improve its efficiency.

TABLE 13. Hypothetical evolution of the percentage of GNP accounted for by public expenditure on education, 1975–2000

	1975	2000
Africa	4.8	10.56
Latin America	3.3	5.48
Asia	3.8	5.24

The projection for Asia and Latin America appears more hopeful, since the targets would be obtained in those regions without exceeding 5.5 per cent of GNP. However, aside from the fact that this is in itself a very large percentage, progress would not be spectacular in Asia, since Unesco's projections were based on the trend during the previous period, when growth was particularly slow in that region. Only Latin America could meet relatively satisfactory targets at a more or less acceptable cost.

We shall not dwell on the case of the developed countries. The slowing down of total public expenditure on education is more marked there than elsewhere, so much so that it is tending to level off and even to drop in some countries. However, basic literacy requirements have by and large been long since satisfied, and the young all spend approximately ten years at school. Only higher education can give cause for concern, in view of the fact that in many countries public expenditure at that level has declined in real terms for several years, whereas the demand continues to increase. Finally, there is an enormous expansion in the demand for adult education, but it is financed from a whole range of sources, public funds accounting for a very small share of the costs.

The future of education is therefore beset by serious problems, particularly in the developing countries. Is there any way of speeding up the growth of educational services?

PROSPECTS FOR MOBILIZING NEW RESOURCES AND FOR MAKING MORE USE OF EXISTING ONES

We shall consider in turn the new financial resources that might be solicited, the possibility of developing the human and material resources needed in education, the possibility of increasing efficiency in the harnessing of these resources and the limitations of such an increase.

Possibility of increasing the means of financing education

Financial resources for education may derive from any of six sources: central government; regional or local communities; those enrolling in education and/or their families; private benefactors; business enterprises; or external aid.

The first two sources are public, as is the last, essentially. We noted in the first part of this study that public sources have increased enormously over the past twenty years, but that for various reasons they are now tending to increase less rapidly. It would therefore seem vain to expect their share in the total financing of education to increase, except possibly external aid in the case of a few developing countries.

The amount contributed by private benefactors is marginal and will of necessity remain so.

The financing of education by those who receive it is generally regarded as a backward step. At first sight, it may appear undemocratic to ask families to provide a large proportion of the finance for a service which is regarded as vital, and which would thereby be allocated principally in accordance with the resources of those applying for it, though also, it is true, in accordance with their preferences. This is undoubtedly true of primary education and of the entire field of compulsory education, since if enrolment fees were charged, the poorest families would be forced to sacrifice other essential items of expenditure.

However, the same is not necessarily true of higher education. Research has shown that it is much more costly than primary and secondary education and that its financing is in most cases regressive, that is, that those whose children do not usually have a higher education contribute most to its financing through the taxes they pay. In all countries in which the financing of higher education is mainly undertaken by the public authorities, consideration must therefore be given to raising the fees substantially—a course which some countries are seriously beginning to contemplate—while at the same time offering a grants system to provide more substantial scholarships for the least wealthy.

Finally, there is financing by business enterprises, which may appear logical when the intention is to provide initial or further vocational training which will be of direct use to employers. There is, however, one proviso: that the community maintain supervision over the content of the training, in order to avoid the danger of 'made-to-measure' training courses that would make retraining impossible.

Possibility of mobilizing new human and material resources

At present, educational activities are essentially in the hands of establishments that form part of a structured system whose human and material resources represent a considerable financial burden. However, this virtual monopoly is a relatively recent one, dating back in most formerly colonized developing countries no more than two decades. It is a cumbersome system, it is very difficult to adapt to new situations, and it cannot mobilize new human and material resources unless it receives new funds.

However, this type of organization is beginning to be seriously challenged. It is extremely ill-suited for adult training schemes, which take a variety of forms and are generally of a sporadic nature. Many people consider that it fails to cater for developing countries' requirements, because it transmits a culture that is both urban and permeated by foreign influences. Moreover, the services of full-time professional teachers are extremely expensive, as they are of necessity persons of a high educational level, whose remuneration must be commensurate with their qualifications if they are to be expected to remain in the teaching profession.

The conclusion is therefore clear. New human and material resources must be found outside the established educational systems. This is perfectly possible. We shall consider only the problem of literacy teaching, this being by far the most urgent and important problem. It concerns both children and adults.

As regards adults, the situation is clear. The traditional school is not suited to teaching them literacy skills, first because they see schools as places to which children are sent, where a language is spoken that they understand imperfectly, if at all, and where they do not feel at ease; second, and more importantly, because adult literacy teaching must be of a functional kind, that is, besides teaching the basic intellectual skills (the three Rs) it must seek to relate these skills to the needs of everyday life—managing farms, using fertilizers and pesticides, reading works on farming that are intended for the general public. It is not humanly or financially possible to perform these considerable tasks successfully unless available local resources are mobilized without direct cash payments, for example by using premises belonging to the local community and enlisting the services of educated persons. Such a scheme is difficult to organize and there are many obstacles in the way of the long-term mobilization of human and material resources. However, there are instances of successful literacy campaigns that can be studied and adapted to other situations, and this would seem to be the only effective approach to the problem.

The situation is less simple as regards children, since the aim must be, at least in the case of some of them, to lay sound foundations which will enable them to continue their education. In all cases, however, if a building erected by villagers working together is made available to the school, and if the most advanced pupils are used to supervise and assist beginners and backward pupils, the development of satisfactory primary schooling will be facilitated. But there may be new and more effective educational methods to which recourse might be had.

Possibility of making more effective use of educational resources

By tradition, education is a service that is skilled-labour intensive rather than capital intensive. It is therefore an activity in which increases in productivity are slight and whose costs per unit produced are high and are tending to increase as workers' living standards rise.

These conditions of production are due to the fact that the message containing the information (knowledge, skills, attitudes) to be transmitted is conveyed by a person, the teacher, who is in direct contact with the 'receivers', the pupils. The spectacular development of telecommunications media has impelled educational specialists to explore the practical possibilities of using such media (radio, television, cassettes, computers) to transmit the educational message and thereby to replace the teacher, at least to some extent.

We shall not attempt to give an account of all the research carried out on this subject. Our direct concern is to find out whether the use of modern media of instruction enables the cost of educational services to be reduced or the volume of services provided at a given cost to be increased.

Generally speaking, the main conclusions to emerge from current research work may be summarized as follows: the introduction of the media into the conventional educational system often increases its costs without making much difference to its results; and distance teaching may substantially improve the cost-benefit ratio in the use of resources for education, on two conditions: first, that those who listen or view really want to learn, and second, that the instruction concerns a specific field, preferably one with a technical content and of direct interest to the listeners or viewers.

This means that the media can enable better use to be made of resources in the teaching of basic skills to adults who want to learn and in the technical training of interested young people in a specific field. In all other cases, the use of the media improves the cost-benefit ratio little if at all, even where it is the sole means of providing schooling for groups of people who have hitherto been denied access to education, because they live too far away from a school or are unable to attend school for some other reason.

Finally, it may reasonably be supposed that there are still situations in which the cost per pupil can be lowered by economies of scale without any change in the methods of transmitting the educational messages. This is true in particular of higher education, which calls for costly equipment and therefore entails high fixed costs which should be shared by a large number of users. An analysis of costs per student in African countries, which are four to five times higher on average than in other developing countries, suggests that the universities are frequently too small and too widely dispersed over the continent. However, economic logic, which would argue in favour of their being grouped together, runs up against political imperatives that are no less restrictive, and which lie outside the scope of this study.

We shall conclude by stressing that educational needs are still enormous. Despite the priority accorded to education, it is doubtful whether ambitious targets for developing existing educational systems can be attained in present circumstances, in view of the limited resources available. In some regions of the developing world it is even to be feared that past progress will prove impossible to maintain at the same rate, which has nevertheless been judged too slow, in the next two decades. However, new resources can and must be found, as the tasks of education are defined anew in accordance with a new conception of the organization of educational activities, in order to gear them more closely to the overall needs of contemporary societies and their development requirements.

Educational resources

Jean-Pierre Jallade

THE PRESENT SITUATION OF THE PUBLIC FINANCING OF EDUCATION

In 1978, public spending on education in the developing countries accounted for 4.1 per cent of their GNP, as compared with 2.3 per cent in 1960. Over the same period, in the industrialized countries, this percentage rose from 4.0 to 5.9 per cent. Therefore we could say that the former were in roughly the same position in 1978 as were the latter in 1960.

A 'typical' developing country today allocates 3.5 per cent of its GNP and between 15 and 25 per cent of its total public spending to education. Can these figures be increased substantially? Technically speaking, it is perfectly feasible, and in fact there are countries which assign a much greater proportion of their GNP and budget to education, for example the Ivory Coast, Nigeria, Malaysia, Algeria, Costa Rica, among others. Unfortunately, the problem is of a political rather than a technical nature. What may have been possible in the past is no longer possible today, for the present economic crisis is making governments act with great caution.

In many countries the continuing increase in public spending on education is beginning to come up against increasingly severe political and economic constraints. The priority unquestioningly given to the education sector in the 1960s began to decline in the 1970s, as new needs, just as pressing, appeared—particularly in the fields of health and rural development. The difficulty experienced by school-leavers in finding employment, the brain drain, and the irrelevance of some courses to the economic and social situation prevailing in the developing countries, have all weakened the traditional economic justification of expansionist ideas about educational policy.

HUMAN RESOURCES FOR EDUCATION: THE LIMITATIONS OF ACTION TODAY

In most developing countries, the rise in school enrolments has been accompanied by a remarkable increase in the provision made for teacher training. The teaching profession enjoys considerable prestige and guarantees security of employment and income, which is important in countries where underemployment is endemic. There are therefore plenty of applicants for teacher training, who need no encouraging. While this problem has been largely solved (or is in the process of being solved) with respect to the training of teachers for general education, there are chronic shortages of teachers in some disciplines at the secondary and higher education levels. The use of foreign teachers, which is very common in Africa and some Arab countries, offers a solution to this problem, but can only be considered as a temporary palliative. These countries have a long way to go before they completely 'nationalize' their teaching personnel.

Most countries, in recruiting teachers, come up against budgetary constraints which are directly related to the economic situation. Teacher recruitment thus lags somewhat behind the growth of the school population. The situation of secondary and higher education, in which pupil-teacher ratios are often quite satisfactory, is in marked contrast with that of primary education, in which overcrowded classes are still the rule rather than the exception: ratios of fifty or even sixty pupils to one teacher are common, especially in Asia and Africa.

In addition to this budgetary constraint, most countries are faced with serious problems concerning the geographical distribution, the use and the quality of teachers. The geographical distribution of teachers is such that urban areas are clearly favoured to the detriment of rural areas, which are often given too few teachers, or teachers whose training is inferior to that of those in urban areas. These rural teachers often work in difficult conditions of isolation, with no chance to update their knowledge and lacking sustained contacts with inspectors.

Teaching personnel are not always used as intensively as they could be, especially at the primary level, where in many countries the length of the school day does not exceed four hours. Teaching therefore becomes part-time employment, so that the teacher can hold a second job. At the secondary and particularly at the higher education level, many teachers teach their subject for only a few hours a week, a waste of manpower that is difficult to stop, because of the force of custom.

Finally, the quality of teaching personnel depends above all on the quality of teacher training, which is often unsatisfactory. In the overwhelming majority of developing countries, teacher training is merely a matter of obtaining a diploma prior to recruitment, and there is no organized system of continuing education or in-service training. As a result, the knowledge and teaching methods of teachers are not usually kept up to date, and they are unable to adapt to change, so that it is difficult to mobilize them with a view to carrying out educational reforms.

Over the past twenty years, the training of teachers has tended to monopolize the attention and energy of the authorities, perhaps to the detriment of the training of education administrators at all levels—school principals, inspectors, regional and national directors. These people are rarely able to discharge their responsibilities fully, sometimes because they are given no clear-cut directives or lack the necessary financial means, but also because they have not been properly trained. There is therefore room for a real manpower development strategy for educational systems.

MATERIAL RESOURCES FOR EDUCATION

There is still an enormous shortage of school buildings and teaching materials, although much determined effort has been put into providing them. In many countries the 'model school' is still an isolated teacher working in a decrepit, unsuitable building, without any back-up teaching materials. Moreover, school buildings are often rented, which makes it hard to convert them into proper classrooms. School building projects have, of course, been started in many places, often with funding from bilateral and multilateral co-operation agencies. But while international co-operation may be of great value in the early stages of a school construction programme, it is no substitute for national action, which is all too often lacking. Most countries spend little more than 5 per cent of their total education budgets on school building. High construction costs are often an obstacle to the implementation of school building programmes.

In many rural schools even the most elementary materials such as books and school supplies are completely lacking, although so many studies emphasize their importance in the learning process. In such cases the obstacles are both technical and economic. The technical obstacle lies in the fact that many educational systems continue to use imported printed materials because they are unable or unwilling to develop materials adapted to the national context and printed in local languages. The economic problem is that, while expenditure per pupil is relatively small, overall expenditure is considerable because of the number of pupils enrolled. Another important point is the quality of the educational materials used in all too many Third World schools at secondary and higher education levels, particularly in scientific and technical disciplines. The linguistic barrier is of major relevance in this connection. The political and technical difficulties which stand in the way of the production and distribution of textbooks in various national languages tend to promote the distribution of outdated foreign publications, which are unsuited to the cultural environment of the country concerned and to the educational level of the students. Very few countries have drawn up overall strategies in these areas in order to deal with a deplorable situation.

Jean-Pierre Jallade

PROSPECTS FOR THE FUTURE:
SHOULD WE SPEND MORE,
OR MORE WISELY?

It is to be expected that government authorities, faced with the rising tide of budgetary constraints, will feel compelled to take economy measures and to do everything possible to improve the efficiency of their sector, in other words, that they will try to spend 'more wisely'. Their aim will therefore be to continue to expand education while keeping public spending on education within reasonable limits. In order to do this, governments will be obliged to make a number of choices with regard to educational policy. The principal choices will be concerned with the dilemma of quantity versus quality, the structure of the educational pyramid, and the internal efficiency of the educational system.

Quantity versus quality

Public spending on education can be determined by multiplying the number of pupils enrolled by expenditure per pupil, and it is theoretically possible to give one of these factors priority over the other. Thus, the number of pupils can be increased and unit costs stabilized or even lowered, by increasing pupil–teacher ratios, overloading the capacity of school buildings, decreasing the supply of educational materials, and cutting down general administrative staff for the educational system. Conversely, quality can be enhanced by limiting the growth of enrolments, which will make it possible to increase expenditure per student and consequently to improve the quality of teaching.[1] There will be fewer pupils per teacher, smaller and better-equipped classes and an efficient system of inspection and administration.

All countries necessarily make choices of this kind, either implicitly or explicitly. The choice is obviously a matter of educational policy, and it must be made carefully, in the light of each country's situation. Partial studies indicate that in the recent past many countries have chosen quantity rather than quality. For instance in fourteen out of a sample of nineteen African countries for which data are available, expenditure per pupil at the primary level dropped between 1970 and 1977; it remained unchanged in three others, and increased in only two countries [1, p. 32].

Other indices, such as an increase in the number of pupils per teacher, confirm this point. In addition, when we consider that the level of expen-

---

1. For the sake of simplicity, we shall assume that the higher the expenditure per pupil the better the quality of education, and vice versa. The relation between expenditure per pupil and quality is, of course, much more complex than this. However, at the level of the teachers in question, this simplification is immaterial. Moreover, it has the advantage of putting the problem in terms which can be easily understood by decision-makers.

diture was in any case very low at the outset, such an increase in the pupil–teacher ratio cannot fail to have a bad effect on the quality of teaching.

In such conditions, in future it would be inadvisable to economize on the quality of education. But public spending on education will probably continue to increase, not only because of an increase in enrolment, but also because of the foreseeable increase in costs per pupil. The real danger with regard to the latter is that expenditure will continue to diminish as a result of budgetary constraints. In the present circumstances, a change of policy on this point would require a clear-cut political decision.

The structure of the educational pyramid

We know that in many developing countries secondary and higher education, which is expensive, has developed more rapidly than primary education, which is not. If policy on this matter were changed, educational systems could adopt a less costly growth model, and thus pursue their expansion in spite of financial constraints. Of course, this entails an extremely important decision on educational policy, which may be taken for reasons other than financial ones. For the rapid expansion of secondary and higher education, however necessary it may have been during the 1960s because of the need to train the nation's leaders, now benefits the wealthy social classes living in urban areas more than anyone else. Secondary and higher education has been expanded to the detriment of primary education, for which the enrolment figures are rising very slowly, while a varying proportion of children in the 6–11 age-group are not yet attending school.

Readjusting the growth of educational systems in favour of the primary level—and also of adult education and vocational training—is therefore justified for both social and financial reasons. Increasingly serious budgetary constraints may facilitate a change of this nature.

Improving the internal efficiency of educational systems

At the primary level, the question of the internal efficiency of the educational system arises at once if we decide to discuss the matter in terms of pupils who have completed the primary course and in terms of the number of pupil-years really required to complete it, rather than in terms of the numbers entering school. If the internal efficiency of the system is to be improved the number of repeats and drop-outs must be reduced, in order to reduce the number of pupil-years required to complete the course, which is at the present time, on average, 60 per cent more than the number of years required by law. It goes without saying that unless the quality of education is improved the repeat and drop-out rates will continue to rise. Better trained teachers, appropriate educational materials and suitable school buildings are therefore needed, which inevitably means increased expenditure per pupil.

Improving internal efficiency may therefore lead to higher costs in the short term. In the long term, however, it is the only way to provide an effective education for all children in the 6 to 11 age-group without causing budgetary waste, which would weaken the political position of the educational sector in relation to that of other sectors competing for public funding.

Are there then any feasible means of ensuring that public funds assigned to the educational sector will be spent more efficiently? An examination of three aspects of educational policy that have an immediate impact on total public spending on education shows that the range of choice is limited.

First, there can be no reasonable expectation of achieving substantial economies in the quality of primary education. On the contrary, efforts should tend towards an improvement of that quality, which is still low in many countries.

Second, the need to improve the internal efficiency of educational systems at the primary level confirms, if that is necessary, the urgent need for a policy of enhancing their quality at this level. In this connection, we must not forget that good primary education is the essential foundation on which high-quality secondary and higher education can be developed.

Third, in view of present budgetary difficulties, a policy of this kind may not be adopted unless public expenditure on education is redistributed in favour of primary education, which will in turn entail keeping the growth of expenditure for secondary and higher education down to a lower rate than in the past.

ADDITIONAL RESOURCES FOR EDUCATION

Most of the public money assigned to education comes from the overall state budget, which in turn is drawn from fiscal revenue. If the portion of the budget assigned to education cannot be increased, other financial resources which would not necessarily come from the overall state budget might be mobilized. Also, unused resources which had been set aside for the organization of society could be made available for education.

Additional financial resources

It may safely be predicted that the progressive industrialization of the developing countries will bring with it the sustained development of vocational training at all levels. In some countries, the financial contribution of industry to the development of vocational training has taken the form of a special one per cent tax on the wage bill, to help finance vocational training. At least twelve Latin American countries have already adopted this system, which raises considerable amounts of money, and has financed the education of nearly 2 million students.

Similarly, literacy and vocational training in rural areas could be financed by a special tax on agricultural exports. In Colombia, for example, a special tax is levied on coffee exports, part of which is used to finance training programmes. Luxury goods could also be taxed to raise additional funds for education.

The financing of education on the basis of fiscal revenue would also be more socially equitable if a more strictly graduated system of taxation were adopted. Care should be taken that people in the middle and high income brackets do not receive more in the form of educational subsidies for their children than they pay in taxes. In cases where this happens, the problem of educational financing can be solved by reforming the tax system in order to make people in the medium and higher income brackets pay more [2].

Resources latent in the organization of society

Apart from the question of supplementary tax revenue, certain resources latent in the organization of society which have been little used until now can be mobilized, such as 'self-help' methods, a 'national teaching service' and the use of modern communications media for educational purposes. Village participation in building schools has been developed in a number of African countries. This sort of self-help can cover a range of extremely diverse situations, from the financing by the village of the construction of classrooms, using local materials, to the provision by the villagers of a construction site or a number of work days for school building, the contractor being the Ministry of Education or its representatives.

Teachers' salaries account for the largest proportion of expenditure on education at all levels. If people who are qualified but do not hold a diploma are used as teachers (being paid little or nothing), urgent situations can be faced without going to unacceptable expense. Many literacy campaigns, in Cuba and Nicaragua in particular, have been carried out with the assistance of unpaid volunteers or of people paid at much lower rates than teachers, and in this way substantial economies have been effected. In other countries, in East Africa for example, steps have been taken to set up a 'national teaching service', in which those holding the secondary school leaving certificate, or university students, will be asked to work as primary-school teachers in rural areas for a set period before completing their studies and obtaining their diploma. This kind of 'national service' makes it possible to mobilize human resources for education at costs far below teachers' salaries. This is unquestionably a policy that many countries could copy.

REFERENCES

1. UNESCO. *Dépenses publiques d'éducation et taux de scolarisation en Afrique* (provisional version). Paris, Unesco, 1981. (Unesco doc. STE/FIN/3; ST-81/WS/1.)
2. JALLADE, Jean-Pierre. Éducation et répartition du revenu en Amérique latine. *Revue Tiers-Monde* (Paris), Vol. XIX, No. 76, October–December 1978, pp. 771–99.

Appendix I

School enrolment trends and projections by level of education and by age[1]
(Totals for the world and by region 1960–2000, as assessed in 1982)

This appendix is concerned with the past and future development of school enrolment in relation to population growth. Based on annual enrolment data compiled by level of education, age-group and sex, covering the years from 1960 to 1980, it examines the implications of these trends as extrapolated over the next twenty years.

The purpose of the analysis is to highlight some of the characteristic features of the quantitative development of education. Obviously the quantitative expansion of educational systems is only one (and not necessarily the most important) dimension of the past and future development of education. The increase in student numbers during the last two decades was, in practically all countries, accompanied by comprehensive or partial changes in the structure and content of education as well as changes in teaching methods. As a result, educational systems have become better structured and their content has been made more relevant to national and regional aspirations. The management of education has been strengthened, moreover, to cope with the growing complexity of the educational sector. There can be no doubt that such changes will be even more pronounced during the next two decades in response to the increasing levels of unemployment prevalent in many countries among school leavers and graduates. These aspects of educational development are, however, outside the scope of the present report, as are considerations regarding teaching staff and the costs of education, as well as the impact of the development of the educational sector on the economic and cultural development of a country.

TRENDS IN EDUCATION DURING THE PERIOD 1960–80

As a consequence of a vigorous policy in favour of education, most countries can look back from the 1980s on two decades characterized by a growth in pupil numbers unparalleled in history. This is particularly true for the developing countries and especially for those which gained their independence during the early 1960s. These new nations had inherited modestly-developed educational

---

1. This appendix has been prepared as part of the study on the basis of a document drawn up by Unesco, *Trends and Projections of Enrolment by Level of Education and by Age, 1960–2000*, Paris, Unesco, 1983. (Current Studies and Research in Statistics.) (Unesco doc. CSR-E-46.)

systems, producing school leavers and graduates often ill-adapted to development needs. The last two decades saw most of the developing countries, including those newly independent, committed to universal primary education, the eradication of illiteracy and the production of qualified manpower. In the developed, industrialized countries the enrolment pressure was on secondary and higher education and the main efforts of governments were directed towards meeting this demand in a way that would promote greater equality of educational opportunities between different groups of the population.

Enrolment growth

Table 1 shows the development of enrolment by level of education between 1960 and 1980. The table illustrates clearly the enrolment explosion which took place during the past two decades, particularly in the developing countries, where the enrolment in primary education increased by 139 per cent, that of secondary education by 343 per cent, and that of higher education by 538 per cent. Although the enrolment in secondary and higher education in the developed, industrialized countries also increased considerably during this twenty-year period, the increase in total enrolment at all levels was only 31 per cent for these countries, compared with 177 per cent for developing countries. As a consequence, the share of the developing countries in total enrolment for all countries covered in Table 1 increased from 45 per cent in 1960 to 63 per cent in 1980.

Examining in greater detail the enrolment growth for each of the five major regions we note the following salient features.

Primary education

The figures given in the last four columns of Table 1 show that, for developing countries as a whole, the increase in enrolment (measured in absolute terms) was considerably lower during the period 1965–70 than during any of the three other periods covered. This comparatively lower enrolment growth during the last half of the 1960s was caused by the slow-down in South Asia, whereas the increased growth at this level during the 1970s was due mainly to a marked increase in Africa. The rapid expansion of primary-school enrolment in Africa is a noteworthy aspect of the development of education in developing countries during the last decade. It is to a large extent explained by sustained efforts to implement universal primary education on the part of some of the most populous states, such as Kenya, Nigeria and the United Republic of Tanzania. The somewhat lower increase in pupil numbers in Latin America and the Caribbean in the 1970s compared with the period 1965–70 is attributable to the fact that many countries in this region have already reached, or are approaching, universal primary education (see 'Progress towards universal primary education by 1980' below).

The development of primary-school enrolment in the industrialized countries followed a quite different pattern, characterized by an increase during the 1960s followed by a decrease of similar magnitude during the 1970s. These fluctuations were caused by corresponding fluctuations in the population of primary-school age (see 'Trends in enrolment ratios' below). As a consequence, the number of primary-school pupils in the industrialized countries in 1980 exceeded the 1960 figure by barely one per cent, compared to an increase of 139 per cent during the same period in the developing countries. In turn this led to an increase in the

Appendixes

Region[1]	Level of education	Number of pupils enrolled (thousands)					Average annual rates of growth			
		1960	1965	1970	1975	1980	1960-65	1965-70	1970-75	1975-80
World (including China)	Primary	339 850	416 591	447 334	529 025	563 693	4.2	1.4	3.4	1.3
	Secondary	83 087	113 446	149 102	197 101	233 963	6.4	5.6	5.7	3.5
	Higher	13 186	20 185	28 190	39 471	47 643	8.9	6.9	6.9	3.8
	Total	436 123	550 222	624 626	765 596	845 299	4.7	2.6	4.1	2.0
World (excluding China)	Primary	246 059	300 381	342 054	378 085	417 423	4.1	2.6	2.0	2.0
	Secondary	68 217	99 126	122 622	151 731	177 185	7.8	4.3	4.4	3.2
	Higher	12 224	19 511	28 142	38 970	46 482	9.8	7.6	6.7	3.6
	Total	326 501	419 018	492 818	568 786	641 090	5.1	3.3	2.9	2.4
Industrialized countries	Primary	124 078	133 730	137 711	131 220	125 455	1.5	0.6	−1.0	−0.9
	Secondary	46 429	63 051	70 519	79 503	80 574	6.3	2.3	2.4	0.3
	Higher	9 599	14 916	21 105	27 154	29 719	9.2	7.2	5.2	1.8
	Total	180 105	211 696	229 335	237 877	235 747	3.3	1.6	0.7	−0.2
Developing countries[2]	Primary	121 982	166 651	204 343	246 866	291 968	6.4	4.2	3.9	3.4
	Secondary	21 788	36 075	52 104	72 228	96 611	10.6	7.6	6.7	6.0
	Higher	2 625	4 595	7 037	11 816	16 763	11.9	8.9	10.9	7.2
	Total	146 395	207 322	263 483	330 909	405 343	7.2	4.9	4.7	4.1
Africa[3]	Primary	19 312	26 304	33 372	45 345	61 284	6.4	4.9	6.3	6.2
	Secondary	1 885	3 270	5 353	8 781	13 798	11.6	10.4	10.4	9.5
	Higher	185	311	479	902	1 366	10.9	9.0	13.5	8.7
	Total	21 382	29 884	39 204	55 027	76 448	6.9	5.6	7.0	6.8
Latin America and the Caribbean	Primary	27 601	36 209	47 062	56 252	64 549	5.6	5.4	3.6	2.8
	Secondary	3 039	4 978	7 528	12 391	17 655	10.4	8.6	10.5	7.3
	Higher	573	913	1 638	3 654	5 156	9.8	12.4	17.4	7.1
	Total	31 212	42 101	56 229	72 297	87 361	6.2	6.0	5.2	3.9
South Asia	Primary	73 595	101 631	121 296	143 593	164 854	6.7	3.6	3.4	2.8
	Secondary	16 196	26 745	37 439	48 188	61 561	10.6	7.0	5.2	5.0
	Higher	1 811	3 305	4 821	7 086	9 819	12.8	7.8	8.0	6.7
	Total	91 602	131 682	163 556	198 867	236 234	7.5	4.4	4.0	3.5
China	Primary	93 790	116 210	105 280	150 940	146 270	4.4	−2.0	7.4	−0.6
	Secondary	14 870	14 320	26 480	45 370	56 778	−0.7	13.1	11.4	4.6
	Higher	962	674	48	501	1 161	−6.9	−41.1	59.8	18.3
	Total	109 622	131 204	131 808	196 811	204 209	3.7	0.1	8.3	0.7

1. See Table 12 for composition of regions referred to in this Appendix.
2. Not including China, the Democratic People's Republic of Korea or Namibia.
3. Not including Namibia.

265

latter countries' share of primary-school enrolment for the world from 50 per cent in 1960 to 70 per cent in 1980.

Comparing the average annual rates of growth given in Table 1 we note that while South Asia had the highest growth rate of the three major developing regions during the period 1960–65 and Latin America and the Caribbean during the period 1965–70, during the 1970s the growth rates for Africa exceeded by far those of the other two regions.

Secondary education
The number of additional pupils enrolled in secondary education increased considerably in Africa as well as in Latin America and the Caribbean during each of the four periods covered. This differs from the situation in South Asia where the increments during the first three periods were about equal and markedly lower than that registered between 1975 and 1980. The industrialized countries showed a sharp increase in the additional number of secondary-school pupils between 1960 and 1965. The increments observed during each of the following two five-year periods were only about half those of the period 1960–65, while the decline between 1975 and 1980, owing to a drop in the population of secondary school age, was even sharper. As a result, the developing countries' share of the global secondary school enrolment increased from 32 per cent in 1960 to 55 per cent in 1980.

With regard to the relative increase in enrolment, we note that the growth rates for secondary education exceeded those of primary education for each of the five major regions included in Table 1 during all four periods. It is also interesting to note that Africa during the 1960s as well as during the period 1975–80 achieved higher rates of growth in secondary education than did Latin America and the Caribbean and South Asia. During the third period, 1970–75, Africa had a level of growth approximately equal to that of Latin America and the Caribbean, but considerably larger than that achieved by South Asia. In fact, apart from the period 1960–65, South Asia's rates of growth were markedly lower than those of Latin America and the Caribbean and indeed lower than those of Africa.

Higher education
The marked increments in the number of students enrolled in higher education in Africa as well as in Latin America and the Caribbean during each of the two periods 1960–65 and 1965–70 were followed by even sharper increases between 1970 and 1975. During the last half of the 1970s, this trend changed markedly. In South Asia, the rates registered during the two decades clearly reveal the trend towards a decline. For the industrialized countries the increments of between 5.3 and 6.2 million achieved during each of the first three periods were reduced by more than half during the period 1975–80. By 1980 the share of the developing countries in total higher education had increased to 36 per cent from 21 per cent in 1960.

It is noteworthy that for developing countries as a whole, as well as for industrialized countries, the growth rates for higher education exceed those of secondary education which in turn exceed those of primary education for each of the four periods covered. However, this generalization does not hold true when we take each of the four developing regions separately. For example, secondary level enrolment increased more rapidly than enrolment in higher education in Africa during the 1960s. The same was true of Latin America between 1960 and 1965.

Appendixes

TABLE 2.   Girls as a percentage of total enrolment by level of education, 1960-80

Region	First level 1960	First level 1970	First level 1980	Second level 1960	Second level 1970	Second level 1980	Third level 1960	Third level 1970	Third level 1980
Industrialized countries	49	49	49	49	49	50	35	41	46
Developing countries	39	42	44	28	34	39	24	29	34
Africa	36	40	44	29	32	38	17	23	27
Latin America and the Caribbean	48	49	49	47	48	50	30	35	44
South Asia	36	40	41	25	31	36	24	27	31

Disparity in enrolment between boys and girls

Table 2 shows the percentage that the enrolment of girls constituted of total enrolment in each of the three levels of education in 1960, 1970 and 1980. For industrialized countries the representation of girls in primary and secondary education was about equal to that of boys for each of the three years shown. The proportion of girls in higher education in these countries increased considerably during the two decades covered, from 35 per cent in 1960 to 46 per cent in 1980.

For the developing countries, the enrolment of girls in 1980 was markedly lower than for boys, particularly in secondary and higher education, in spite of considerable improvement during the previous twenty-year period. There were, however, fairly large differences between the three developing regions. In Latin America and the Caribbean the representation of girls in primary and secondary education was already practically equal to that of boys in 1960, while girls' participation in higher education increased rapidly, from 30 per cent in 1960 to 44 per cent in 1980. As regards Africa and South Asia, the enrolment of girls was still markedly lower than that of boys in 1980, particularly in secondary and higher education, and this in spite of quite significant increases since 1960.

Trends in enrolment ratios

The data and projections relating to enrolment ratios for the period 1960-80 are shown in Table 3 for the five major regions and for the thirty-one countries classified by the United Nations as the 'least developed countries'.

The two types of enrolment ratios given in Table 3 offer two complementary measurements of the development of enrolment as compared with population growth during the period 1960-80. The figures given in this table reveal a whole range of disparities of paramount importance for the analysis of future trends.

Disparities in enrolment ratios between industrialized and developing countries
Enrolment capacity of *primary schools* in the industrialized countries was more than sufficient, throughout the last two decades, to take in all children of primary-school age. In the developing countries, by contrast, despite a quite remarkable

Appendixes

TABLE 3. Percentage enrolment ratios by level of education and by age-group, 1960–80

Region	Year	Adjusted gross enrolment ratios[1] First level	Adjusted gross enrolment ratios[1] Second level	Adjusted gross enrolment ratios[1] Third level	Enrolment ratios by age-groups[2] 6–11 years	Enrolment ratios by age-groups[2] 12–17 years	Enrolment ratios by age-groups[2] 18–23 years
Industrialized countries	1960	106	55	12.8	91	70	14.8
	1965	106	65	19.6	91	77	23.9
	1970	106	70	23.4	92	80	26.6
	1975	105	76	28.3	93	82	30.5
	1980	107	78	30.0	93	83	32.2
Developing countries	1960	60	13	2.0	47	21	3.7
	1965	70	18	3.3	55	27	5.4
	1970	74	22	4.3	58	31	6.9
	1975	80	26	6.1	63	35	9.4
	1980	86	31	7.4	68	39	11.2
Africa	1960	44	5	0.7	34	16	1.9
	1965	52	8	1.1	41	21	2.8
	1970	57	11	1.6	43	26	4.2
	1975	67	16	2.5	52	32	6.3
	1980	78	21	3.2	63	37	7.9
Latin America and the Caribbean	1960	73	14	3.0	58	37	5.8
	1965	82	19	4.2	64	43	8.1
	1970	92	25	6.3	72	51	11.3
	1975	98	35	11.8	76	59	18.1
	1980	104	44	14.3	81	64	22.2
South Asia	1960	62	15	2.2	48	19	3.8
	1965	72	21	3.7	56	25	5.5
	1970	74	24	4.6	58	28	6.6
	1975	79	27	5.6	62	30	8.0
	1980	83	31	6.7	66	32	9.1
Least developed countries	1960	29	4	0.2	21	9	0.7
	1965	34	6	0.4	25	12	1.0
	1970	39	9	0.9	29	16	1.9
	1975	51	13	1.2	38	21	2.6
	1980	57	15	1.7	43	24	3.3

1. The gross enrolment ratios are the more accurate indicators of the coverage of a particular level of education. The ratios for primary and secondary education are adjusted to national structures. For example, for primary education the ratio for a particular region is obtained by dividing the region's total enrolment at this level by a population equalling the sum of the primary-school age populations according to national definitions for all countries comprising this region. This ratio may thus be interpreted as an indicator of the 'capacity' of the region's primary schools measured in terms of the 'number of available places' in relation to the primary-school age population. However, this ratio is not without its drawbacks. First, it does not take account of the fact that the number of children actually enrolled is determined not only by the availability of educational opportunities but also by the demand for education and the use made of the opportunities offered. Second, this enrolment ratio gives at best an indication of the potential school capacity, no account being taken of repetitions or of late entries. Third, the enrolment figures used in calculating enrolment ratios refer to registration at the start of the school year and, as a result, frequently overestimate to a considerable extent the actual attendance of pupils at school. Fourth, the adjusted gross enrolment ratios disregard the fact that in some regions where the primary cycle is shorter the school capacity required in order to attain universal primary education is less than that needed in other regions where the cycle is longer.
2. The age-specific enrolment ratios are purely demographic indicators, showing the proportion of given age-groups enrolled at school; they should not be used as indicators of enrolment at any particular level of education. This is especially true for most developing countries where, owing to late entrants and repeaters, a considerable proportion of the pupils enrolled are 'over-aged'.

boom since 1960, there were still primary-school facilities for only some 86 per cent of the school-age population in 1980. Since the rate of repetition is lower in industrialized countries than in developing countries, even though the level of attendance is higher (owing to compulsory schooling), the gap in the percentages of primary-school enrolments between these two groups of countries is actually greater than that indicated by the figures shown in Table 3. For example, as regards repetition, if we take an average for all developing countries, we find that 12–14 per cent of their primary-school pupils are repeaters, as compared with about 2 per cent in the industrialized countries (see 'Projections for out-of-school youth' below). Thus at the start of the 1980s, the numbers enrolled in the developing countries, net of repeaters, corresponded to about three-quarters of their population of primary-school age. Owing to the high drop-out rate common to most developing countries this means that more than three-quarters of the population of entry age were admitted to school but that a considerably lower proportion actually completed primary education. In fact data on enrolment in the first grade of primary education show that, in general, for each of the three regions—Africa, Latin America and the Caribbean, and South Asia—the number of pupils in this grade exceeds the number of children of admission age. The paradox resides in the fact that a part of this 'capacity' is occupied by repeaters. More important than this is the statistic showing that in developing countries about 15 per cent of those admitted to Grade 1 do not reach Grade 2.

Enrolment in *secondary schools* grew quickly in both industrialized and developing countries during the last two decades. However, while for primary education the gap in enrolment ratios between these two groups of countries was reduced in both absolute and relative terms, this was not the case for secondary education where the gap (in absolute terms) widened from 42 percentage points in 1960 (55 per cent for industrialized countries compared to 13 per cent for developing countries) to 47 points in 1980 (78 per cent compared to 31 per cent). The real gap in secondary school 'capacity' between these two groups of countries is even higher than that suggested by these two figures, since the level of repetition is higher in developing countries than in industrialized countries (see 'Trends in grade repetition and withdrawal in primary education' below).

Enrolment in *higher education* increased at an exceptionally rapid rate both in developed and developing countries over the last two decades. Thus, between 1960 and 1970 the enrolment ratio in the developing countries more than doubled (from 2.0 per cent to 4.3 per cent) while that of the industrialized countries almost doubled (from 12.8 to 23.4 per cent). During the 1970s the ratios for both groups of countries continued to increase, although the rate of increase of enrolment slowed down, particularly in industrialized countries and especially during the second half of the 1970s. However, in spite of this comparatively more rapid growth in developing than in industrialized countries, the gap between the enrolment ratios in higher education for these two groups of countries widened appreciably during the twenty-year period, going from 10.8 percentage points in 1960 to 19.1 points in 1970 and to 22.6 points in 1980. Thus, the enrolment ratio achieved in higher education in 1980 in the developing countries (7.4 per cent) was only slightly over half that achieved in the industrialized countries in 1960 (12.8 per cent), i.e. before the start of the enrolment explosion at this level in the latter group of countries.

A study of the expansion of higher education during this twenty-year period will show that, particularly in the industrialized countries, important changes took place in the choices made by students as regards fields and duration of studies, and also in the socio-economic background, age and sex of the student population. These changes can unfortunately not be studied in a generalized report such as this one. Suffice it to mention here the very rapid increase, observed in many countries, of enrolments in higher education of the short cycle type; even faster expansion, in many cases, of non-university as compared with university higher education (although the distinction between the two sectors is becoming increasingly blurred); the increased access of girls and women; and changes in the social origin of students.

Disparities in enrolment ratios between developing regions
The average enrolment ratios for the developing countries mask large differences between countries and regions. The country differences in primary education is examined below (see 'Progress towards universal primary education by 1980'). As regards differences between the three major developing regions, Table 3 shows that in 1980 the enrolment ratios at all three levels of education were markedly higher in Latin America and the Caribbean than in South Asia and Africa. For example, Latin America and the Caribbean's ratio of 44 per cent for secondary education in 1980 was more than twice that of Africa and about 1.4 times that of South Asia. It was during the 1970s that Latin America and the Caribbean began to outstrip South Asia, the two regions having had secondary-school enrolment ratios of about the same magnitude during the 1960s. At the third level, the enrolment ratio for Latin America and the Caribbean in 1980 was more than four times that of Africa and more than twice that of South Asia.

With regard to the differences in enrolment ratios between Africa and South Asia, it is interesting to note that the gap of 18 percentage points which existed in primary education in 1960 was reduced only slightly during the 1960s (17 points in 1970) but then fell very sharply during the 1970s to reach a difference of only 5 percentage points in 1980.

We note also from Table 3 that although the least developed countries doubled the enrolment 'capacity' of their primary schools during the last two decades, their enrolment ratio at this level was only 57 per cent in 1980, while that for the secondary level barely reached 15 per cent.

Differences in enrolment ratios by level of education and by age
An analysis of enrolment ratios by age-groups reveals that the industrialized countries at the beginning of the 1980s had already attained close to universal enrolment for the 16–17 age-group, and that as much as a third of the 18–23 age-group was in attendance, mainly at institutions of higher learning. The enrolment ratio for the developing countries was about three-quarters of that of the industrialized countries for the 6–11 age-group, half for the 12–17 age-group, and a third for the 18–23 age-group.

With respect to the differences between the two sets of ratios, the gross enrolment ratios for primary education is, for all regions, higher than the ratio for the 6–11 age-group, while the gross enrolment ratios for secondary and higher education are lower than the ratios for, respectively, the 12–17 and 18–23 age-groups. However, the magnitude of the differences between the two sets of ratios varies considerably from one region to another, reflecting corresponding regional differences in educational structures as well as in the age distribution of the pupils enrolled. These regional differences in the gap between the two sets of ratios are particularly marked when we compare the ratios for secondary education and the 12–17 age-group for South Asia with those for Latin America and the Caribbean; i.e. a difference of only one percentage point for the former region in 1980 as compared with 20 percentage points for the latter. Therefore the warning given earlier as regards the danger of interpreting the enrolment ratio for the 12–17 age-group as an indicator of secondary education coverage cannot be sufficiently stressed.

In the case of the industrialized countries, the difference between the enrolment ratios for primary education and the 6–11 age-group is explained partly by the fact that the age for admission to primary education differs from country to country, and partly by data classification variations in some federal states. As regards the former aspect, the ratio for the 6–11 age-group excludes 5-year-old pupils enrolled in primary education while the denominator of the adjusted gross enrolment ratio excludes 6-year-old children in countries where 7 is the official age of admission. Both of these factors tend to lower the ratio for the 6–11 age-group as compared with that of primary education.

The differences between the two sets of ratios for Africa and Latin America and the Caribbean are mainly explained by the fact that a large proportion of the primary-school pupils in these two regions are more than 11 years old and a large proportion of the secondary-school pupils are older than 17 years. This disparity is caused partly by grade repetitions and late entrants, and partly by the fact that primary education in some populous countries starts at the age of 7 and has more than six grades.

Lastly, the difference between the ratios for primary education and the 6–11 age-group for South Asia is mainly due to the large number of 5-year-olds enrolled in Bangladesh, India and Pakistan and because these three populous countries have only five grades of primary education. These two factors also explain why only a comparatively small proportion of primary-school pupils are aged 12 years or above, and why the enrolment ratio for the 12–17 age-group is only marginally larger than the gross enrolment ratio for secondary education.

Progress towards universal primary education by 1980

During the last two decades most developing countries have established the achievement of universal primary education (UPE) as one of their priority targets for national development.[1] Unesco has encouraged this process by convening a

1. In quantitative terms a country is generally said to have achieved UPE when its gros enrolment ratio for this level attains 100 per cent, i.e. when the number of primary-school pupils equals the number of children of primary-school age. However, since enrolment ratios are inflated by the inclusion of repeaters and late entrants and depressed by drop-outs, this is not a precise yardstick. High repetition may, for example, cause enrolment ratios exceeding 100 per cent even in cases where not all children enter school. Conversely, a high level of wastage may depress enrolment ratios below 100 per cent even in cases where everybody enters school. The regional targets for UPE were also defined as the attainment of a gross enrolment ratio of 100 per cent. Applied at the regional level, this definition has an additional ambiguity caused by the considerable diversity in the duration of primary education found within most regions.

Appendixes

TABLE 4. Developing countries classified according to gross enrolment ratio (national systems) in primary education and percentage of region's population of primary-school age, 1980

Region	Gross enrolment ratios for primary education								
	Below 50%	50–59%	60–69%	70–79%	80–89%	90–94%	95–99%	100% and above
Africa (41 countries)	Burkina Faso, Burundi, Chad, Ethiopia, Gambia, Guinea, Mali, Mauritania, Niger, Senegal, Sierra Leone, Somalia	Sudan	Benin, Liberia, Malawi, Rwanda, Uganda	Central African Republic, Egypt, Ghana, Ivory Coast, Morocco, Zimbabwe	Equatorial Guinea, Nigeria	Zaire	Algeria, Guinea-Bissau, Kenya, Mozambique, Zambia	Botswana, Cameroon, Lesotho, Madagascar, Mauritius, Swaziland, Togo, Tunisia, United Republic of Tanzania
(100%)	18.8%	4.2%	8.6%	20.6%	16.5%	6.8%	13.9%	10.6%
Latin America and the Caribbean (26 countries)			Guatemala, Haiti		Bolivia, El Salvador, Honduras	Brazil, Nicaragua, Trinidad and Tobago	Guyana, Jamaica	Argentina, Barbados, Chile, Colombia, Costa Rica, Cuba, Dominican Republic, Ecuador, Mexico, Panama, Paraguay, Peru, Puerto Rico, Suriname, Uruguay, Venezuela
(100%)			3.4%		4.7%	39.9%	0.8%	51.1%
South Asia (28 countries)	Afghanistan, Bhutan, Yemen	Pakistan	Bangladesh, Oman, Saudi Arabia	India	Burma, Nepal, Yemen Democratic Republic	Malaysia	Kuwait, Lao People's Democratic Republic, Sri Lanka, Syrian Arab Republic, Thailand	Bahrain, Indonesia, Islamic Republic of Iran, Iraq, Lebanon, Philippines, Qatar, Singapore, Turkey, United Arab Emirates, Viet Nam
(100%)	2.3%	6.5%	7.4%	47.0%	3.2%	1.1%	6.1%	26.4%
Oceania (2 countries)			Papua New Guinea					Fiji
(100%)			78.2%					21.8%
Total (97 countries)	15 countries	2 countries	11 countries	7 countries	8 countries	5 countries	12 countries	37 countries

number of regional conferences which, *inter alia*, have urged the participating nations to attain this goal within a specific time limit. Thus, at the 1960 Karachi conference, 1980 was set as the target year for achieving UPE in most Asian countries. The same target year was agreed upon by the African States (in Addis Ababa, 1961) and the Arab States (in Tripoli, 1966), while the Santiago conference in 1962 called upon the Latin American and the Caribbean countries to achieve this objective by 1970.

Looking at the progress made towards UPE by 1980, it can be seen from Table 3 that the adjusted gross enrolment ratios reached in this year were 78 per cent in Africa, 83 per cent in South Asia and 104 per cent in Latin America and the Caribbean. These aggregate figures are of course heavily affected by the level of enrolment in the most populous countries in each region. Table 4 provides some information on disparities in the development of primary education within each of the three major developing regions.

Although Table 4 reveals that many countries did not achieve the regional targets of universal primary education by 1980, it is none the less true that these targets made a useful contribution towards mobilizing resources for education in the developing countries. By doing so, they also doubtless did much to enhance the value of human resources in the Third World and, as a result, to foster the democratization of education.

Trends in grade repetition and withdrawal in primary education

The figures given in Table 3 suggest that, on average, for all developing countries, enrolment in primary schools corresponded in 1980 to about 86 per cent of their population of primary-school age. However, since enrolment ratios are affected by repetition and dropping out, they at best give a very approximate picture of the proportion of a region's primary-school population which actually completes this level of education. For example, a country with a low drop-out rate, but high repetition, may have an enrolment exceeding the population of primary-school age even if a large percentage of this age-group never enters school. Conversely, a country where all children enter school may have an enrolment ratio well below 100 per cent, owing to a high drop-out rate. In the next section a brief review will be given of the level of repetition and dropping out in primary education towards the end of the 1970s.

Dropping out
The performance of an educational system should be measured in terms of the quantity as well as the quality of its output. Although output is difficult to define in meaningful, measurable terms, for primary education it may be assumed that the main objective in the early grades is to give pupils the rudiments of instruction. To attain this goal, it is not only necessary that children enter the first grade of primary education, but also that they remain enrolled for a sufficient number of years. Dropping out during primary education is obviously not compatible with the attainment of that objective, particularly if it occurs before the child has acquired literacy skills.

Table 5 shows rates of survival up to the final grade of primary school, should

Appendixes

TABLE 5.   Classification of countries according to level of drop-out prior to the final grade of primary education, cohorts starting school around 1978–79

Region	Drop-out range	Median drop-out	50% and above	Between 49% and 25%	24% and below	Total
Africa	6–72%	33%	6	19	10	35
Latin America and the Caribbean	12–70%	34%	6	10	4	20
Asia and Oceania	0–75%	10%	4	4	20	28
Europe	0–28%	5%	0	1	16	17
Total	0–75%	25%	16	34	50	100

(Number of countries where the percentage of the cohort dropping out prior to the final grade is)

the promotion, repetition and drop-out rates observed around 1978–79 remain stable in the future.[1] The first two columns give, for four major regions, the range and the median[2] value of the percentage of the cohort dropping out prior to the final grade of primary education, while the following three columns distribute countries according to their wastage level.

The figures shown in Table 5 illustrate the relatively high drop-out level in the developing regions as well as the considerable disparity in drop-out between as well as within regions. Thus the proportion of the cohort dropping out for the countries covered prior to the final grade of the cycle ranged from 0 to 75 per cent. The median level of drop-out was 5 per cent in Europe, 10 per cent in Asia and Oceania, 33 per cent in Africa and 34 per cent in Latin America and the Caribbean. The median value for all the hundred countries covered was 25 per cent. The figures on wastage levels show that while sixteen out of seventeen European countries had a drop-out level below this median value, only slightly more than one-third of the developing countries could boast as much.

Repetition

Table 6 shows the percentage of primary-school enrolment constituted by repeaters in 113 countries and territories. The data refer to the years around 1978–79. The considerable disparities in the level of repetition between developing countries are most striking in this table. These disparities are particularly large in Africa where the level of repetition ranged from 0 per cent (United Republic of Tanzania) to 47 per cent (Sao Tome and Principe). Although high, the range between countries was somewhat lower in the three other regions.

1. All estimates concerning survival and dropping out presented in this section are derived by means of the 'reconstruction cohort method'. Using data on promotion, repetition and drop-out rates, this method permits us to estimate the progression of a cohort throughout a cycle of education, on calculating for each grade and year the number of pupils who repeat a given grade, are promoted to the following grade or drop out.
2. The median value indicates the position of the 'middle case' when countries are ranked according to their wastage level prior to the last grade of the cycle under consideration.

TABLE 6. Percentage of repeaters in primary education, latest year available (generally 1978 or 1979)

Region	Below 5%		5-9%		10-14%		15-19%		20-24%		25-29%		30% and over	
Africa	United Republic of Tanzania	0	Kenya	6	Uganda	10	Libya	15	Benin	20	Comoros	25	Central African Republic	30
	Seychelles	1	Rwanda	6	Liberia	11	Lesotho	16	Zaire	20	Congo	26	Morocco	30
	Zambia	1	Egypt	8	Swaziland	11	Senegal	16	Tunisia	21	Mali	27	Togo	31
	Ghana	2			Algeria	12	Malawi	17	Guinea	22	Burundi	29	Guinea-Bissau	33
	Botswana	3			Gambia	13	Burkina Faso	17	Madagascar	24	Cameroon	29	Gabon	35
					Mauritania	14	Djibouti	19					Chad	38
					Niger	14	Ivory Coast	19					Sao Tome and Principe	47
							Réunion	19						
Latin America and the Caribbean	Antigua and Barbuda	2	Cuba	5	Argentina	10	Guatemala	15	Brazil	20	Suriname	26		
	Jamaica	4	Guyana	7	Mexico	10	Uruguay	15	Haiti	21				
			Costa Rica	8	Grenada	11	Peru	16						
			El Salvador	8	Chile	13	Guadeloupe	17						
			Venezuela	9	Ecuador	13	Martinique	17						
					Panama	13	Nicaragua	17						
					Paraguay	14	Dominican Republic	18						
Asia and Oceania	Cyprus	0	Solomon Islands	5	Sri Lanka	10	Qatar	15			Afghanistan	29		
	Japan	0	Tonga	5	Thailand	10	Saudi Arabia	16						
	Republic of Korea	0	Kuwait	7	Turkey	12								
	Malaysia	0	Singapore	7	Oman	12								
	Norfolk Island	1	Viet Nam	7	Bhutan	13								
	Mongolia	2	Indonesia	8	Brunei	14								
	Philippines	2	Syria	8										
	Jordan	3	United Arab Emirates	9										
	Fiji	4												
	Hong Kong	4												
	Kiribati	4												
Europe and the USSR	Denmark	0	Luxembourg	6			Portugal	17						
	Norway	0	France	9			Belgium	19						
	Sweden	0												
	United Kingdom	0												
	USSR	0												
	Czechoslovakia	1												
	Greece	1												
	Italy	1												
	Bulgaria	2												
	Federal Republic of Germany	2												
	Hungary	2												
	Poland	2												
	Switzerland	2												
	Yugoslavia	2												
	Austria	3												
	Netherlands	3												
	Malta	4												

Appendixes

EDUCATION PROJECTIONS FOR THE PERIOD 1980-2000

In this section, some of the consequences of allowing these trends to continue along their main lines for the coming two decades will be analysed, with the reminder that the projections presented below are very much of a conditional nature. Their results are heavily qualified by the data available on past trends; by the projections regarding future changes in the population of school age; by the hypothesis and the projection model chosen to quantify the implications of continuing these trends and projections; as well as by the long period covered. There is therefore no doubt that actual future development, particularly for the years beyond 1990, could be quite different from that suggested by these extrapolations. Indeed, the main purpose of conditional projections is to serve as an early warning signal for the competent authorities, by indicating a need for policy decisions which would change prevailing trends in cases where their continuation would lead to results contradictory to national educational objectives. Concerted actions would have to be taken by many countries in order to bring about a future development different from that suggested by the results shown below.

Projections of enrolment ratios

Table 7, covering the period 1980-2000, sets out data and projections regarding enrolment ratios for the three age-groups 6-11, 12-17 and 18-23 years in the major regions and subregions and the adjusted gross enrolment ratios for the first, second and third levels of education. The table shows that continuation of the enrolment trends of the last two decades would imply that enrolment in the developing countries' *primary schools* would correspond to about 96 per cent of their primary-school age population in the year 2000. Latin America and the Caribbean, which in 1980 already had an enrolment ratio at this level exceeding 100 per cent, would see a further small increase while Africa and South Asia would both pass the 90 per cent mark. In the least developed countries, enrolment in primary schools would correspond to about four-fifths of their population of primary-school age. As discussed above, the 'real' coverage of primary education as compared to the developing countries' population of primary-school age is lower than that suggested by these enrolment ratios, which are inflated by repeaters and because a number of the pupils registered in the beginning of the school year drop out during the year. Thus, although continuation of past trends would imply a notable progress towards universal primary education during the next two decades, Africa and South Asia would, by the end of this century, still be a good distance from that goal.

To continue past trends would lead to a substantial increase in enrolment in *second level education* in the developing countries, and the enrolment would be equal to about half of their population of secondary-school age in the year 2000, up from about one-third in 1980. Notwithstanding this considerable increase, implying a growth in enrolment at this level of 124 per cent between 1980 and 2000, the secondary-school enrolment ratio at the turn of the century would be below the 55 per cent achieved by the industrialized countries in 1960.

The disparities in secondary-school enrolment ratios between the three major

Appendixes

TABLE 7. Percentage projections of enrolment ratios by level of education and by age-group, 1980–2000

Region	Year	Adjusted gross enrolment ratios			Enrolment ratios by age-groups		
		First level	Second level	Third level	6–11 years	12–17 years	18–23 years
Industrialized countries	1980	107	78	30.0	93	83	32.2
	1985	107	83	31.5	93	89	33.3
	1990	106	85	34.2	93	91	36.4
	1995	106	86	35.6	93	90	37.9
	2000	105	87	37.6	93	90	39.8
Developing countries[1]	1980	86	31	7.4	68	39	11.2
	1985	89	37	8.7	72	43	13.0
	1990	92	42	9.9	75	46	14.6
	1995	94	46	10.9	77	49	16.1
	2000	96	49	11.8	79	51	17.3
Africa[2]	1980	78	21	3.2	63	37	7.9
	1985	84	29	4.2	69	44	10.0
	1990	88	35	5.1	74	48	12.0
	1995	91	39	5.9	77	52	13.9
	2000	93	43	6.4	80	54	15.1
Latin America and the Caribbean	1980	104	44	14.3	81	64	22.2
	1985	106	53	17.6	84	69	25.9
	1990	107	59	21.0	86	73	29.5
	1995	109	64	23.6	87	76	32.7
	2000	109	67	25.9	89	77	35.2
South Asia	1980	83	31	6.7	66	32	9.1
	1985	86	35	7.7	70	35	10.3
	1990	89	40	8.5	72	38	11.3
	1995	91	43	9.3	75	40	12.4
	2000	93	47	10.1	77	42	13.4
Least developed countries	1980	57	15	1.7	43	24	3.3
	1985	64	19	2.6	49	28	4.7
	1990	71	23	3.1	55	32	5.7
	1995	77	28	3.8	59	36	7.0
	2000	82	32	4.4	63	40	8.1

1. Not including China, the Democratic People's Republic of Korea or Namibia.
2. Not including Namibia.

developing regions would continue to be considerable, ranging from a ratio of 43 per cent in the year 2000 for Africa to 67 per cent in the same year for Latin America and the Caribbean. In spite of the fact that Africa would double its enrolment ratio at the second level during the next two decades, by the year 2000 that continent's ratio would still be slightly lower than that achieved in Latin America and the Caribbean in 1980. The second level enrolment ratio for South Asia would increase from 31 per cent in 1980 to 47 per cent in the year 2000. Finally, enrolment of secondary schools of the least developed countries would correspond to 32 per cent of their population of secondary-school age, up from 15 per cent in 1980.

If past trends were to continue, the largest increase in enrolment ratios, measured in relative terms, would take place in *higher education*. Thus, the enrolment ratio for Africa would double between 1980 and 2000, while those of Latin America and the Caribbean as well as South Asia would increase by about four-fifths and one-half respectively. Furthermore, at the third level the large disparities existing in 1980 would continue and even widen. We note in particular that Latin America and the Caribbean, in the year 2000, would have an enrolment ratio 2.5 times that of South Asia and four times that of Africa. Notwithstanding this fact, the enrolment ratio for Latin America and the Caribbean in the year 2000 would be lower than that attained by the industrialized countries in 1975. Finally, enrolment in institutions of higher learning in the least developed countries, in spite of an increase of 150 per cent between 1980 and the year 2000, would remain quite modest compared with the other regions and would, by the end of the century, barely surpass the comparatively low value attained by Africa in 1985.

As regards the industrialized countries, continuation of past enrolment trends would imply that the growth in the enrolment ratio for secondary education would level off in the 1980s and that this ratio would remain between 83 and 81 per cent during the period 1985-2000. The enrolment 'capacity' of higher education institutions would continue to increase, though less spectacularly than during the past two decades.

Projections of enrolment

Table 8 shows that although the developing countries' enrolment ratio for *primary education* is projected to increase rather moderately during the next two decades (9 percentage points—see Table 7), in terms of enrolment the increase would be very considerable, going from about 292 million in 1980 to 455 million in the year 2000. This would imply an increase of some 164 million or 56 per cent over the next two decades compared with an increase of some 170 million or 139 per cent over the previous two decades. This is in contrast to the industrialized countries, which would see their number of primary school pupils increase by only some 8 million between 1980 and the year 2000. As a consequence, the share of the developing countries in total primary-school enrolment would increase from 50 per cent in 1960 to 70 per cent in 1980, and further to 77 per cent by the year 2000.

Examining the enrolment increase during each of the four decades covered in Table 8, we note that the number of additional primary-school pupils enrolled in the developing countries was about 82 million between 1960 and 1970, rising to 88 million between 1970 and 1980. It would be 83 million during the 1980s and 81 million during the 1990s.

As regards *secondary education*, the developing countries would see their enrolment at this level increase from 97 million in 1980 to 217 million in the year 2000, i.e. an increase of some 120 million or 124 per cent, compared with an increase of 75 million or 343 per cent during the previous two decades. (This high percentage increase between 1960 and 1980 is naturally related to the comparatively low enrolment in 1960.) The enrolment growth between 1980 and the year 2000 would also at the second level be particularly high in Africa (284 per cent), followed by Latin America and the Caribbean (115 per cent) and South Asia (99 per cent). Thus, all three major developing regions would at least double their secondary-school enrolment during the next two decades.

Appendixes

TABLE 8. Trends and projections of enrolment by level of education, 1960-2000

	Level of education	Number of pupils enrolled (thousands)					Average annual rates of growth			
		1960	1970	1980	1990	2000	1960-70	1970-80	1980-90	1990-2000
Industrialized countries	Primary	124 077	137 711	125 454	130 920	133 702	1.1	—0.9	0.4	0.2
	Secondary	46 429	70 519	80 574	81 087	86 734	4.3	1.3	0.1	0.7
	Higher	9 599	21 105	29 719	31 166	34 955	8.2	3.4	0.5	1.1
	Total[1]	180 105	229 335	235 747	243 172	255 391	2.5	0.3	0.3	0.5
Developing countries[2]	Primary	121 982	204 343	291 968	374 478	455 490	5.3	3.6	2.5	1.9
	Secondary	21 788	52 104	96 611	155 234	216 840	9.1	6.4	4.8	3.4
	Higher	2 625	7 037	16 763	27 942	39 946	10.4	9.1	5.2	3.6
	Total[1]	146 395	263 483	405 342	557 653	712 276	6.0	4.4	3.2	2.5

1. Totals and sub-totals may not necessarily add up correctly due to rounding of figures.
2. Not including China, the Democratic People's Republic of Korea or Namibia.

The high growth in developing countries contrasts with the situation in industrialized countries where, despite a significant increase in the enrolment ratio, the number of secondary-school pupils would decrease by approximately 3 per cent between 1980 and 1990. The data and projections by single calendar year show that this relative levelling-off in secondary-school enrolment starts in the late 1970s and continues until the early 1990s, at which time the enrolment would again start to increase very rapidly. These fluctuations in enrolment, caused by corresponding waves in the population of school age, represent a serious problem in many industrialized countries. Finally, we note that by the end of the century, the share of the developing countries in total enrolment in secondary education in the countries covered here would be some 71 per cent, up from 32 per cent in 1960 and 55 per cent in 1980.

Turning now to *higher education*, we may start by drawing attention to the fact that the aggregated model used to derive the projections presented in this report is probably less well suited for projecting enrolment at this level than for primary and secondary education. The results shown here should therefore be interpreted with the utmost caution. Bearing this reservation in mind, we note that these projections portend an increase in the developing countries of 11.2 million students during the 1980s (67 per cent) and 12 million during the 1990s (43 per cent), compared with an increase of 4.4 million (168 per cent) during the 1960s and 9.7 million (138 per cent) during the 1970s. During the whole period 1980–2000 the enrolment in higher education would increase by some 274 per cent in Africa, 166 per cent in Latin America and the Caribbean and 113 per cent in South Asia.

Thus, the continuation of past trends would imply a substantial increase of student numbers in developing countries during the coming two decades. In view of factors such as the high unit costs of higher education, the widening gap in many countries between requirements and resources available for education, the efforts to give priority to some basic education for all and the increasing levels of unemployment for graduates, one may well question whether developing countries can manage to follow the growth path indicated by past trends. On the other hand, in interpreting these figures, one should not lose sight of the fact that these projections imply an enrolment ratio for higher education of only 11.8 per cent for the developing countries in the year 2000, i.e. less than the 12.8 per cent attained by the industrialized countries in 1960.

The growth in student numbers at the third level in the developed countries would be very modest during the 1980s (1.4 million) and somewhat higher during the 1990s (3.8 million). The waves in the school-age population will also affect the development of enrolment at this level (see 'Growth in the school-age population' below). By the end of this century, developing countries' share in the total enrolment in highere ducation would be 53 per cent, up from 21 per cent in 1960 and 36 per cent in 1980. Taking into account the enrolment at all levels of regular education, and excluding China, some 74 per cent of the world's pupils would be in the developing countries in the year 2000, compared with 45 per cent in 1960 and 63 per cent in 1980. Including the enrolment for China, the number of students worldwide will exceed 1,000 million by the end of the 1980s.

Appendixes

Growth in the school-age population

The enrolment projections presented above are largely determined by demographic trend forecasts regarding the school-age population. The enrolment projections included in this report correspond to the 'medium' variant of the population projections established by the United Nations Population Division. The United Nations considers that this variant 'represents future demographic trends that seem more likely to occur considering observed past demographic trends, expected social and economic progress, ongoing government policies and prevailing public attitudes towards population issues'.[1]

In addition to the medium variant, the United Nations also prepares a 'low' and a 'high' variant. These two variants 'indicate the plausible, but not exhaustive, range of future deviations from the medium variant projections because future fertility, mortality and migration rates could take alternative courses under various conditions'.[2]

Table 9 shows the percentage by which the population aged 5–14 years would increase between 1980 and 2000 according to the three population variants. Using the development of this age-group as a proxy for the development of the population of primary-school age we note the following salient features.

The considerable margin of uncertainty associated with the projections of the future population of school age. Thus, depending on how fertility and mortality rates develop, the developing countries' population of primary-school age in year 2000 could be between 25 and 51 per cent greater than that of 1980.

The marked difference in projected future population growth between developed and developing countries. For example, according to the medium variant, the increase in the primary-school age population between 1980 and 2000 would be more than twenty times higher in the latter than in the former countries.

The considerable differences in the projected growth between the three developing regions. We note in particular the high rates of growth in Africa for all three variants. For example, the percentage growth implied for the low variant in Africa is of the same magnitude as that implied by the high variant for Latin America and the Caribbean.

TABLE 9. Percentage increase in population aged 5–14 between 1980 and 2000, by population variant[1]

Region	Low variant	Medium variant	High variant
Industrialized countries	—9.3	1.9	10.7
Developing countries	24.7	40.1	50.7
Africa	47.7	84.6	95.4
Latin America and the Caribbean	26.5	37.9	48.9
South Asia	17.2	26.4	36.7

1. Not including China.

1. See 'World Populations Prospects as Assessed in 1980', New York, United Nations. (ST/ESA/SER.A/78.)
2. Ibid.

Appendixes

To summarize the figures set out in Table 9, it can be said that in order to keep pace with population growth, that is, to maintain in the year 2000 the primary-school enrolment ratios attained in 1980, the developing countries would have to increase their primary-school enrolment by some 25 per cent according to the low population variant, by 40 per cent according to the medium variant, and by 51 per cent according to the high variant. To increase the enrolment ratio would, of course, imply even higher growth. Thus, to attain a projected ratio of 95 per cent by the year 2000, developing countries would (under the medium variant) have to increase their enrolment by 55 per cent between 1980 and 2000, while this increase would have to be of the order of 63 per cent if they were to achieve 100 per cent enrolment.

The high enrolment growth required in the developing countries even to maintain their comparatively lower enrolment ratios is in stark contrast with the situation in the industrialized countries which, according to the medium variant, would be able to maintain their universal enrolment at this level by a 2 per cent increase in enrolment during this twenty-year period. Enrolment could even decrease if the low variant were to hold true. This does not, however, mean that population factors will not also play an important role in future educational development in industrialized countries. This is particularly so because of the fluctuations which occur in their population of school age.

These 'waves' in the age-groups have their source in the way demographic variables evolved three decades ago. After the Second World War, fertility and births increased in most industrialized countries. Known as the post-war baby boom, the phenomenon lasted for varying periods, depending on the particular country. Total births generally peaked in the late 1950s or early 1960s, and therefore throughout the 1960s the 6–11 age-group increased, peaking late in the decade. At the beginning of the 1970s, the fertility rate dropped, and with it the number of births. One repercussion was a decrease in the 6–11 age-group, so that it is now smaller than it was in 1960.

Of course, the other age-groups undergo the same ups and downs, but with six- and twelve-year time lags. The oldest age-group, 18–23, dropped noticeably from 1960 to 1963, reflecting the decreased birth rate and the number of children who died during the Second World War. The augmentation in this age-group after 1965 clearly reflects the post-war baby boom.

Progress towards universal primary education by the year 2000

As shown in Table 7, continuation of the enrolment trends of the last two decades would, according to the projections presented in this report, result in an adjusted gross enrolment ratio for primary education in the developing countries in the year 2000 of about 6 per cent of their population of primary-school age. The corresponding figure would be 93 per cent both for Africa and South Asia. However, in interpreting these global averages we should keep in mind that they mask very different levels of development of primary education within as well as between different developing nations. The purpose of this and the following section is to highlight some aspects of these differences.

In the first place, some of the school facilities are taken up by repeaters and,

Appendixes

as Table 6 shows, the level of repetition varies quite considerably from one country to another. Even if the level of repetition were to decline more rapidly in the future than during the past ten to fifteen years and reach, say, about half of the level observed around 1978, this would still mean 5-7 per cent repeaters in Africa and South Asia, reducing their enrolment ratio, net of repetition, to approximately 85 per cent.

Secondly, the enrolment ratios for primary education set out in Table 7 refer to both sexes together and thus conceal quite important (although declining) differences in enrolment between boys and girls. At the level of primary school, such differences are almost exclusively limited to countries in Africa and South Asia. The detailed projections for the year 2000 yield a primary-school enrolment ratio of 88 per cent for girls, compared with 98 per cent for boys, in Africa; and 85 per cent for girls, compared with 100 per cent for boys, in South Asia. Thus, in the aggregate, one of the main obstacles to the attainment of universal primary education by the year 2000 in these two regions appears to be the comparatively low enrolment of girls.

Thirdly, as regards the attainment of universal primary education, the main concern for most developing countries during the past two decades has been to increase access to education by providing more schools. However, in the 1980s, when most countries have achieved enrolment ratios exceeding 80 per cent (see Table 4), the main concern should be to improve the internal efficiency of the educational system and to enrol population groups which traditionally have enrolment ratios below the national average. As regards the former aspect, the persistently high wastage rates in developing countries are a serious obstacle to the attainment of universal primary education. Clearly, the high drop-out rate at this level of education is a major obstacle to the achievement of such national development targets, also the elimination of illiteracy and equality of educational opportunity for the various population groups. If the drop-out rate does not decline substantially during the next decades, even a considerable increase in enrolment will not in itself be sufficient to cope with the growth of the population and enable the developing countries to win the battle that most of them are now waging against illiteracy.

The improvement of enrolment ratios projected in this study obviously presupposes a constantly diminishing level of drop-out, although no explicit hypothesis on this point can be applied to the type of overall model used to draw up the projections in question. However, it is equally clear that, just as the enrolment ratio gives no indication as to the qualitative performance of an educational system or the percentage of pupils who will complete a given level of instruction, similarly the figures for enrolment ratios in the first year of primary education, for drop-out rates, and for school-leaving certificates awarded, may vary considerably from the ratios projected for the year 2000.

As regards equal access to education, one aspect of this problem has already been mentioned above, namely the disparities in enrolment ratios between boys and girls. Another aspect is the availability of educational opportunities to population groups which, because of their area of residence, ethnic origins and/or socio-economic background, have hitherto been educationally disadvantaged compared with other groups. It should be noted that in many countries, the segment of the child population which has so far not been enrolled is also the segment which will be most difficult, and possibly also most costly, to enrol in future.

Appendixes

TABLE 10. Distribution of the least developed countries by gross ratios of enrolment in primary schools, as projected for the year 2000

Percentage enrolment ratio	Countries	Percentage of the LDC's primary-school age population[1]
Less than 50	Bhutan, Burkina Faso	2.9
50–59	Afghanistan, Chad, Guinea, Mali, Niger	15.9
60–69	Burundi, Gambia	1.8
70–79	Ethiopia, Uganda, Yemen	20.2
80–89	Bangladesh, Malawi, Rwanda, Sudan	39.3
90–99	Benin, Central African Republic, Haiti, Somalia, Democratic Yemen	6.9
100 and above	Botswana, Guinea-Bissau, Lao People's Democratic Republic, Lesotho, Nepal, United Republic of Tanzania	13.0
		100.0

1. Not including Cape Verde, the Comoros, Maldives or Samoa.

To serve these groups may require special measures, such as boarding schools for nomads and populations living in sparsely-populated areas; efforts to reduce the direct as well as substitution costs that must be borne by parents who send their children to school; adapting curricula to the special needs of certain population groups; and so on.

Fourthly and lastly, the average enrolment ratios shown in Table 9 do not reveal the fact that the failure to achieve universal primary education by the target year 2000, if past trends continue, would mainly be attributable to a comparatively slow enrolment growth in some countries. These countries would be in Africa and South Asia, and most of them would belong to the group of least developed countries. Thus, among the developing countries twenty-three would in the year 2000 have primary enrolment ratios below 90 per cent (as compared with 43 per cent in 1980), and eighteen of these twenty-three would be among the least developed countries group. The gross enrolment ratios in primary education for this group in the year 2000 would be as shown in Table 10. Thus the continuation of past enrolment trends would mean that 83 per cent of the primary-school age population of the least developed countries would be living in countries with enrolment ratios below 90 per cent at the dawn of the next century.

Projections for out-of-school youth

Table 11 shows that the number of children aged 6–11 who are not enrolled at school in the industrialized countries would change only marginally between 1980 and 2000, while the number of out-of-school youths aged 12–17 years would continue to decrease. The existence of out-of-school children aged 6–11 years in these countries is mainly explained by the fact that the admission age to primary education is 7 in some of them, for example the USSR. As regards the 12–17 age-

Appendixes

TABLE 11. Out-of-school youth (millions)

Region	6–11 age-group 1960	1980	2000	12–17 age-group 1960	1980	2000
Industrialized countries	9.9	7.4	7.9	28.0	19.0	12.0
Developing countries	113.0	114.0	103.0	136.0	191.0	222.0
Africa	28.0	29.0	29.0	30.0	39.0	55.0
Latin America and the Caribbean	14.0	10.0	9.0	17.0	18.0	16.0
South Asia	70.0	76.0	66.0	89.0	133.0	152.0

group it should be recalled that the enrolment figures cover only full-time regular education, and thus exclude part-time vocational education, which is relatively important in some industrialized countries. It should also be borne in mind that at these ages most of the out-of-school youth of industrialized countries have completed primary and a part of secondary education as well.

Table 11 also shows that the number of out-of-school children aged 6–11 years in the developing countries increased by 1 million between 1960 and 1980 and would gradually decrease between 1980 and the year 2000. According to the data for the past two decades, the number of out-of-school children in this age-group had remained practically constant between 1960 and 1980. For the 12–17 age-group, the number of young people not in school increased by 55 million between 1960 and 1980, and would increase by another 31 million between 1980 and the year 2000. Thus, while the percentage of developing countries' youth aged 12–17 not attending school would decline from 61 per cent in 1980 to 49 per cent in the year 2000, the absolute number of out-of-school adolescents in this age-group would increase by some 16 per cent. Looking at the data by regions we see that this increase would take place almost entirely in Africa and South Asia.

The very large number of out-of-school children shown for the developing countries includes five main categories: (a) those who have never entered school; (b) those who have begun their primary education but have dropped out before completing this level; (c) those who have completed primary schooling, but who have not begun their secondary education; (d) those who have begun secondary school but have dropped out before completing this level; and (e) those who have completed their secondary education before age 17 but who have not gone on to higher education.

Unfortunately, the data available for developing countries do not allow us to divide the out-of-school youth shown in Table 11 into these five categories on a regional basis. The problems presented by each of these groups can, therefore, only be sketched here.

In category (a) are children for whom opportunities to enter school are not available; either there are not enough places in schools within their reach, or places are available but their families cannot afford to send them to school. There are also children for whom there are places but whose parents are prejudiced against schooling. Furthermore, there are children who have not yet entered school but who will enter later, such as 6-year-olds in a system where the starting age is 7.

Appendixes

In categories (b) and (d) are children who are rejected by the school as failures, who are withdrawn by the parents or who drop out, or who are disillusioned by school and drift from truancy into drop-out. As discussed above, this group is probably quite large.

In category (c) are children whose parents regard basic literacy and numeracy as being sufficient school-based training and perhaps as conferring a right to gainful employment, and still others for whom places in second-level education are not available. This latter group is no doubt quite large in many countries, and it is growing rapidly.

In category (e) are those young people who have not been able, or have not wanted, to enter higher education. As we are here only considering those under 18 years of age, this category includes a relatively small number.

The problem for the out-of-school youth in the categories (c) to (e) is particularly serious in countries where there is a lack of employment opportunities.

TABLE 12. Composition of major areas and regions[1]

AFRICA

Eastern Africa
Burundi
Comoros
Ethiopia
Kenya
Madagascar
Malawi
Mauritius
Mozambique
Réunion
Rwanda
Somalia
Uganda
United Republic of Tanzania
Zambia
Zimbabwe

Middle Africa
Angola
Cameroon
Central African Republic
Chad
Congo
Equatorial Guinea
Gabon
Zaire

Northern Africa
Algeria
Egypt
Libyan Arab Jamahiriya
Morocco
Sudan
Tunisia

Southern Africa
Botswana
Lesotho
Namibia
South Africa
Swaziland

Western Africa
Benin
Burkina Faso
Cape Verde
Gambia
Ghana
Guinea
Guinea-Bissau
Ivory Coast
Liberia
Mali
Mauritania
Niger

1. Following the practice of the United Nations, the industrialized countries include all European countries, Union of Soviet Socialist Republics, Canada, United States of America, Israel, Japan, South Africa, Australia and New Zealand. All other countries are classified as developing countries. The least developed countries are: Afghanistan, Bangladesh, Benin, Bhutan, Botswana, Burkina Faso, Burundi, Cape Verde, Central African Republic, Chad, Comoros, Democratic Yemen, Ethiopia, Gambia, Guinea, Guinea-Bissau, Haiti, Lao People's Democratic Republic, Lesotho, Malawi, Maldives, Mali, Nepal, Niger, Rwanda, Samoa, Somalia, Sudan, Uganda, United Republic of Tanzania, Yemen.

TABLE 12 *(continued)*

Nigeria
Senegal
Sierra Leone
Togo

LATIN AMERICA AND THE CARIBBEAN

Caribbean

Barbados
Cuba
Dominican Republic
Guadeloupe
Haiti
Jamaica
Martinique
Puerto Rico
Trinidad and Tobago
Windward Islands
Other Caribbean

Middle America

Costa Rica
El Salvador
Guatemala
Honduras
Mexico
Nicaragua
Panama

Temperate South America

Argentina
Chile
Uruguay

Tropical South America

Bolivia
Brazil
Colombia
Ecuador
Guyana
Paraguay
Peru
Suriname
Venezuela

NORTH AMERICA

Canada
United States of America

EAST ASIA

China

Japan

Other East Asian

Democratic People's Republic of Korea
Hong Kong
Mongolia
Republic of Korea

SOUTH ASIA

Eastern South Asia

Burma
Democratic Kampuchea
East Timor
Indonesia
Lao People's Democratic Republic
Malaysia
Philippines
Singapore
Thailand
Viet Nam

Middle South Asia

Afghanistan
Bangladesh
Bhutan
India
Islamic Republic of Iran
Nepal
Pakistan
Sri Lanka

Western South Asia

Bahrain
Cyprus
Democratic Yemen
Iraq
Israel
Jordan
Kuwait
Lebanon
Oman
Qatar
Saudi Arabia
Syrian Arab Republic
Turkey
United Arab Emirates
Yemen

TABLE 12 *(continued)*

EUROPE	Netherlands
	Switzerland
Eastern Europe	
Bulgaria	OCEANIA
Czechoslovakia	
German Democratic Republic	*Australia–New Zealand*
Hungary	Australia
Poland	New Zealand
Romania	
	Melanesia
Northern Europe	New Caledonia
Denmark	Norfolk Islands
Finland	Papua New Guinea
Iceland	Solomon Islands
Ireland	Vanuatu
Norway	
Sweden	*Micronesia–Polynesia*
United Kingdom	Micronesia
	Guam
Southern Europe	Kiribati
Albania	Nauru
Greece	Niue
Italy	Pacific Islands
Malta	Other Micronesia
Portugal	Polynesia
Spain	American Samoa
Yugoslavia	Cook Islands
	Fiji
Western Europe	French Polynesia
Austria	Samoa
Belgium	Tonga
Federal Republic of Germany	Wallis and Futuna Islands
France	
Luxembourg	UNION OF SOVIET SOCIALIST REPUBLICS

Appendix II
Bibliographical notes on the authors

Malcolm Adiseshiah
Educator, President of the Madras Institute of Development Studies. President of the International Council on Adult Education and Chairman of the Governing Board of the International Institute for Educational Planning. Former Deputy Director-General of Unesco. Author of several works on education.

Ivan T. Berend
Historian, Professor at the Karl-Marx University in Budapest, Member of the Planning Commission and President of the Public Education Committee of Hungary.

Oleg K. Dreier
Specialist in African history, which he teaches at Patrice Lumumba University, Moscow. Author of books and articles on educational problems in developing countries.

Jean-Claude Eicher
Economist, Director of the Institute for Research on the Economics of Education and Professor at the University of Dijon, France. Author of several books on the economics of education and on educational resources.

Ingrid Eide
Professor of Sociology at the University of Oslo. Researcher and writer on sociology, educational policy, and on research. Former Deputy Minister of Education and former Deputy in Norway.

Torsten Husén
Educator, Member of the Swedish Royal Academy for Sciences, Director of the Institute of International Education at the University of Stockholm. Chairman of the Governing Board of the International Institute for Educational Planning from 1970 to 1980. Researcher specialized in the reform of educational systems, author of more than fifty books on education.

Jean-Pierre Jallade
Economist, researcher on the economics of education and the relation between education, training and employment, at the European Institute of Education and Social Policy at the University of Paris (Dauphine).

Appendixes

Mircea Malitza
Former Romanian Minister of Education and Professor at the Mathematics Faculty of the University of Bucharest. Author of several works on education and on mathematics. Co-author of *No Limits to Learning: Bridging the Human Gap*.

Asok Mitra
Professor at the Centre for Regional Development at Jawaharlal Nehru University, New Delhi. Secretary to the Minister of Information and Broadcasting and Member of the Planning Commission of the Indian Government.

Ivan F. Obraztsov
Member of the USSR Academy of Sciences, Minister of Secondary, Specialized and Higher Education of the Russian Soviet Federative Socialist Republic.

Denis G. Osborne
Physicist, Professor in the Department of Physics and Astronomy of the University College of London. Author of several books on the future development of basic science and of education.

Jean Pliya
Historian and geographer. Vice-Rector of the National University of Benin, in charge of putting into practice the programme for educational reform. Former Minister of Education and Culture.

Germán W. Rama
Uruguayan historian and sociologist, Director of the Division of Social Development of the United Nations Economic Commission for Latin America.

Shapour Rassekh
Economist and sociologist. Doctor of Sociology at the Faculty of Economic and Social Sciences at the University of Geneva. Former consultant with the International Institute for Educational Planning.

Pierre Schaeffer
Professor at the National Music Conservatory and member of the French National Advisory Council for Audiovisual Affairs, Paris. Composer, writer and researcher in audio-visual fields.

Harold G. Shane
Educator and Professor of Education at the University of Indiana. Author of several works on the future development of education.

Andrzej Sicinski
Head of the Department of Social Research and Long Term Planning at the Institute of Philosophy of the Polish Science Academy.

Luis Ricarte Soto
Chilian researcher on socio-economic development in the Third World.

Appendixes

Michel Souchon
Head of Studies at the Department of Futures Research at the National Audiovisual Institute of Paris. Author of several books on the sociology of communication and on the media.

Juan Carlos Tedesco
Argentine educator, specialist in educational science, with the Unesco Regional Office for Education in Latin America and the Caribbean.

Nissanka Wijeyeratne
Minister of Justice and Head of Sri Lanka relations with Unesco, former Minister of Education.

[II 80] ED.85/D.146/A